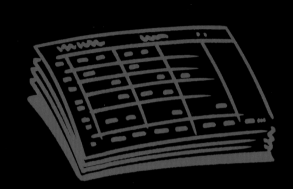

easy
Microsoft® Office 2000

M000104684

See it done

Do it yourself

que®

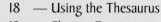

Part ▶ 4: Advanced Word Features

Part ▶ 5: Excel 2000 Basics

Part 6: Working with Excel Worksheets

Part 7: PowerPoint 2000 Basics

Copyright© 1999 by Que® Corporation

Library of Congress Catalog No.: 98-86834

ISBN: 0-7897-1835-9

02 01 00 99   6 5 4 3 2 1

Interpretation of the printing code: The rightmost double-digit number is the year of the book's printing; the rightmost single-digit number, the number of the book's printing. For example, a printing code of 99-1 shows that the first printing of the book occurred in 1999.

Trademarks

All terms mentioned in this book that are known to be trademarks or service marks have been appropriately capitalized. Que cannot attest to the accuracy of this information. Use of a term in this book should not be regarded as affecting the validity of any trademark or service mark.

Screen reproductions in this book were created using Collage Plus from Inner Media, Inc., Hollis, NH.

About the Author

Nancy Warner is a private consultant in the computer and publishing arenas currently focusing on freelance writing and development editing. She graduated from Purdue University in Computer Information Systems and has worked as an end user specialist and data access analyst. Along with the numerous computer books she has developed and edited, she has written or contributed to *Easy Excel 2000*, *Office 2000 Quick Ref*, *Word 2000 Quick Ref*, *Excel 2000 Quick Ref*, *Easy Office 97, Second Edition*, *Special Edition Using Office 97*, *Platinum Edition Using Office 97*, *Sams Teach Yourself Office 97 in 10 Minutes*, *Easy Windows NT Workstation 4.0*, and *How to Use Access 97*.

Acknowledgments

I would first like to thank Jamie Milazzo for getting me started on these "easy" books. I really appreciate all your help! I would also like to thank Jill Byus for all her work on this project. I would again like to thank Jim Grey for his development and technical editing on this book. Thanks for all your helpful suggestions.

A special thanks to Damon Jordan for all his hard work on completing this project (and making me laugh). In addition, I would like to thank Kitty Jarrett for all her final edits.

Dedication

To my parents (John and Pauline) for all their love, support, and encouragement.

Executive Editor
Jim Minatel

Acquisitions Editor
Jill Byus

Development Editor
Jim Grey

Managing Editor
Thomas F. Hayes

Project Editor
Damon Jordan

Copy Editor
Kitty Jarrett

Proofreader
Sheri Replin

Indexer
Chris Wilcox

Book Designer
Jean Bisesi

Cover Designer
Anne Jones

Production Designer
Trina Wurst

Illustrations
Bruce Dean

How to Use This Book

It's as Easy as 1-2-3

Each part of this book is made up of a series of short, instructional lessons designed to help you understand basic information that you need to get the most out of your computer hardware and software.

① Each step is fully illustrated to show you how it looks onscreen.

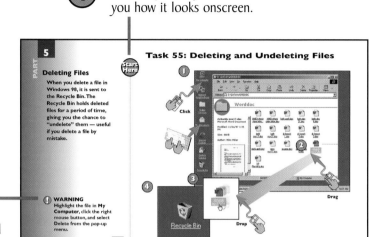

Click: Click the left mouse button once.

Double-click: Click the left mouse button twice in rapid succession.

 Tips and Warnings give you a heads-up for any extra information you may need while working through the task.

Right-click: Click the right mouse button once.

② Each task includes a series of quick, easy steps designed to guide you through the procedure.

Pointer Arrow: Highlights an item on the screen you need to point to or focus on in the step or task.

③ Items that you select or click in menus, dialog boxes, tabs, and windows are shown in Bold. Information you type is in a special font.

Selection: Highlights the area onscreen discussed in the step or task.

Drag

Drop

Click & Type: Click once where indicated and begin typing to enter your text or data.

How to Drag: Point to the starting place or object. Hold down the mouse button (right or left per instructions), move the mouse to the new location, then release the button.

Next Step: If you see this symbol, it means the task you're working on continues on the next page.

End Task: Task is complete.

Introduction to Office 2000

Easy Microsoft Office 2000 will help you learn the tasks to work efficiently and effectively in Microsoft Office 2000 applications. More specifically, you will learn about each of the following software applications:

- *Word*. Create documents such as a one-page memo, a newsletter with graphics, or a 500-page report.

- *Excel*. Generate impressive financial statements, charts, and graphs.

- *PowerPoint*. Create exciting slides and printouts that will help you give a memorable and informative presentation.

- *Outlook*. Manage your time and projects with an electronic mail client, daily planner, calendar, contacts list, and a to-do list.

- *Publisher*. Create and edit different types of publications and insert design gallery objects too.

- *FrontPage*. Create a new Web page, Web site, and upload information to your Web site. Because Microsoft Office 2000 is an integrated suite, you will find that many of the tasks in this book apply to other applications in the suite. For example, the Web-related features you find in Part 10 are applicable to all the Office applications.

Tell Us What You Think!

As the reader of this book, *you* are our most important critic and commentator. We value your opinion and want to know what we're doing right, what we could do better, what areas you'd like to see us publish in, and any other words of wisdom you're willing to pass our way.

As the executive editor for the General Desktop Applications team at Macmillan Computer Publishing, I welcome your comments. You can fax, email, or write me directly to let me know what you did or didn't like about this book—as well as what we can do to make our books stronger.

Please note that I cannot help you with technical problems related to the topic of this book, and that due to the high volume of mail I receive, I might not be able to reply to every message.

When you write, please be sure to include this book's title and author as well as your name and phone or fax number. I will carefully review your comments and share them with the author and editors who worked on the book.

Fax: 317-581-4666
Email: **office_que@mcp.com**
Mail: Executive Editor
    General Desktop Applications
    Que Corporation
    201 West 103rd Street
    Indianapolis, IN 46290 USA

Office 2000 Basics

Part I introduces you to Microsoft Office 2000 basics. You need to know some fundamental things about Microsoft Office before you start working with its applications.

Ensure that Microsoft Office is installed on your hard disk so that it appears in your Windows Programs menu. To install Microsoft Office, follow the installation instructions on the CD-ROM and on screen.

The tasks in this part are common to all Microsoft Office applications. If you learn how to perform these tasks in one Office application, you can perform them the same way in all Office applications.

Tasks

Starting an Office 2000 Application

When an application is installed, a copy of the application icon is placed in the Programs menu by default. From this menu, you can launch the applications you have installed. If an application doesn't show up in your Programs menu, it probably wasn't installed.

✅ **The Office Assistant**
If this is the first time you have opened an Office application since you installed it, you might see the Office Assistant on your screen. You can leave the Office Assistant open, or close it by following the Closing the Assistant tip in Task 7, "Getting Help with the Office Assistant."

✅ **Starting an Application from a File**
Another way to start an Office application is to double-click an Office document (in a Windows 98 Explorer window, for example).

Task 1: Starting an Application

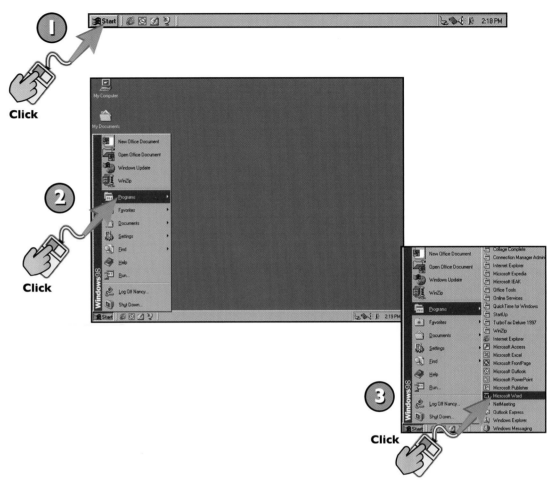

Start Here

Click

(1) Click the **Start** button in the taskbar.

(2) Move the mouse pointer to **Programs**.

(3) Move the mouse pointer over and choose the application you want to start (for example, **Microsoft Word**).

End Task

Task 2: Using the Office Shortcut Bar

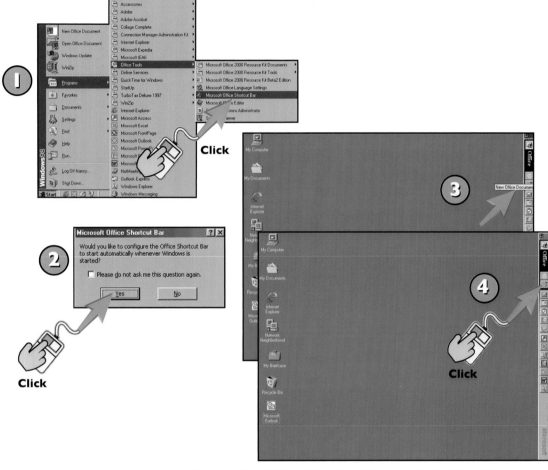

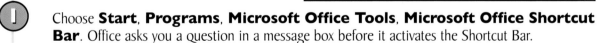

Activating the Office Shortcut Bar

If Office 2000 has just been installed, you might not have activated the Shortcut Bar yet. The Shortcut Bar enables you to open applications with the click of a button, instead of using the Start menu. There are other buttons that also let you quickly create new Office documents, open Office documents, and perform Office tasks.

☑ **Moving the Shortcut Bar**
You can move the Shortcut Bar just as you can any other toolbar. You can place it along the side of the desktop, or it can be a *floating toolbar* in your workspace. See Task 4, "Using Toolbars," for more information.

☑ **Office 2000 Disk**
You might be asked to insert your Office 2000 disk into the CD-ROM for this task.

① Choose **Start**, **Programs**, **Microsoft Office Tools**, **Microsoft Office Shortcut Bar**. Office asks you a question in a message box before it activates the Shortcut Bar.

② Click **No** if you simply want to review the Shortcut Bar; click **Yes** if you want the Shortcut Bar to start automatically each time you start Windows.

③ Move the mouse pointer over the Office Shortcut Bar buttons to view the ScreenTips.

④ Click an Office Shortcut Bar button (for example, **Open Office Document**) to start the application.

Working with Regular and Personalized Menus

The menu bar is just below the title bar and varies from application to application. You select commands on the menu to perform operations such as saving a file, formatting text, and printing a document. *Personalized menus* are a new feature in Office 2000. Personalized menus change, depending on what you are trying to accomplish in the application. They hide infrequently used commands so that it's easier for you to find the ones you use a lot. In addition, if you have personalized menus turned on, every time you execute a command that's on the hidden portion of the personalized menu, it becomes one of the commonly available commands.

Task 3: Using Menus

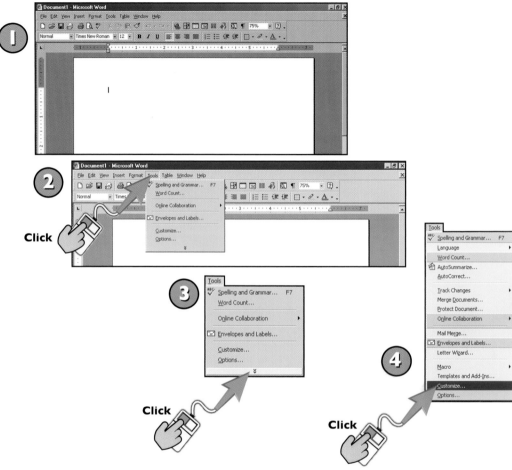

1. Start Microsoft Word using the instructions in Task I, "Starting an Application."

2. Choose **Tools** in the menu bar, which opens the adaptive Tools menu.

3. Click the double-down arrow at the bottom of the menu to expand the menu.

4. Choose **Tools**, **Customize**.

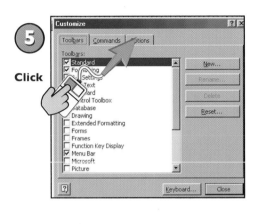

Click

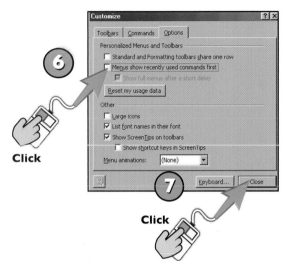

Click

Click

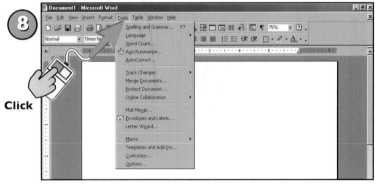

Click

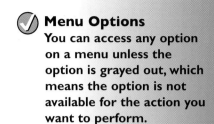

Menu Options
You can access any option on a menu unless the option is grayed out, which means the option is not available for the action you want to perform.

Short Delay
Another option on the Options tab of the Customize dialog box is **Show Full Menus After a Short Delay**. If you uncheck this option, you must click the double-down arrow on an adaptive menu instead of just moving the mouse pointer over the double-down arrow.

Customizing Menus
Keep in mind that you must set your customized menu options in each Office application. Changing the defaults in one location doesn't apply to other Office applications. However, you can access the Customize dialog box in each application the same way: by choosing **Tools, Customize.**

⑤ Click the **Options** tab on the Customize dialog box.

⑥ Uncheck the **Menus Show Recently Used Commands First** option in the **Personalized Menus and Toolbars** section.

⑦ Click the **Close** button in the Customize dialog box to close it and accept any changes.

⑧ Choose **Tools** in the menu bar to open the complete Tools menu.

Working with the Standard and Formatting Toolbars

To perform tasks, you can click a toolbar button with your mouse pointer. Doing so is faster than using a menu command, especially for frequent or repetitive tasks. The Standard toolbar contains buttons for the most common commands. The Formatting toolbar contains lists and buttons for the most common formatting commands. Keep in mind that the Standard and Formatting toolbars are similar—but not identical—in all Office applications. In addition to moving a *docked toolbar*, you can add and delete the command buttons on a toolbar. This feature has been simplified in Office 2000; the option is now part of a command, called **More Buttons,** on each toolbar.

Task 4: Using Toolbars

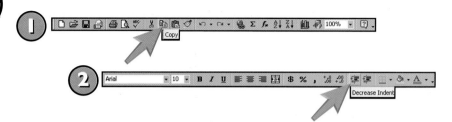

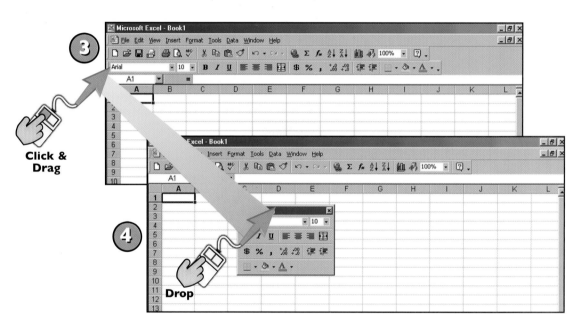

Click & Drag

Drop

① Move the mouse pointer over each of the buttons on the Standard toolbar without wiggling the pointer. If you pause for a second, you see a descriptive ScreenTip for the nearest button.

② Move the mouse pointer over each of the buttons on the Formatting toolbar without wiggling the pointer. If you pause for a second, you see a descriptive ScreenTip for the nearest button.

③ Press and hold down the left mouse button on the vertical bar on the leftmost side of the Formatting toolbar, and drag the toolbar somewhere on your desktop.

④ Release the mouse button to drop the toolbar in its new location.

Next Step

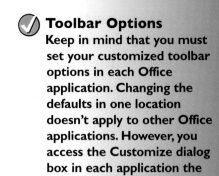

Toolbar Options
Keep in mind that you must set your customized toolbar options in each Office application. Changing the defaults in one location doesn't apply to other Office applications. However, you access the Customize dialog box in each application the same way: by choosing **Tools, Customize**.

Customizing Toolbars
If the command button you want to add to your toolbar isn't located in the **More Buttons** drop-down list, click the **Customize** command. Click the **Commands** tab on the Customize dialog box and scroll through the categories and commands. Click the command you want to add to your toolbar, drag and drop it on the toolbar, and close the dialog box.

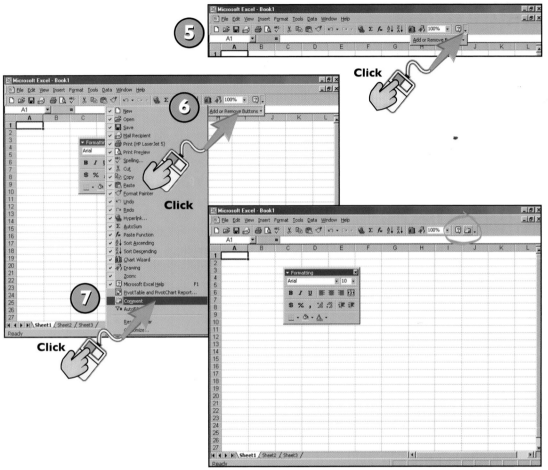

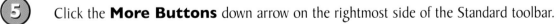

⑤ Click the **More Buttons** down arrow on the rightmost side of the Standard toolbar.

⑥ Click the **Add or Remove Buttons** command.

⑦ Click the command button you would like to add or remove from the Standard toolbar (for example, add the **Comment** button), and it appears on the toolbar.

⚠ WARNING
Be careful not to eliminate commands and options that you use frequently. For the original default commands, choose **More Buttons, Add or Remove Buttons, Reset Toolbar**.

Moving Around in Office 2000

You can have multiple Office applications and documents open at one time and switch between them whenever you want. For example, you might use data in Excel to help create two reports in Word, which you want to immediately send to your manager by using Outlook. You can use the Windows taskbar to quickly move from one open application window or Office document to another.

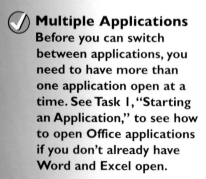

Multiple Applications
Before you can switch between applications, you need to have more than one application open at a time. See Task 1, "Starting an Application," to see how to open Office applications if you don't already have Word and Excel open.

Task 5: Switching Between Office Documents and Applications

Start Here

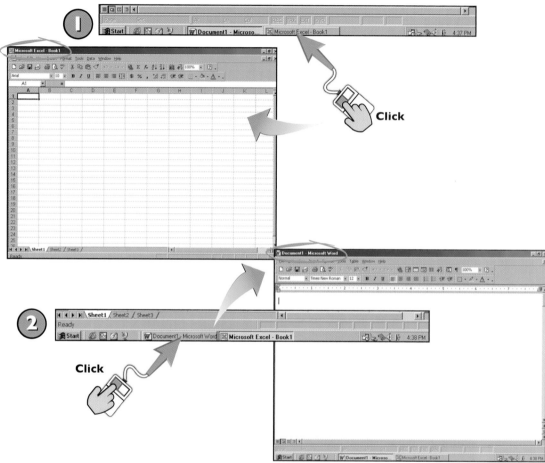

Click

Click

1 Click the **Microsoft Excel - Book1** button on the taskbar, and Excel becomes the active application, with Book1 open.

2 Click the **Document1 - Microsoft Word** button on the taskbar, and Word becomes the active application, open to Document1.

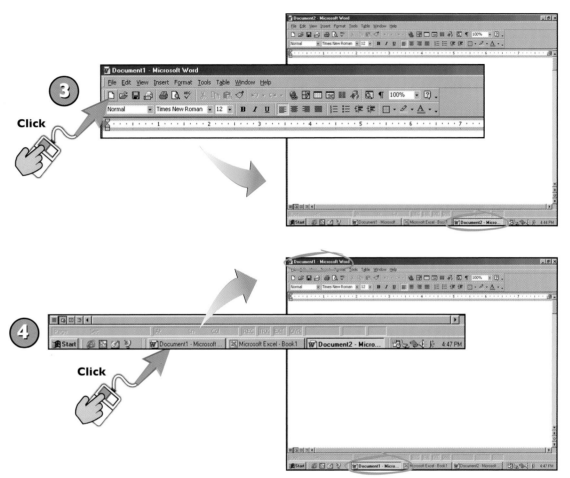

Click

3

Click

4

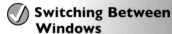

3 Click the **New Blank Document** button on the Standard toolbar; an additional Word document opens and a taskbar button appears as **Document2 – Microsoft Word**.

4 Click the **Document1 - Microsoft Word** button on the taskbar, and Document1 in Word becomes the active application document.

✓ Switching Between Windows

If you have **Office 2000** and **Windows 98**, you can use **Alt+Tab** to switch between open documents *and* applications. You can also keep the **Alt** key pressed while you press the **Tab** key to toggle through the open windows. Like the taskbar, the **Alt+Tab** key allows you to switch between open documents and applications, not just applications, using **Office 2000**.

✓ Resizing Application Windows

If your application windows aren't maximized, you can resize them to view multiple windows on the desktop. Do this by placing the mouse pointer on the window border, where the pointer turns into a double-headed arrow. Then click the left mouse button and drag the window until it's the desired size.

End Task

Task 6: Using the Right Mouse Button

Using Shortcut Menus

When you right-click an item in your workspace, a *shortcut menu* (also known as a *pop-up* or *context menu*) appears. Shortcut menus include the commands you use most for whatever is currently selected—text, cells, charts, pictures, and so on. The menu's commands vary, depending on your selection. For example, you might use a shortcut menu instead of a toolbar to quickly edit or format text.

✓ **Closing a Shortcut Menu**

Sometimes you display a shortcut menu that doesn't have the command you want to use. To leave a shortcut menu without making a selection, press the **Esc** key or click elsewhere on the desktop.

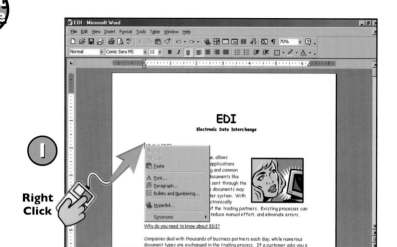

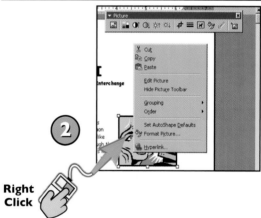

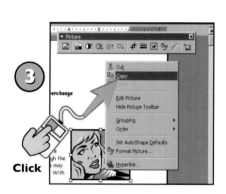

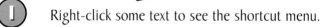

1. Right-click some text to see the shortcut menu.

2. Right-click a different object (a table or picture) to see the shortcut menu.

3. Choose a command (for example, **Copy**) on the shortcut menu. The action is performed, and the shortcut menu disappears.

Task 7: Getting Help with the Office Assistant

Start Here

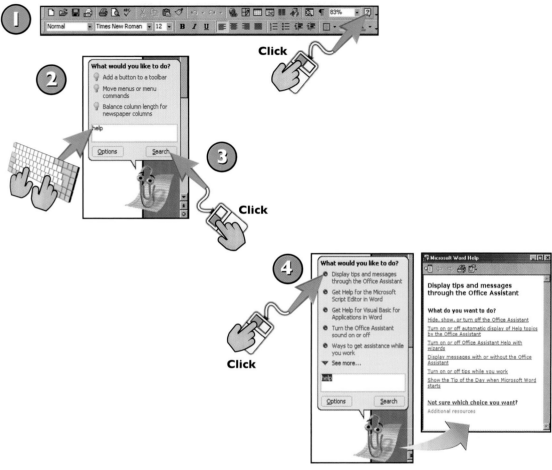

Click

Click

Click

Click

Using the Office Assistant

Office 2000 offers many ways to get help. By default, the Office Assistant is in your workspace and ready for your questions. If it is not visible, choose Help, Show the Office Assistant. The Office Assistant helps you quickly search for help on a particular topic and find shortcuts in Word, PowerPoint, Excel, and Outlook. It helps you find instructions and tips for getting your work done more easily.

 Closing the Assistant
When you finish reading the Help information, click the Close (×) button in the upper-right corner of the Help window to close the window. If you don't want to use the Office Assistant, you can turn it off and use the regular Office 2000 Help. To do this, right-click the Assistant and choose Options. Uncheck the Use the Office Assistant option and click the OK button.

---

(1) Click the **Office Assistant** button on the Standard toolbar (or click the Assistant itself, if it is already visible).

(2) Type the topic or question you want help on; for example, type **help** in the text box.

(3) Click the **Search** button to view the list of Help topics.

(4) Click the Help topic you want information on. The Help window appears with more detailed options about the topic you selected.

End Task

Task 8: Asking Office What's This?

Using What's This? Help

There are times when a ScreenTip for a command doesn't give you enough information for you to know what the command does. Or maybe you don't want to search for the information in Help, but you would like to know what the command is for. Office 2000 gives you the What's This? option for these situations.

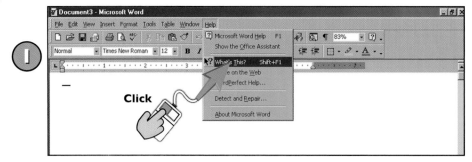

Click

Click

✓ **What's This? in a Dialog Box**
If you are unsure of an option in a dialog box, you can click the **What's This?** (?) button to the left of the **Close** (×) button. You can then click the option to activate a What's This? pop-up.

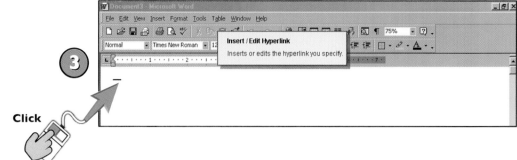

Click

① Choose **Help**, **What's This?** (the mouse pointer now has a **?** on it).

✓ **Using What's This? Fast**
You can simultaneously press the **Shift+F1** shortcut key to activate the What's This? option.

② Click the command or object you want explained (for example, the **Insert Hyperlink** button) and read the **What's This?** pop-up.

③ Click anywhere in your workspace to clear the pop-up information.

Task 9: Exiting an Application

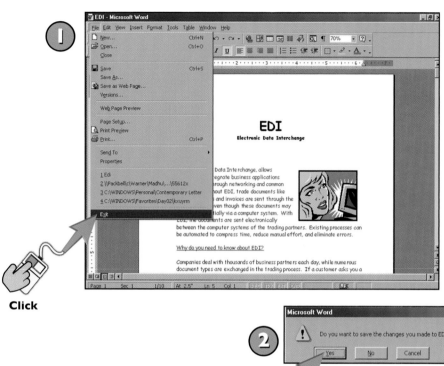

Click

Click

Exiting an Office 2000 Application

When you no longer want to work in an application, you need to exit the application and return to the Windows desktop. The best practice is to exit all applications before you turn off your computer.

1 Choose **File**, **Exit**, and the application closes. If you are working in a document and have not yet saved your work, the application asks you to save.

2 Click the **Yes** button if you want to save your work. Click the **No** button if you don't want to save your work. Click the **Cancel** button if you want to return to working in the document without saving or exiting.

✓ **Taskbar**
Notice that after you close an application, the taskbar no longer has a button for that application.

✓ **Quick Closing**
You can close all open documents without exiting the application. Press the Shift key and choose **File**, **Close All**.

PART 2

Word 2000 Basics

Most Word documents are much larger to work with than one screen can display at a time. When you're relocating text from one area of the document to another, you must be able to move to the desired locations. To help you do this, Word provides a ruler to show you your text positioning within specified *margins*. The *ruler* also shows any *tabs* and *indents*.

Word also provides information in the *status bar*, which tells you the exact position of your *cursor* within the document. For example, in a 17-page document, you might be on page 7, section 1, at 3.9 inches from the top of the document, on line 14 and *column* 33.

The cursor shows your *insertion point* in a document, represented by a flashing vertical bar (called an *I-beam*) that appears in the document window. Text you type appears at the insertion point.

Any time you are working in a document, you're inserting text into that document. You use simple editing features—including *insert mode* and *overtype mode* (typing over text)—to add text to an existing document. To add text to any document, you either type new text or use text from another document or location.

The tasks in this part teach essential skills for beginning to work with Word 2000.

Tasks

Task 1: Entering Text

Begin Typing Your Words

When you open Word, you can begin entering text in a document immediately. Notice that Word always begins with a default document called Document1, with the cursor at the top of the document where text you type will appear. A new feature in Word 2000 is that it allows you to begin entering text anywhere in the document, not just the top left, when you are in Print Layout view (see Task 8, "Changing the Document View," for more information). Word enters *carriage returns* above the new text you enter and allows you to enter text that is aligned to the left, center, or right (see Part 3, Task 9, "Changing Alignment," for more information). When you have entered enough text for one line, the cursor automatically wraps (moves) to the next line. If you want to begin a new paragraph, press the **Enter** key on the keyboard.

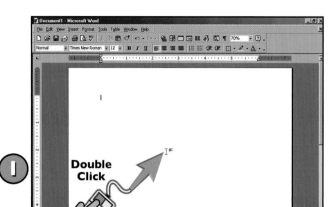

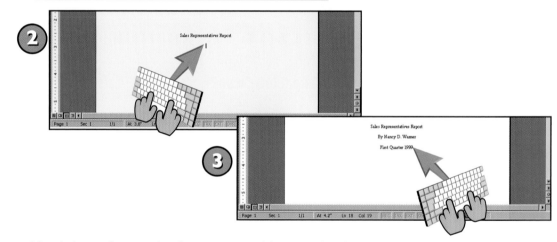

 Double-click anywhere in the document to add text at that location. Notice that the I-beam includes an alignment indicator that depends on where you are in the document.

 Type one line of text (for example, **Sales Representatives Report**) and press the **Enter** key to begin a new paragraph.

3 Continue entering text until you are familiar with how Word displays the text on screen.

Task 2: Moving Around a Document

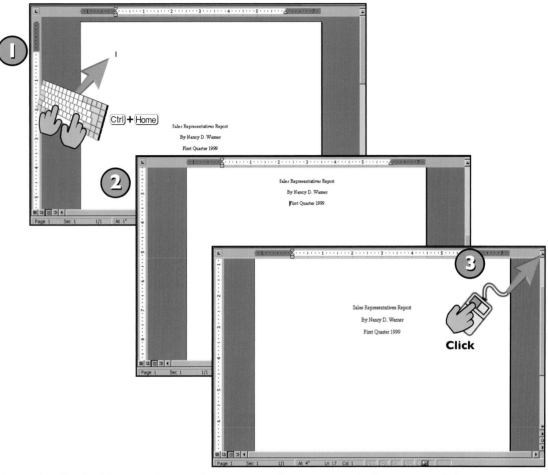

Navigating Your Text

At times you want to move through your document and place the cursor in different locations to add text. You can click the scrollbars to move the view of the document; you can press the keys on the keyboard to move the cursor through the document.

✓ Keyboard Shortcuts

Use the following keys on the keyboard to move through a document:

To Move	Press
Right one character	→
Left one character	←
Up one line	↑
Down one line	↓
Previous word	Ctrl+←
Next word	Ctrl+→
Beginning of a line	Home
End of a line	End
End of document	Ctrl+End

① Press the **Ctrl+Home** shortcut key to move the cursor to the beginning of the document.

② Press the ↑ and ↓ keys to get the feel of how the cursor moves. Also press the **Page Up** and **Page Down** keys.

③ Click the scrollbar arrows to move the document view up or down.

Task 3: Saving a Document

Storing a Document on Disk

Save the document you are working on to store it on disk. A good practice is to save your documents frequently as you work on them. After you save a document, you can retrieve it later to work on again. The Save As dialog box includes a Places bar that includes icons to immediately take you to recently saved history files, personal files, files on your desktop, files in your Favorites folder, and Web folders.

✓ Changing Dialog Box Views

You can view different file information in the Save As dialog box (and the Open dialog box in Task 6, "Opening a Document") by clicking on the Views button on the dialog box's toolbar.

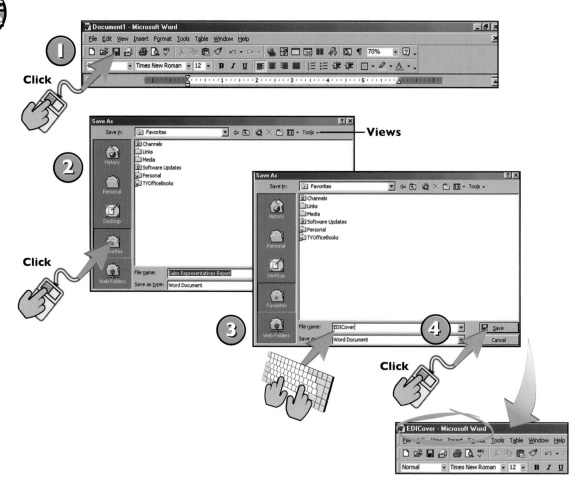

1. Click the **Save** button on the Standard toolbar; the Save As dialog box appears, with a default file name.

2. Click the **Favorites** icon on the Places bar.

3. Type a different document name in the **File name** list box if you want (for example, EDICover).

4. Click the **Save** button, and the document saves. The file name you assigned now appears in the title bar.

Task 4: Closing a Document

Start Here

Click

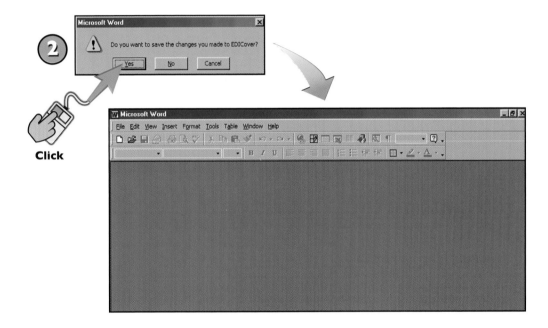

Click

Exiting Your Work

When you finish working on a document, you can close it and continue to work on other documents. You can close a file with or without saving changes. If you have been working in a document and you try to close it, Word asks you whether you want to save the document before it closes.

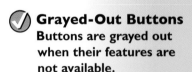

✅ **Grayed-Out Buttons**
Buttons are grayed out when their features are not available.

✅ **No Save**
If you don't want to save your document when Word asks you, two options are available. If you decide you want to continue working in the document, click **Cancel**. Click **No** if you want to close your document but don't want to save your changes; in this case the document reverts to the previously saved version.

I Click the **Close (×)** button. If you changed the document, Word asks you whether you want to save it.

2 Click the **Yes** button to save your changes. Word then closes the document.

End Task

Task 5: Creating a New Document

Starting a Blank Document

Word presents a blank document each time you start the application. You can create another new document at any time. For example, after you save and close one document, you might want to begin a new one.

✓ Sample Documents and Wizards

You can create a new document using a sample or a wizard. Choose **File, New,** and peruse the tabs in the **New** dialog box. Double-click a sample document, and make changes accordingly. Double-click a document wizard and follow its steps. You can tell samples and wizards apart because a wizard's icon includes a magic wand with stars around it.

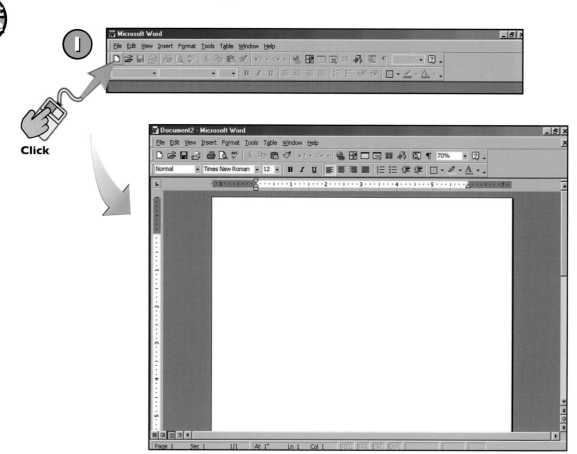

Start Here

Click

Click the **New** button on the Standard toolbar, and Word opens a new document.

Task 6: Opening a Document

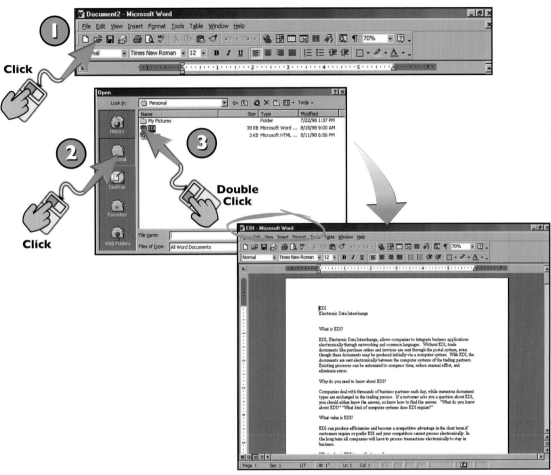

Click

Click

Double Click

Returning to Saved Work

Each time you want to work with a document, you need to open it by using the Open dialog box. The Open dialog box includes a Places bar with icons that immediately take you to recently saved history files, personal files, files on your desktop, files in your Favorites folder, and Web folders.

✓ Changing Dialog Box Views

You can view different information about the files in the Open dialog box (and the Save As dialog box, as you learned in Task 3, "Saving a Document") by clicking on the Views button on the dialog box's toolbar.

✓ Alternate Look-In Locations

If necessary, click the **Look In** drop-down arrow and select the folder from the list. To move up a folder level, click the **Up One Level** button on the Open toolbar. If you double-click a subfolder, its contents appear in the list of files and folders.

1 Click the **Open** button on the Standard toolbar, and the Open dialog box appears.

2 Click the **Personal** icon on the Places bar (you might have a **My Documents** icon instead).

3 Double-click the file you want to open (for example, **EDI**), and Word opens the document.

Task 7: Viewing Multiple Documents

Looking at More Than One Document

If you don't want to constantly switch between documents, you can view multiple Word documents at one time. This can be a convenient feature if you are comparing two documents or working on two documents at the same time. You can also resize each document's window. The document displaying a darker title bar is considered the *active document*; when you type, text goes in the active document.

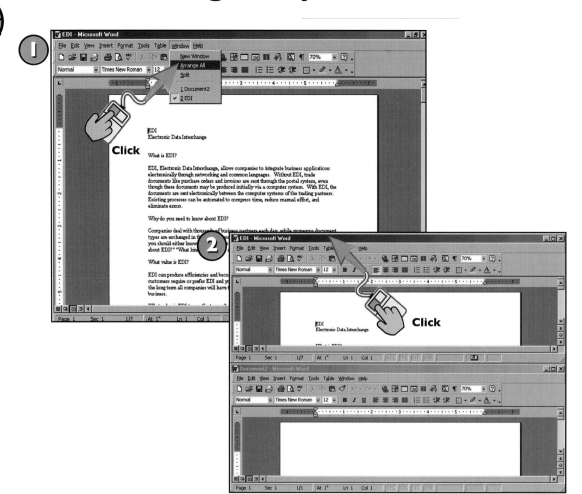

✓ Returning to One Document

To return to viewing only one entire document, double-click the title bar of the document you want to work in.

Choose **Window**, **Arrange All**.

Click the title bar or in the body of the document you want to work in.

End Task

Task 8: Changing the Document View

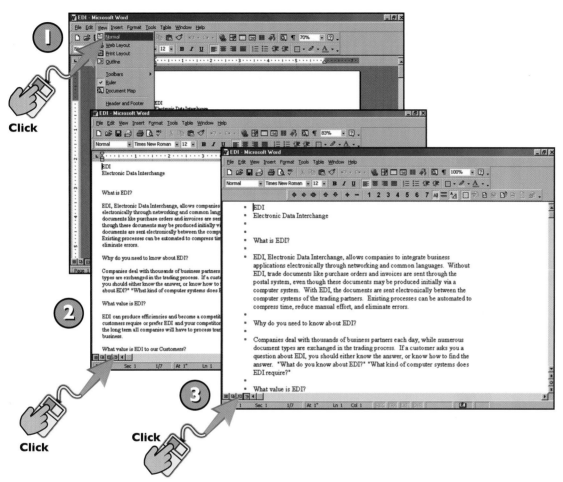

Click

Click

Click

Working with Views

Word provides many ways to view documents—each view has its purpose. The two most common views are **Normal and Print Layout**. Normal view (Word's default view) shows text formatting in a simplified layout of the page so you can type and edit quickly. In Print Layout view (called **Page Layout** view in previous versions of Word), you see how objects will be positioned on a printed page.

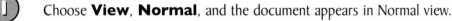

1	Choose **View**, **Normal**, and the document appears in Normal view.
2	Click the **Outline View** button to see Outline view.
3	Click the **Print Layout View** button to return to Print Layout view.

✓ Alternative Views

Other views you can select from are **Web Layout**, which optimizes the layout to make online reading easier, and **Web Page Preview** (we will cover this view and more information on Web pages in Part 4, "Advanced Word Features").

Task 9: Inserting Text

Adding Information to Your Document

When you insert new text into a document, Word automatically moves the existing text to the right or down a line, depending on what you type. Word also lets you insert a blank line, which moves lines down so you can begin another paragraph.

✓ **Dividing Paragraphs**
You can split a paragraph into two paragraphs by moving the cursor to where you want to divide the paragraph and pressing the **Enter** key.

✓ **Undoing Changes**
If you decide you don't want to insert the text you added after all, you can undo your insertion by clicking the **Undo** button on the Standard toolbar. See Task 12, "Undoing and Redoing Changes," for more information.

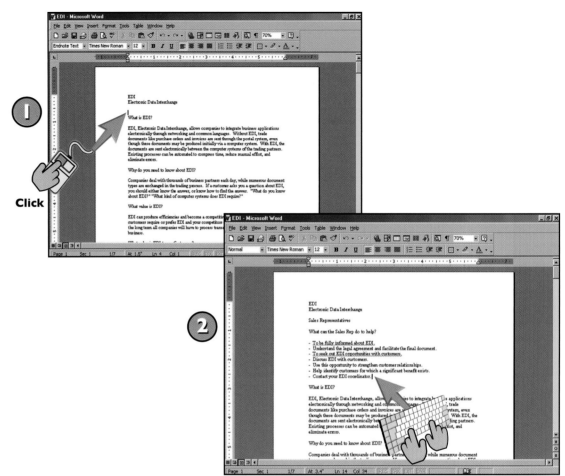

Click

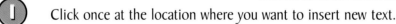

1 Click once at the location where you want to insert new text.

2 Type the text to insert into your document.

Task 10: Selecting Text

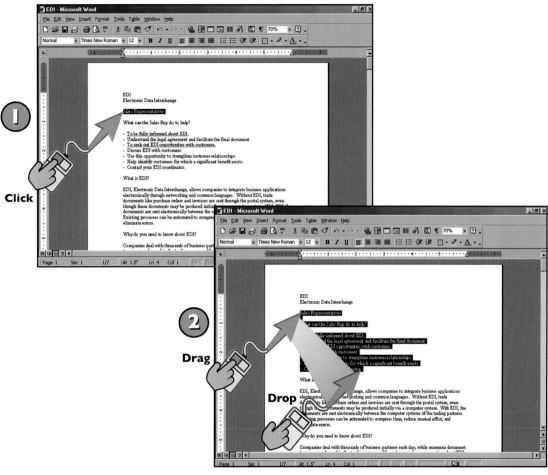

Click

Drag

Drop

Choosing Text to Work With

Selected text appears highlighted in the document. You select text when you want to do something to it, such as formatting. A fast way to select an entire word is to double-click the word. A fast way to select an entire paragraph is to triple-click in the paragraph.

✓ **Keyboard Shortcuts**

Use the following keys to select document text:

To Do This	Press
Select entire document	**Ctrl+A**
Move right one character	**Shift+→**
Move left one character	**Shift+←**
Move right one word	**Shift+Ctrl+→**
Move left one word	**Shift+Ctrl+←**
Move to beginning of paragraph	**Shift+Ctrl+↑**
Move to end of paragraph	**Shift+Ctrl+↓**
Move to end of document	**Shift+Ctrl +End**
Move to beginning of document	**Shift+Ctrl +Home**

① Click at the end or beginning of the text you want to select (click in the left margin if you want to select the entire line).

② Press and hold down the left mouse button while you drag the pointer over the text you want to select. Then release the mouse button where you want the text to appear.

End Task

Task 11: Cutting, Copying, and Pasting Text

Working with up to 12 Different Items

You can share information within and between documents in Word by copying and pasting information. This feature can save you time you would spend retyping or re-creating work you have already completed. A great new feature in Office 2000 is the ability to cut, copy, and paste up to 12 different items at a time. For example, if you need to copy two different paragraphs from the beginning of a document to two different locations toward the end of a document, you can do it in fewer steps using the *Clipboard*.

✓ **Cut Versus Copy**
The Cut option removes the selected text from the old location; whereas, the Copy option keeps the text in its old location and moves it to the new location (or locations) that you select.

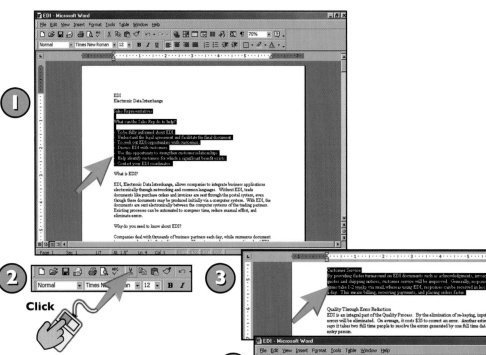

Start Here

Click

Click

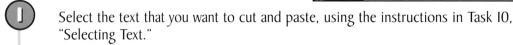

① Select the text that you want to cut and paste, using the instructions in Task 10, "Selecting Text."

② Click the **Cut** button on the Standard toolbar.

③ Select a paragraph that you want to copy and paste.

④ Click the **Copy** button on the Standard toolbar; notice that the Clipboard toolbar appears.

Next Step

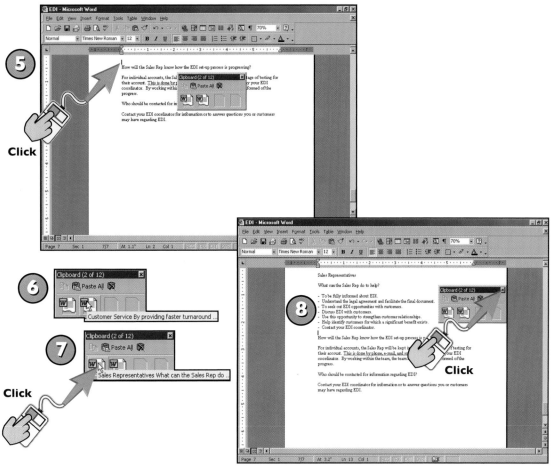

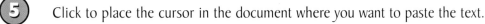

✓ **Using the Clipboard**
If you want to clear all the items copied to the Clipboard, click the **Clear Clipboard** button. If you want to copy all the items saved to the Clipboard in one location, click the **Paste All** button. If you don't want to use the Clipboard window, click the **Close** button when it appears.

✓ **Keeping the Clipboard Open**
You can keep the Clipboard window open and use the buttons while you work. It might be easier to move the Clipboard window out of the way by dragging and dropping it as you would a toolbar (see Part 1, Task 4, "Using Toolbars," for more information).

⑤ Click to place the cursor in the document where you want to paste the text.

⑥ Move the mouse pointer over the Clipboard items, and a ScreenTip displays what is contained in each copied clip (unless the clip is extensive, in which case only part of it displays).

⑦ Click the clip button on the Clipboard toolbar of the item you want to paste; either the cut or copied text.

⑧ Click the **Close** (✕) button to return to the document.

Task 12: Undoing and Redoing Changes

Fixing Mistakes

At times you make changes to text and then decide you don't want the change after all—maybe you made a mistake, or maybe you are experimenting with your document. Whatever the reason, instead of starting over, you can undo and redo your changes. The Undo and Redo options are convenient when you want to see how your document looks with and without the change.

Start Here

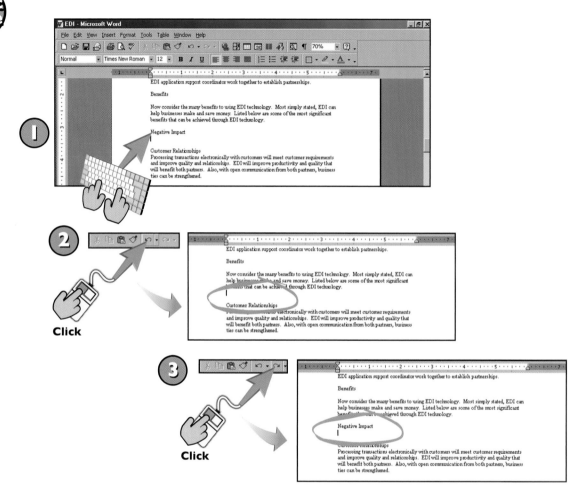

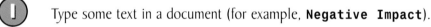

Click

Click

✓ Multiple Undo

You can click the Undo button multiple times to undo changes as far back as when you first opened the document. In addition, you can click the Redo button multiple times after you have used Undo multiple times.

1 Type some text in a document (for example, **Negative Impact**).

2 Click the **Undo** button on the Standard toolbar, and the text disappears.

3 Click the **Redo** button on the Standard toolbar, and the text reappears.

End Task

Task 13: Overwriting and Deleting Text

Start Here

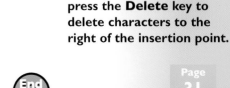

Removing Unnecessary Text

At times, you need to alter or delete text in a document. You can do this in many different ways in Word. A couple of the easiest ways are to overwrite text and to delete it with the **Delete** command. Overwriting replaces the existing text with new text as you type. Deleting completely removes the text from the document.

① Select the text you want to overwrite, using the instructions in Task 10, "Selecting Text."

② Type the text with which you want to overwrite the previous text.

③ Select the text you want to delete.

④ Press the **Delete** key to remove the text.

✓ **Backspace and Delete**
If you make a mistake when typing text, press the **Backspace** key to delete characters to the left of the insertion point, or press the **Delete** key to delete characters to the right of the insertion point.

End Task

Task 14: Moving Text

Rearranging Your Document

You can reorganize text in a Word document by moving items as you work. This method is faster than cutting and pasting text. For example, if you are working on a report, you can use this technique to quickly play around with the order in which you present information.

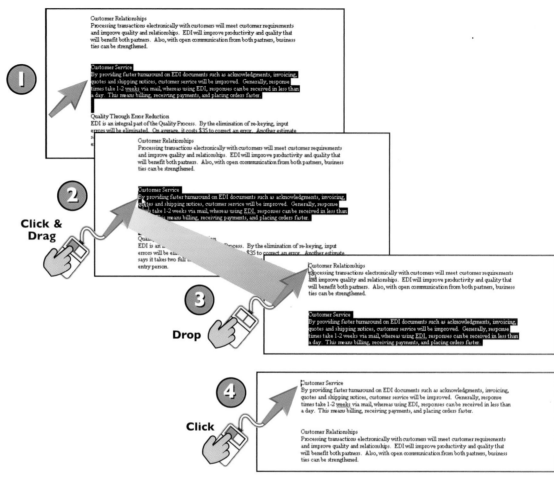

Start Here

Click & Drag

Drop

Click

✓ Undoing Actions

If you accidentally release the mouse button before you place the insertion point at your desired location, click the Undo button to remove the inserted text. Then try the Move command again.

1 Select the text you want to move, using the instructions in Task 10, "Selecting Text."

2 Press and hold down the left mouse button over the selected text, and drag the pointer to the new location.

3 Release the mouse button to drop the text in the new location.

4 Click anywhere in the document to deselect the text.

End Task

Task 15: Finding Text

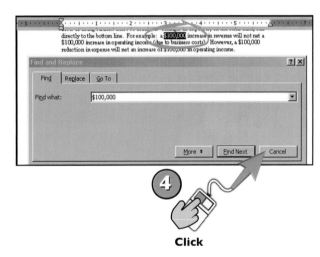

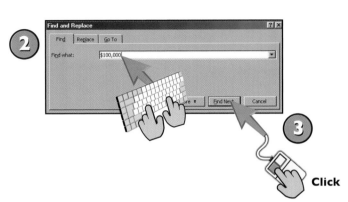

Click

Click

You can use **Word's Find** feature to locate text, characters, paragraph formatting, or even special characters. For example, if you want to determine where your document refers to a specific name or reference, you can search for that text, and **Word** will take you to the location in the document.

✓ Using More

You can click the **More** button on the Find and Replace dialog box to narrow the scope of your search options. For example, if you need to look for a reference to **SCOTT**, in all capital letters, you can select the **Match Case** search option. This way the search will skip over any references to **Scott** and find only **SCOTT**.

1. Choose **Edit**, **Find** to open the Find and Replace dialog box.

2. Type the text you want to locate in the **Find What** text box (for example, **$100,000**).

3. Click the **Find Next** button to search for the first appearance of the specified text. If Word finds the text, Word highlights it.

4. Click the **Cancel** button if you want to cancel the search.

Task 16: Replacing Text

Using Find and Replace

In Word, you can replace text, character and paragraph formatting, and special characters. You use the Replace command to have Word search for and replace all occurrences of a particular bit of text. For example, if you entered a number incorrectly throughout a document, you can search for the number and replace it with the correct number. You can begin a find and replace operation from any location in a document, not just from the beginning.

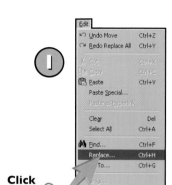

Click

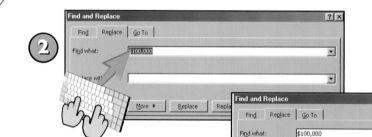

✓ **Special Characters**

If you need to search for special characters in your document, click the **More** button to extend the search options, and then click the **Special** button. You can select the special character (for example, a Tab character) from the pop-up list.

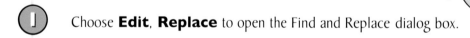

① Choose **Edit**, **Replace** to open the Find and Replace dialog box.

② Type the text you want to locate in the **Find What** text box (for example, **$100,000**). Any text from a previous search will still be in the dialog box.

③ Click in the **Replace With** text box (or press the **Tab** key). Type the text you want to replace it with (for example, **$1,000,000**).

Next Step

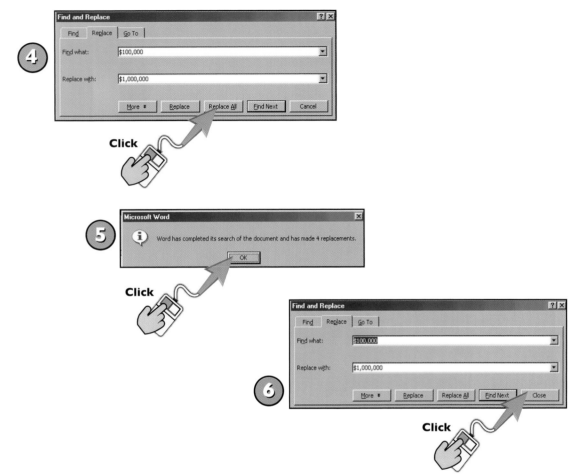

✓ **Using the Find and Replace Dialog Box**
You can search and replace through a document one occurrence at a time by clicking the **Replace** button. If you don't want to replace a specific occurrence, click the **Find** button to move to the next occurrence.

✓ **Using More**
You can click the **More** button on the Find and Replace dialog box to narrow the scope of your search options. For example, if you need to replace all references to **and** with the ampersand (**&**), you can select the **Find Whole Words Only** search option. This way the search will skip any references that contain **and** in any form—such as **candy** or **android**—and find only the whole word **and**.

(4) Click the **Replace All** button to search and replace all the occurrences that satisfy the specified criteria. Or, you can click the **Replace** button to move to each occurence.

(5) Click the **OK** button when Word tells you how many replacements were made.

(6) Click the **Close** button to exit the Find and Replace dialog box.

End Task

Task 17: Checking Spelling and Grammar

Making Sure Your Text Is Well Written

Word 2000 shows red wavy lines under any words it thinks are misspelled and green wavy lines under any sentences it finds grammatically problematic. This enables you to see immediately whether a word you typed is mis-spelled or a sentence is not grammatically correct.

Click

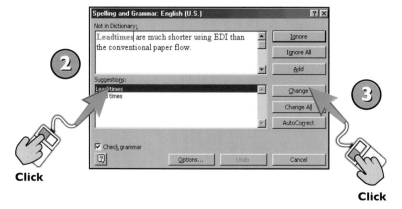

Click

Click

✅ Not in Dictionary

If the correction for the text Word finds to be in error is not one of the options in the Suggestions list box, you can correct the word yourself. Click in the **Not in Dictionary** list box, type the specific correction, and click the **Change** button.

 Click the **Spelling and Grammar** button on the Standard toolbar. The Spelling and Grammar dialog box opens, displaying the first spelling or grammar error it finds.

 Click the appropriate spelling option in the **Suggestions** list box (for example, **Lead-times**).

 Click the **Change** button. Word makes the change in the document and moves to the next error it finds.

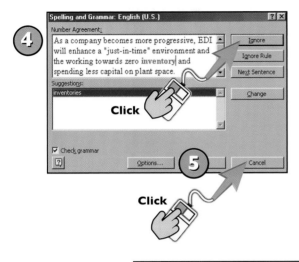

Checking from the Beginning

You don't have to be at the beginning of a document when you check for spelling and grammar errors. If you start in the middle of a document, Word checks until it reaches the end and then automatically asks you whether you want to continue checking at the beginning of the document.

Checker Errors

Keep in mind that Word's spelling and grammar check isn't perfect. For example, it might think a slang word or sentence is an error. Fortunately, you can ignore Word's spelling and grammar suggestions. Furthermore, Word's spelling and grammar check doesn't catch everything, so you still need to proofread your documents.

④ Click the **Ignore** button if Word finds something that shouldn't be altered. Word then moves on to the next error it finds.

⑤ Click the **Cancel** button if you want to quit checking the spelling and grammar; otherwise, continue through the document.

⑥ Click the **Yes** button or the **No** button if Word asks you to continue checking the document.

⑦ Click the **OK** button if Word displays a message telling you that the spelling and grammar check is complete. This means that Word has reviewed all the inaccuracies.

Task 18: Using the Thesaurus

Choosing Synonyms

Word's thesaurus is a convenient tool that helps you replace words with more suitable ones. For example, if you find yourself using a certain word too often, you can substitute another word so your text doesn't sound redundant. The thesaurus is not usually part of the default Office 2000 installation; the first time you try to run it, Word might ask if you want to install the feature.

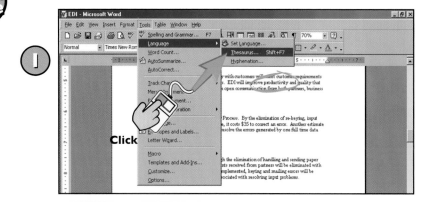

Click

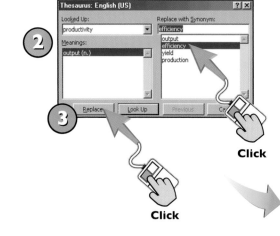

Click

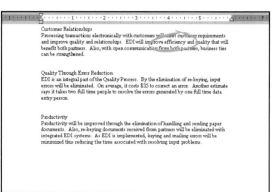

Click

✅ Word Meaning

You can select the specific word meaning in the **Meanings** list box. This is convenient when you want to distinguish between nouns and verbs, for example.

✅ Quick Thesaurus

A quick way to access the thesaurus is to press the **Shift+F7** shortcut key.

① Choose **Tools**, **Language**, **Thesaurus** to look up the word nearest the cursor in the Thesaurus dialog box.

② Click the synonym you like for the word in the **Replace with Synonym** list box.

③ Click the **Replace** button to insert the new word. The word is replaced, and the Thesaurus dialog box disappears.

End Task

Task 19: Sharing Documents

Start Here

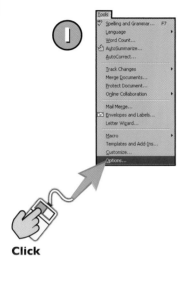

Click

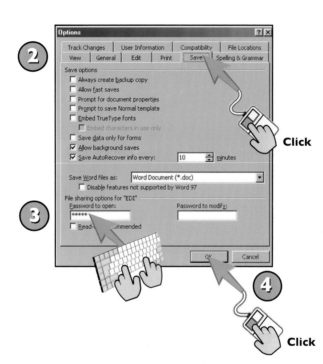

Click

Click

Assigning File Sharing Options

When you share files with multiple users, you might find it useful to protect your documents. You can protect your documents either by restricting access to the document or preventing changes being made within each particular document. You can remove the password by deleting the asterisk.

✓ Alternative File Sharing Options

There are two other file sharing options in Word. Password to modify is where Word lets anyone read the document but lets users change it only if they know the password. Read-only recommended is where any other user can open this document, and Word gives the user the option of opening the document as read-only or with the ability to make and save changes.

---

1 Choose **Tools**, **Options** to open the Options dialog box.

2 Click the **Save** tab.

3 Click and type a password in the **Password to Open** file sharing option. This means that any other user will need to enter the same password to open this document.

4 Click the **OK** button. Have someone else try to open the file with and without the password.

End Task

Task 20: Comparing Documents

Seeing the Difference Between Two Documents

When you make changes to your documents, it is good practice to keep copies of older versions in case you accidentally delete the newer one or need to refer to the old one. But what if you have tried going through both documents and reviewing them for their differences, but you just can't find them? A quick way to find their differences is to do a document compare. After you compare the documents, new text appears in one color, with *underline*, and old text appears in a different color, with *strikethrough*.

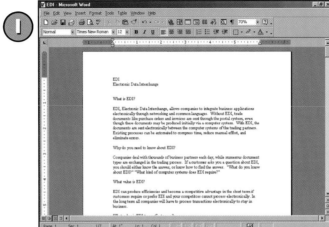

Click

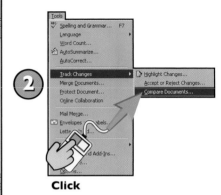

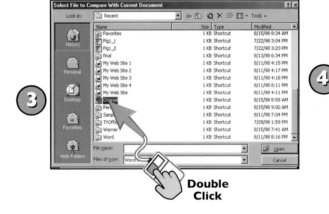

Double Click

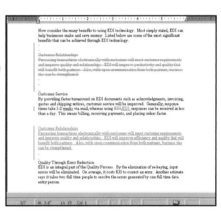

✔ **Accepting or Rejecting the Changes**
To go through the document and determine which tracked changes you want to keep or delete, see Task 22, "Accepting or Rejecting Tracked Changes."

1. Open the document you want to use as your final document (for example, **EDI**). Refer to Task 6, "Opening a Document," if you need help.

2. Choose **Tools**, **Track Changes**, **Compare Documents** to open the Select File to Compare with Current Document dialog box.

3. Double-click the file you want to compare the current document with (you can click the **History** icon to find the file you recently used—for example, **Original**).

4. Press the **Page Down** and **Page Up** keys to review the differences that the compare reveals with tracked changes.

End Task

Task 21: Tracking Document Changes

Start Here

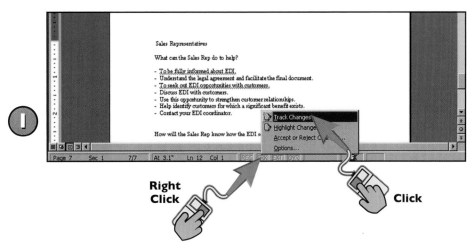

Right Click

Click

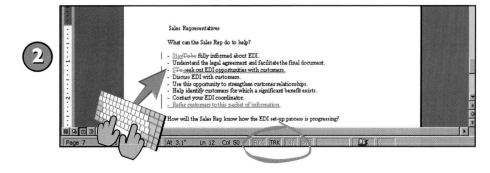

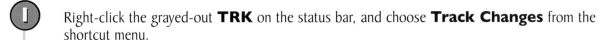

Editing with Revision Marks

Sometimes you find that you have to make corrections in a document, or perhaps you are working on a report in a team environment. To determine who made what changes when, you can track the changes onscreen with *revision marks*.

✔ **Turning Off Track Marks**
You can quickly turn off track marks by double-clicking **TRK** on the status bar.

✔ **Tracking Names**
When you place the mouse pointer over a track mark, the assigned name of the person who made the edit displays in a ScreenTip.

1 Right-click the grayed-out **TRK** on the status bar, and choose **Track Changes** from the shortcut menu.

2 Type some changes in the document. The new text appears as a different color and underlined. A change is flagged by a vertical black bar in the margin next to the line containing the change.

End Task

Reviewing Revision Marks

When you are ready to finalize any tracked changes in a document, you need to determine which changes to accept and which to reject. If you accept a change, Word keeps the text change and removes the revision marks. You can start reviewing track marks at any point in your document.

✅ **Finding Changes**
If you want to skip over a change and review other changes, you can click the ➪ **Find** button to skip to the next revision. If you want to review a change earlier in the document, you can click the ⇦ **Find** button to return to a previous change.

Task 22: Accepting or Rejecting Tracked Changes

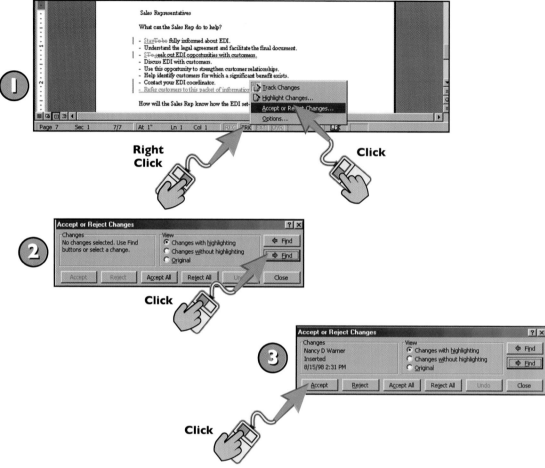

Right Click

Click

Click

Click

① Right-click **TRK** on the status bar and choose **Accept or Reject Changes** from the shortcut menu. The Accept or Reject Changes dialog box opens.

② Click the ➪ **Find** button, and Word searches for, finds, and highlights the first (if any) occurrence of a tracked change.

③ Click the **Accept** button as many times as necessary to accept the changes you want. Word takes you to the next tracked change each time.

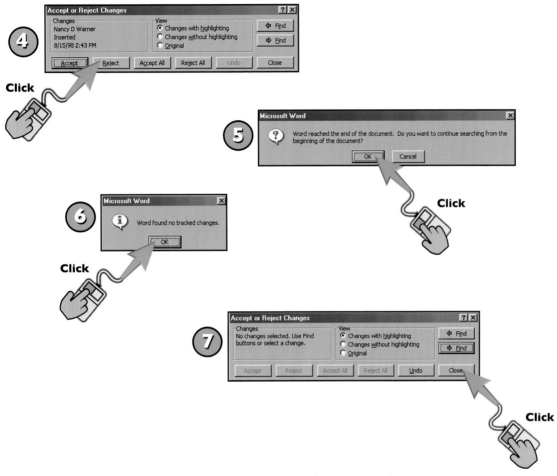

The End of the Document

If you begin reviewing tracked changes at the end of a document, you might see a message box that asks if you want to continue searching for changes from the beginning of the document. Click the **OK** button if you do; click the **Cancel** button if you want to stop searching for changes.

Accept or Reject All

You can use the **Accept All** and **Reject All** buttons in the Accept or Reject Changes dialog box instead of going through the document and accepting or rejecting each change. This can sometimes be dangerous, because you might accept or reject something you didn't want to.

Skipping and Rejecting Changes

If you don't want to accept a change, but you do want to leave the track mark, you can choose to find the next track mark. If you reject a change, Word returns to the original text, deleting the tracked change and removing the track mark.

④ Click the **Reject** button to reject any changes you don't want to keep.

⑤ Click the **OK** button to continue checking from the beginning of the document (if you started anywhere besides the beginning).

⑥ Click the **OK** button to acknowledge that Word found no more changes.

⑦ Click the **Close** button to close the Accept or Reject Changes dialog box.

Working with Word Documents

You can format your documents with Word's formatting tools to make them more attractive and readable.

In addition to applying formatting to your documents, you can insert symbols, graphics, and page information (such as headers and footers).

After you have worked with your document and have it in the format you like, you can preview and print your document to see how it actually looks.

Tasks

Using Basic Formatting Tools

To draw attention to important text in a document, you can make the text any combination of bold, italic, and underlined. For example, perhaps you want to italicize the title of a book or emphasize the word don't by making it bold. In this task, you apply all three formatting options to the same text. You can apply these options individually as well.

✓ Removing Formatting

If you decide you don't want certain text to be bolded, italicized, or underlined, you can select the text and click the appropriate button on the Formatting toolbar again. Notice that the button looks as if it has been pressed and then unpressed. Clicking the button turns the formatting option on and off.

Task 1: Applying Bold, Italics, and Underline

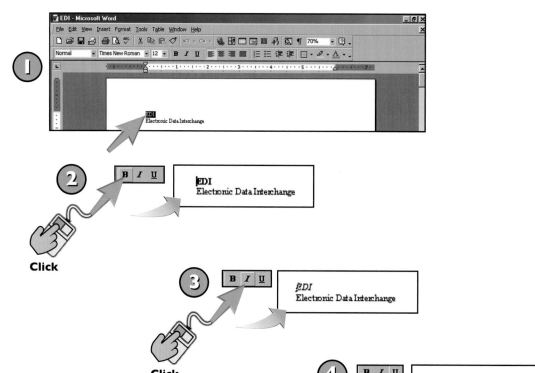

Start Here

Click

Click

Click

1. Select the text you want to format (see Part 2, Task 10, "Selecting Text," for more information).

2. Click the **Bold** button on the Formatting toolbar.

3. Click the **Italics** button on the Formatting toolbar.

4. Click the **Underline** button on the Formatting toolbar.

End Task

Task 2: Changing Text Font

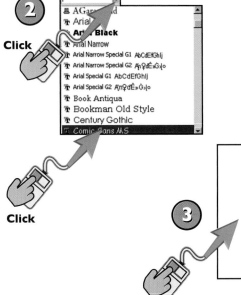

Click

Click

Click

Using a Different Typeface

To draw attention to important words and phrases in a document, you can change the font. You might change the font of a document title, for example, to make the title stand out at the top of the document. There are two different categories of fonts: serif and sans serif. Serif fonts have those little "tails," and sans serif fonts don't. Serif fonts include Times New Roman and Courier. Sans serif fonts include Helvetica and Arial.

① Select the text you want to format, or press **Ctrl+A** to select the entire document (see Part 2, Task 10, "Selecting Text," for more information).

② Click the **Font** arrow on the Formatting toolbar, and click the font (for example, **Comic Sans MS**) from the drop-down list box.

③ Click anywhere in the document to deselect the text.

 Changing the Document Font
To change the font that appears as you type, choose it from the Font drop-down list and start typing. Your new text appears in the font you chose.

Task 3: Changing Text Size

Making Text Bigger and Smaller

Sometimes you want text to unmistakably stand out in a document. One way to do this is to increase the text's size. If you make a word large, it has a pretty good chance of being read. On the other hand, you might want to make text smaller so you can fit more information on a page.

✓ **Typing the Font Size**
Instead of selecting the font size from the Font Size drop-down list box, you can simply click in the text area and type the exact size you would like. For example, you could type 15 even though it isn't in the font list.

✓ **Font Size Variations**
Font sizes can vary, depending on the type of printer you have and the selected font. For example, the only printable font-size options for the Courier font are 10 and 12. (However, the Courier New font is available in a wide range of sizes.)

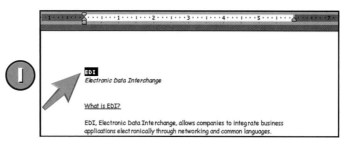

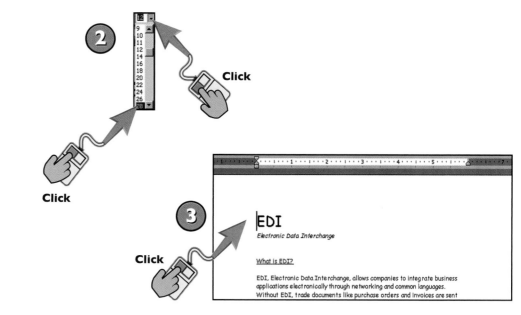

Click

Click

Click

1 Select the text you want to format (see Part 2, Task 10, "Selecting Text," for more information).

2 Click the **Font Size** arrow on the Formatting toolbar and click the font size (for example, **28**) from the drop-down list box.

3 Click anywhere in the document to deselect the text.

End Task

Task 4: Applying Text Color

Start Here

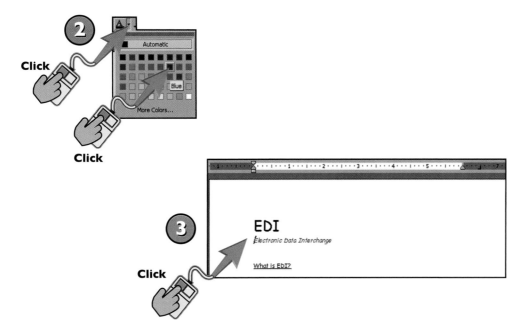

Select the text you want to format (see Part 2, Task 10, "Selecting Text," for more information).

Click the **Font Color** arrow on the Formatting toolbar and click the **Blue** square from the font color selection box.

Click anywhere in the document to deselect the text.

Adding Color to Your Text

Colors can quickly emphasize items in documents. For example, if you are creating a report to show an expense, you might want it to be in red. Or, if you want to compare information in two different plans—Plan A versus Plan B—applying two different colors can help distinguish your nformation.

✓ Typing Text of a New Color

Instead of changing text to a different color after it is typed, you can select a font color and then begin typing. Anything you type is in the color you selected until you change it back to **Automatic** (the default color).

✓ Changing Colors

Sometimes a color doesn't end up looking so good on your text. If you decide you want to change the text color to something else, repeat this task's steps and select a new color.

End Task

Task 5: Highlighting Text

Adding Highlight to Text

When you want to draw attention to important text, highlight it. Highlighting is different from text color because highlighting alters the color of the text's background, not the text itself. Keep in mind that highlight colors print as shades of gray unless you use a color printer; so don't use too dark a highlight color if you are printing to a non-color printer.

✓ **Typing Highlighted Text**
Instead of highlighting text after it is typed, you can select a highlight color and then begin typing. Anything you type is in the highlight color you selected until you change it back to **None** (the default highlight color).

✓ **Highlighting Display Options**
You can display or hide highlighting on the screen and in the printed document by choosing **Tools, Options**. Then choose the **View** tab and clear the **Highlight** checkbox.

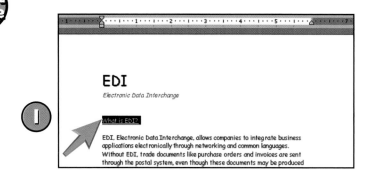

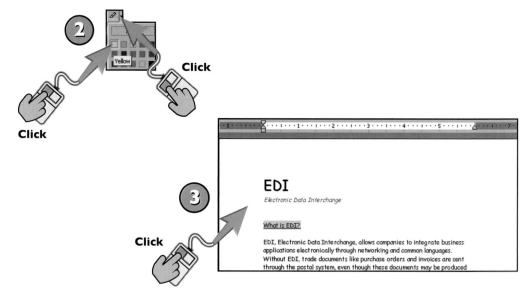

1. Select the text you want to format (see Part 2, Task 10, "Selecting Text," for more information).

2. Click the **Highlight** arrow on the Formatting toolbar and select the **Yellow** square from the highlight color selection box.

3. Click anywhere in the document to deselect the text.

Task 6: Adding a Border to Text

Start Here

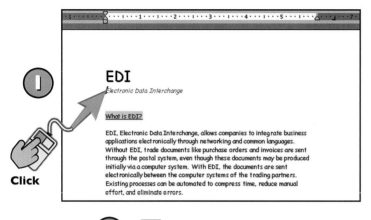

Click

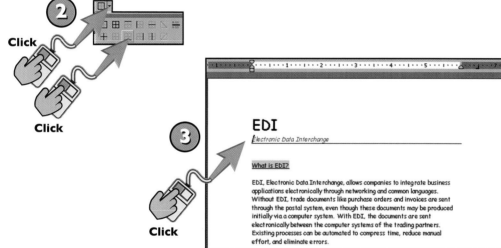

Click

Click

Click

Click

1. Click the line of a paragraph in your document where you want to add a border.

2. Click the **Border** arrow on the Formatting toolbar and select the type of border you want to apply to the document (for example, **Buttom Border**).

3. Click anywhere in the document to deselect the text.

Adding Lines in Your Document

You add a border to any or all sides of a paragraph or selected text in Word. (You can also add borders to tables, but we will cover that in Part 4, "Advanced Word Features.") Borders can accentuate portions of your text, add a clean frame to your entire document, or divide sections of a document.

✓ **More Border Options**
For more border options, choose **Format, Borders and Shading**, and then click the **Page Border** tab.

Task 7: Adding Numbers and Bullets

Working with Lists

With numbered and bulleted lists, you can present a series of information that helps readers visually follow a document's path. If you type a list of three items, for example, you can have Word add bullets or numbers to the items automatically. Numbered lists are useful for presenting a set of items or steps that must be in a particular order. Bulleted lists are useful for presenting a series of items when order doesn't matter.

✓ Multilevel Lists

A new feature in **Office 2000** is that you can automatically create multilevel bulleted and numbered lists by default. When typing text into a list, pressing the **Tab** key automatically indents the list to a new level. A numbered list sequences like an outline (1, 2, a, b, i, ii, and so on); a bulleted list uses different kinds of bullet symbols at each level.

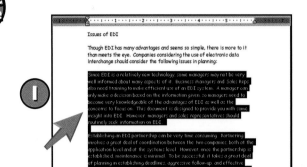

Start Here

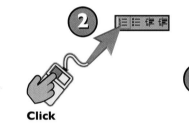

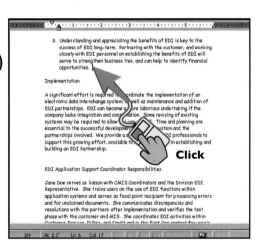

Click

Click

1 Select the text you want to make into a numbered list (see Part 2, Task 10, "Selecting Text," for more information).

2 Click the **Numbering** button on the Formatting toolbar.

3 Move through the document and place the cursor at the end of the last numbered paragraph.

Next Step

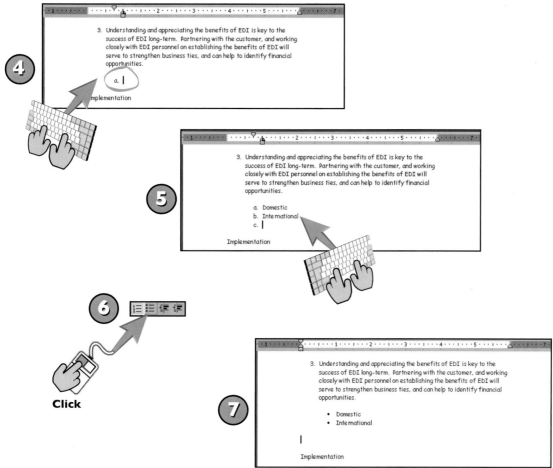

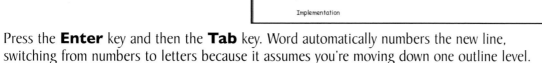

Click

Creating a New List
If you haven't yet created the list you want to make into a numbered or bulleted list, select the **Numbering** or **Bullets** button from the **Formatting toolbar** and then start typing the information. When you press **Enter** to start a new line, Word adds the number or bullet automatically. To stop adding bullets or numbers, press the **Enter** key more than once.

4 Press the **Enter** key and then the **Tab** key. Word automatically numbers the new line, switching from numbers to letters because it assumes you're moving down one outline level.

5 Type your text, and press the **Enter** key at the end of each line to move to the next line.

6 Click the **Bullets** button on the Formatting toolbar to make the list a bulleted list instead of a numbered list.

7 Press the **Enter** key to end the bulleted list and move to the next regular line.

End
Task

Task 8: Inserting Symbols

Using Symbol Characters

The Symbol command enables you to insert special characters, international characters, and symbols such as the registered trademark (®) and trademark (™) symbols. You can easily add these and other special characters to your Word documents. In addition, you can delete symbols and special characters just as you delete any other text—by using the **Backspace** or **Delete** key.

Click

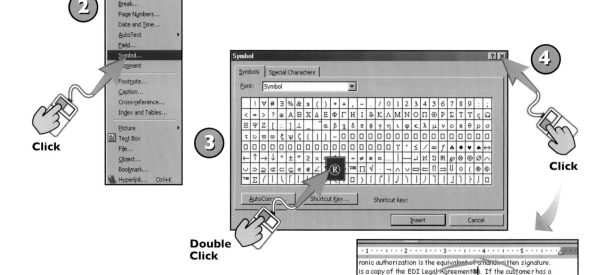

Click

Double Click

Click

✓ **Finding Symbols**
You can locate different symbols and different types of symbols by clicking the **Font** drop-down arrow and selecting from the different fonts. Each font provides you with different symbols to choose from.

① Click the cursor in the text where you want to add the symbol.

② Choose **Insert**, **Symbol** to open the Symbol dialog box.

③ Double-click the symbol you want to insert into your document.

④ Click the **Close** (×) button to close the Symbol dialog box.

End Task

Task 9: Changing Alignment

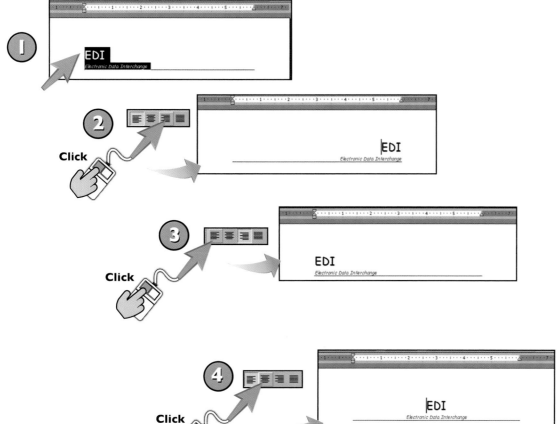

Click

Click

Click

Aligning Text in Documents

When you enter text into a document, the text automatically aligns flush (even) with the left margin. However, you can change the *alignment* of text at any time, before or after you have entered the text. You can center text, make it flush with the right margin, or justify it (make it flush with both margins).

✅ **Clicking and Typing**
Remember that in Word 2000 you can click any-where in your document and type text. The text automatically aligns to the spot where you clicked in the document. See Part 2, Task 1, "Entering Text," for more information.

✅ **Justifying Text**
If you select the paragraph text you want to realign and click the **Justify** button on the Formatting toolbar, the text becomes flush left *and* flush right.

① Select the text you want to realign (see Part 2, Task 10, "Selecting Text," for more information).

② Click the **Align Right** button on the Formatting toolbar.

③ Click the **Align Left** button on the Formatting toolbar.

④ Click the **Center** button on the Formatting toolbar.

Formatting with Indents

You can indent an entire paragraph to the right of the left margin to make it stand out. For example, if you are creating a contract, you might want to indent certain paragraphs to make them subordinate to other text.

✓ Hanging Indents

When you're creating a résumé, you might find it convenient to use hanging indents. With a hanging indent, all but the first line of a paragraph is moved to the right, giving a clean presentation of information with the emphasis on the first line. To create a hanging indent, click a paragraph and choose **Format, Paragraph.** In the Paragraph dialog box, click on the **Indents and Spacing** tab and choose **Hanging** from the **Special** drop-down list.

Task 10: Indenting Paragraphs

Click

Click

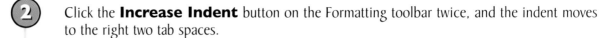

Click

Click somewhere in the paragraph you want to indent.

Click the **Increase Indent** button on the Formatting toolbar twice, and the indent moves to the right two tab spaces.

Click the **Decrease Indent** button on the Formatting toolbar once, and the indent moves to the left one tab space.

Task 11: Setting Tabs with the Ruler

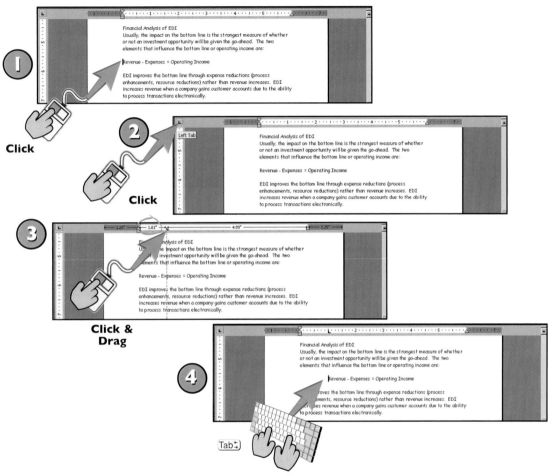

Click

Click

Click & Drag

Tab

Creating Tab Stops

You can set different types of *tab stops*: left (default), right, decimal, or center. Setting tabs is useful for indenting paragraphs at one or more tab stops. Word 2000 displays the exact tab measurements in the ruler when you press the **Alt** key while you click to add the tab stop.

✓ Tab Options

The tab options look like an **L** for a left tab, an upside down **T** for a center tab, a backward **L** for a right tab, and an upside-down **T** with a dot for a decimal tab. You cycle through the tab options each time you click the **Tab Alignment** button.

✓ Removing a Tab Stop

If you want to remove a tab stop, select the text for which you set the tab, point to the tab marker, left-click and drag it off the ruler, and then release the mouse button. The tab stop disappears.

(1) Click in the paragraph where you want to set a tab.

(2) Click the **Tab Alignment** button to choose the type of tab stop you want.

(3) Move the mouse pointer to the place on the ruler where you want the tab stop, and click at the desired size.

(4) Press the **Tab** key to align the text with the tab stop.

Task 12: Changing Line Spacing

Adding Space Between Lines

Have you ever found yourself in a situation where you needed to fill up a page with text but you just couldn't think of any more text to write? Line spacing can be a handy tool that can increase (or decrease, if needed) the amount of vertical space between lines of text—so you can stretch one and a half pages to fill two pages. Word uses single-line spacing by default.

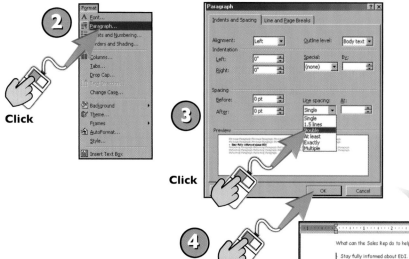

Click

Click

Click

✅ **Spacing Above and Below**

You can also alter the amount of space above or below a line of text by altering the **Above** and **Below** options in the Paragraph dialog box.

① Select the text you want to alter (see Part 2, Task 10, "Selecting Text," for more information).

② Choose **Format**, **Paragraph** to open the Paragraph dialog box.

③ Click the spacing you desire in the **Line Spacing** drop-down list (for example, **Double**).

④ Click the **OK** button, and your selected text has the line spacing you chose.

Task 13: Inserting a Break

Start Here

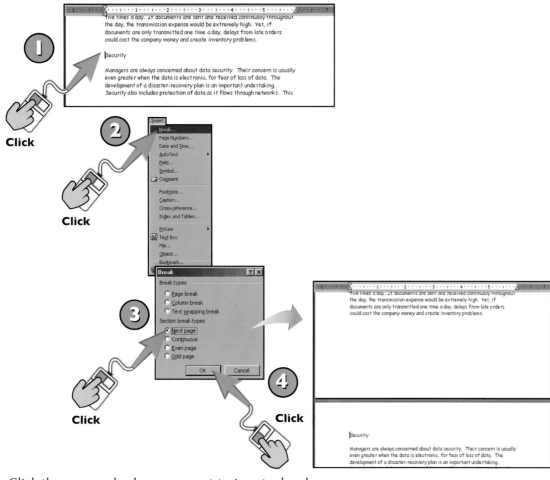

Click

Click

Click

Click

Forcing Text to the Next Page

You can have a break in a page or a section. When a page is filled with text, Word automatically begins a new page by inserting a page break for you; however, there are times when you want to manually insert a page break. For example, if you are writing a report with multiple topic sections, you might want each topic to begin at the top of a new page. Section breaks enable you to format each section separately; for example, different portions of your document can have different margins.

✓ **Quick Page Breaks**
You can press the **Ctrl+Enter** shortcut key to insert the page break in your document. To delete a page break, select the manual page break (by clicking the mouse pointer once on the page break's dotted line in Normal view) and press the **Delete** key.

(1) Click the paragraph where you want to insert a break.

(2) Choose **Insert**, **Break** to open the Break dialog box.

(3) Click the type of section break you would like to insert (for example, **Next Page**).

(4) Click the **OK** button, and the section break appears in the document.

End Task

Task 14: Inserting Graphics

Adding Pictures to Documents

Clip art adds visual interest to your Word documents. With Microsoft *clip art*, you can choose from numerous professionally prepared images, sounds, and movie clips. Once you have added graphics, you can move them around in the document and even assign text *wrapping*.

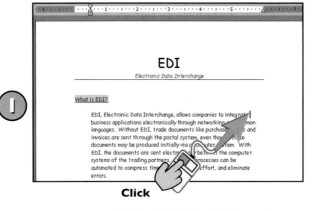

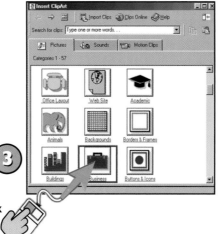

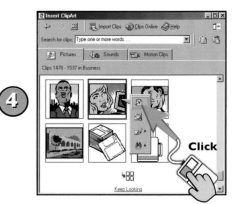

✓ **The Insert ClipArt Dialog Box**
You can leave the Insert ClipArt dialog box open if you need to insert more than one piece of clip art. In addition, you can use this dialog box to add sounds and movie clips.

Click in the document near where you want the clip art to appear.

Choose **Insert**, **Picture**, **Clip Art** to open the Insert ClipArt dialog box.

Click on the category of clip art in the **Pictures** tab (for example, **Business**) and scroll through the options.

Click on the piece of clip art and click the **Insert Clip** icon from the pop-up. Word inserts the clip art into your document.

Next Step

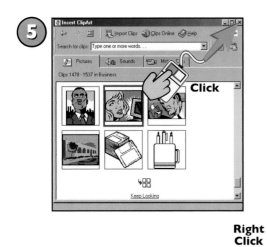

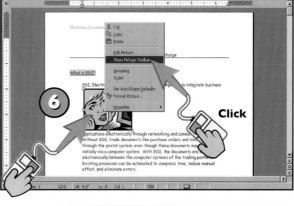

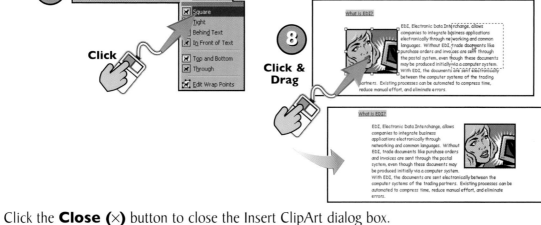

The Picture Toolbar
When you select a picture, the Picture toolbar appears with tools you can use to crop the picture, add a border to it, or adjust its brightness and contrast.

Formatting a Picture
You can double-click on a picture to open the Format Picture dialog box. This allows you to alter the size, layout, colors and lines, and more.

5. Click the **Close (×)** button to close the Insert ClipArt dialog box.

6. Right-click on the clip art and choose **Show Picture Toolbar** to activate the Picture toolbar.

7. Click the **Text Wrapping** button on the Picture toolbar, and then click **Square**. This wraps the text around all sides of the square object bounding box.

8. Click and drag the picture to the exact location you desire in the document.

Task 15: Adding Columns

Creating a Newspaper Layout

You can display text in multiple columns on a page in a Word document. This is convenient when you want to create a brochure or newsletter or even differentiate sections of a document. Keep in mind that you must be in Print Layout view to work with columns in your document. See Part 2, Task 8, "Changing the Document View," for instructions on how to change views.

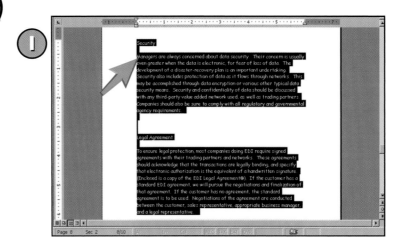

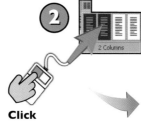

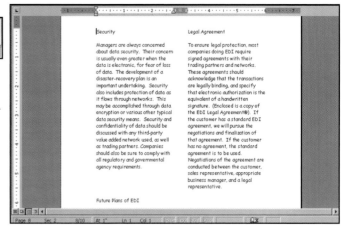

Start Here

Click

✓ Beginning Columns

A good place to begin adding a section of columns is where you have entered a page break (as you did in Task 13, "Inserting a Break"). This adds columns from the point of the cursor down to the end of the document (or another section break) instead of in the entire document.

1 Select the text you want to insert columns (see Part 2, Task 10, "Selecting Text," for more information).

2 Click the **Columns** button on the Standard toolbar and select the number of columns you want.

End Task

Task 16: Inserting Page Numbers

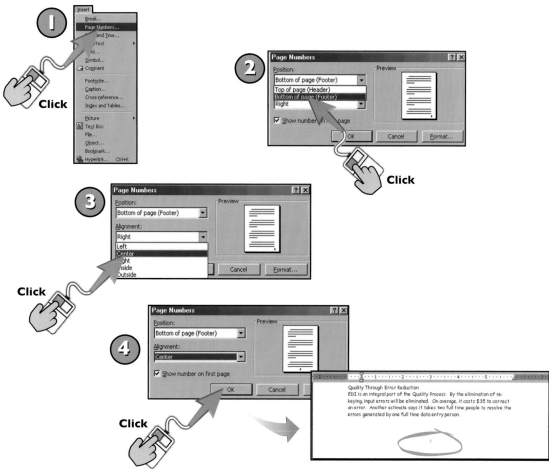

Numbering Pages

Word can automatically insert page numbers in your documents and print the page numbers in the position you specify. That way, you don't have to manually enter and manage the page numbers.

✅ **Showing Numbers on the First Page**

If you don't want a page number on the first page of a document, click to remove the check mark from the **Show Number on First Page** check box of the **Page Numbers** dialog box. This is a good idea when a document's first page is its cover.

✅ **Page Number Formats**

You can alter the page number format to be letters or Roman numerals if you click the **Format** button on the **Page Numbers** dialog box. You can also choose to include the chapter number with the page number (for example, 2-1 for page one of Chapter 2) in this dialog box.

① Choose **Insert**, **Page Numbers** to open the Page Numbers dialog box.

② Click the **Position** drop-down arrow to select whether you want the page number at the top or bottom of the page.

③ Click the **Alignment** drop-down arrow to select whether you want the page number at the left, center, or right side, as well as on either the inside or outside of the page.

④ Click the **OK** button. You can see the page number (grayed out) in Print Layout view.

Task 17: Inserting a Header and Footer

Working with Headers and Footers

Headers and footers are text that prints at the top and bottom of every page in a document—headers at the top, footers at the bottom. For example, you might want to place your name and the date at the top of the document and the document's name at the bottom. You can include any type of text, page numbers, or the current date and time, and you can even apply formatting to the information in a header or a footer.

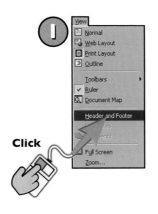

Click

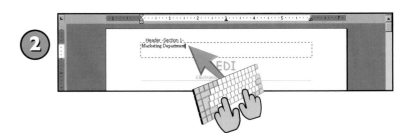

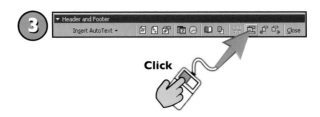

Click

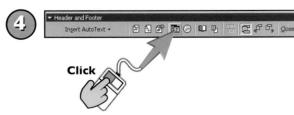

Click

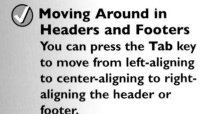

✓ **Moving Around in Headers and Footers**
You can press the **Tab** key to move from left-aligning to center-aligning to right-aligning the header or footer.

① Choose **View**, **Header and Footer** to open the Header and Footer toolbar. Word automatically places the cursor in the header area.

② Type the text you want to print at the top of each page.

③ Click the **Switch Between Header and Footer** button to go from the header to the footer.

④ Click the **Insert Date** button to add the date to the footer.

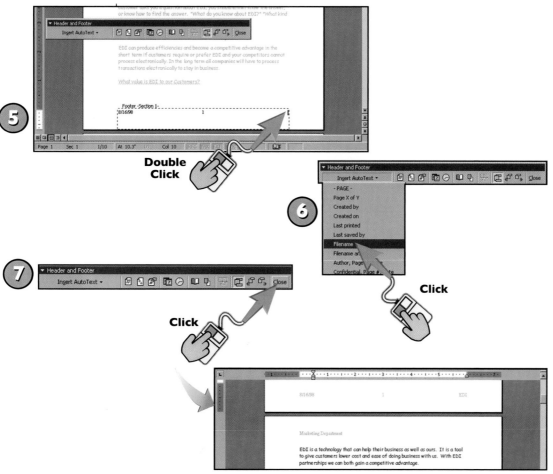

Double Click

Click

Click

Click

5. Double-click on the right side of the footer section to insert the cursor, aligned to the right.

6. Click **Filename** from the **Insert Autotext** drop-down list to add the file name to the footer.

7. Click the **Close** button to return to the main document.

✓ **Print Layout View**
The only view where you can see a header or footer in the document is Print Layout view. If you are in a different view—for example, **Normal view**—choose **View, Print Layout**. See Part 2, Task 8, "Changing the Document View," for more information.

✓ **Switching Between the Header and Footer**
You can click the **Switch Between Header and Footer** button on the Header and Footer toolbar as many times as you need to review your edits.

End Task

Task 18: Inserting Footnotes

Adding Footnotes

You can use footnotes to add comments and references to a document. You might use a footnote at the end of a page to tell the reader what the source of your information was. A footnote consists of the note reference mark and the corresponding note text, which are linked together.

✓ Viewing Footnotes

If you want to view footnotes, place the mouse pointer on the note reference mark in the document. The text you typed appears in a pop-up above the reference mark.

✓ Endnotes

If you want to insert an endnote instead of a footnote, click the **Endnote** option on the Footnote and Endnote dialog box. You might use endnotes to cite references for a research paper.

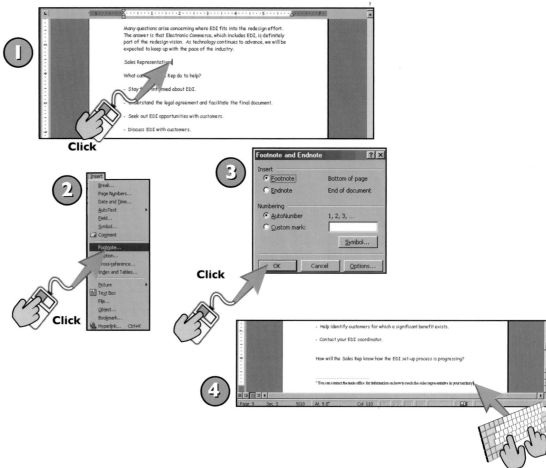

Click

① Click the cursor where you want to insert a footnote.

② Choose **Insert**, **Footnote** to open the Footnote and Endnote dialog box.

③ Click the **OK** button to accept the default option of a **Footnote** with **AutoNumber**. Word automatically places the cursor at the end of the page and numbers the footnote.

④ Type the text you want to appear in the footnote.

End Task

Task 19: Inserting Comments

Start Here

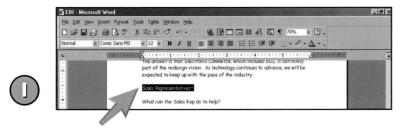

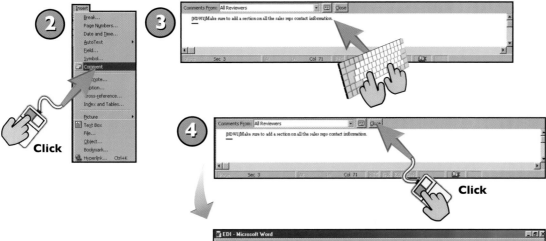

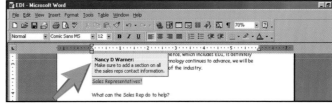

Click

Click

Adding Notes in Documents

You might find that you need to add a note in your document to remind yourself to check on something or verify some information when you work on the document later. Instead of adding the note directly into the text, you can add a comment. This can also be convenient when you are sharing documents with other people in a workgroup, in order to let them know specifics about information in a document. You can add, edit, or delete comments at any time.

✓ Editing a Comment

You can edit your comments by selecting the highlighted area of the comment with the mouse, right-clicking on the comment, and choosing **Edit Comment** from the shortcut menu. You can then make any changes and click the **Close** button to return to the document.

① Select the text where you want to insert a comment.

② Choose **Insert**, **Comment** to open the comments area at the bottom of the workspace.

③ Type the text you want to appear in the comment.

④ Click the **Close** button to return to the document. Now when you move the mouse pointer over the highlighted area, the comment appears in a ScreenTip.

End Task

Task 20: Setting Page Margins

Adjusting Margins

You can adjust the top, bottom, left, and right margins for a single page or for your entire document. For example, you might need to fit a large amount of text on one page and therefore need to increase the margins for the document's printable area. Word's default margins are 1 inch for the top and bottom and 1.25 inches for the left and right.

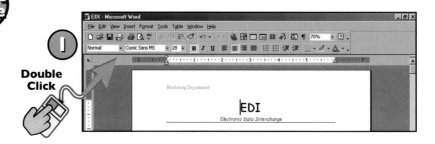

Double Click

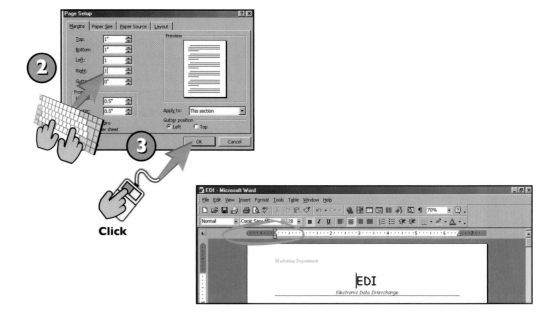

Click

✓ Portrait and Landscape

If you need to alter your page from portrait to landscape or increase the size of your document (for example, to legal size—8.5 by 14 inches), modify the **Paper Size** tab on the Page Setup dialog box.

Double-click the gray area—where the ruler does not extend—to open the Page Setup dialog box. Or, choose **Edit**, **Page Setup**; **Margins** tab if not in Print Layout view.

Type the new margin settings (for example, 1 inch in the **Left** drop-down box and 1 inch in the **Right** drop-down box).

Click the **OK** button. You can view the new page margins applied in the document by looking at the new locations of the indent markers on the ruler.

Task 21: Previewing a Document

Start Here

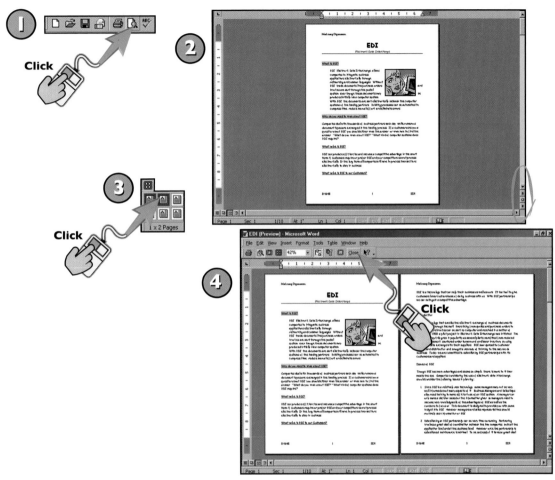

Reviewing Before You Print

Print Preview enables you to see document pages on screen as they will appear printed on paper, displaying page numbers, headers, footers, fonts, font sizes and styles, orientation, and margins. Previewing your document is a great way to catch formatting errors such as incorrect margins. You save paper and time by previewing your documents before you print.

✓ **Editing in Print Preview**

If you find a small typo while viewing your document in Print Preview, there's no need to go back to Normal or Print Layout view to fix it. Just click the Magnifier button on the Print Preview toolbar. Then you can click anywhere in the document and make your edits.

1. Click the **Print Preview** button on the Standard toolbar.

2. Press the **Page Up** and **Page Down** keys to navigate through each page of your document.

3. Click the **Multiple Pages** button on the Print Preview toolbar and click the number of pages you want to view at a time.

4. Click the **Close** button on the Print Preview toolbar to return to the document's Normal view.

End Task

Getting a Closer Look at Your Text

If you want to zoom in and get a closer look at text in your document while you are previewing it, you can select a higher percentage of magnification. On the other hand, if you want to zoom out so more of the page—or even the whole document—shows on the screen at one glance, you can select a lower percentage of magnification.

✓ Zoom Control

When zooming in on a document, the mouse pointer becomes a magnifying glass with a minus sign (–); when zooming out it becomes a magnifying glass with a plus sign (+).

✓ Viewing Pages

If you want to zoom a document while you are viewing multiple pages, you can click the **One Page** button on the Print Preview toolbar to return to viewing one page at a time.

Task 22: Zooming a Previewed Document

Start Here

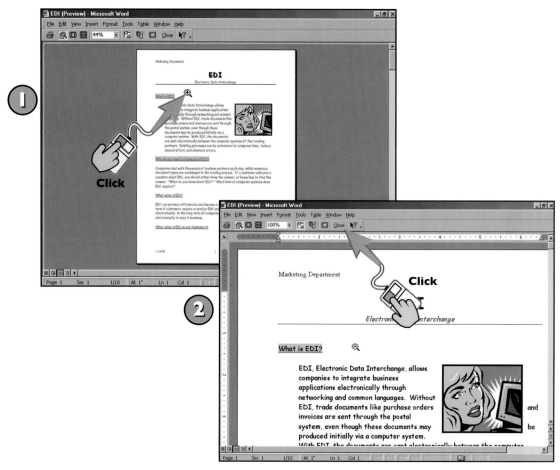

Preview the document by using the steps in Task 21, "Previewing a Document." Then click once directly on the document to magnify the text to 100%.

Click the **Close** button to exit Print Preview.

Task 23: Printing a Document

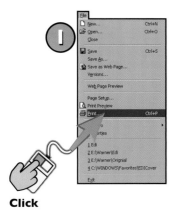

Click

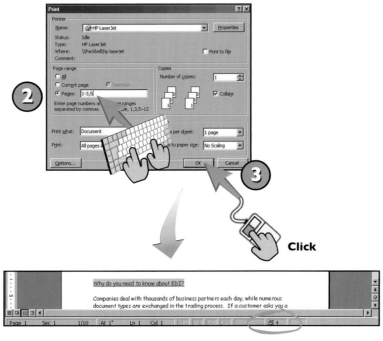

Click

Putting Words to Paper

Word makes it easy to print a document and enables you to select the printer and font settings. You can print the whole document, a single page, specific page ranges, specific separate pages, or selected text. You can also specify the number of copies to print, and you can collate the copies as you print.

✓ **Automatically Printing with Defaults**
If you click the **Print** button on the Standard toolbar, Word prints the document, using its default settings, and skipping the Print dialog box.

✓ **Canceling a Print Job**
You can double-click the Printing indicator on the status bar to immediately cancel a print job.

1 Choose **File**, **Print** to open the Print dialog box.

2 Type or select printing options (for example, choose to print pages **1-3,5**).

3 Click the **OK** button, and the document pages print. You can tell Word is printing the document because of the Printing indicator on the status bar.

Advanced Word Features

You are probably already working with some of Word's advanced features, but this part shows you exactly what you are doing. To begin, you will learn how to apply and create a **style**. Styles are formatting features that you can apply automatically to your text.

You often do certain tasks over and over again. When this happens, you can create a **macro**. Many people are afraid that macros are for programmers and too hard to understand. They can be complicated, but as you will see in this part, they can also be simple and convenient.

When you work on a document, you might find that you want to organize your data and perform some simple calculations. This would be a good time to add a Word table. In a table, you can organize information in a row-and-column format. Each entry in a table, called a **cell**, is independent of all other entries. You can have almost any number of rows and columns in a table. You also have a great deal of control over the size and formatting of each cell.

When you have completed all the features up to the point of creating tables, you are ready to develop **Web pages**. In Word 2000, all you have to do is save your document as a Web page and apply any feature that you want, such as frames, backgrounds, and themes. **Frames** are ways to navigate through documents, **backgrounds** allow you to colorize your documents, and **themes** help you add consistent visuals to your documents.

Tasks

Task 1: Assigning a Style to Text

Applying Styles

Word 2000 has numerous default styles for you to choose from when formatting text. Instead of applying a particular format to text—for example, section headings—you can apply a style that formats the text the same way each time. This way you won't accidentally format things differently each time.

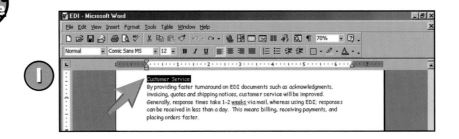

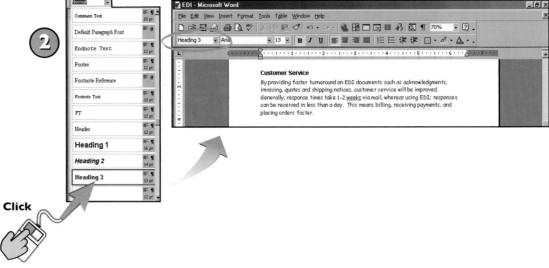

Click

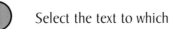

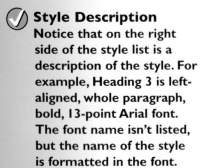

✓ **Style Description**
Notice that on the right side of the style list is a description of the style. For example, Heading 3 is left-aligned, whole paragraph, bold, 13-point Arial font. The font name isn't listed, but the name of the style is formatted in the font.

① Select the text to which you would like to apply the style.

② Click the **Style** drop-down list and select the style (for example, **Heading 3**). The text is formatted accordingly.

Task 2: Creating a New Style

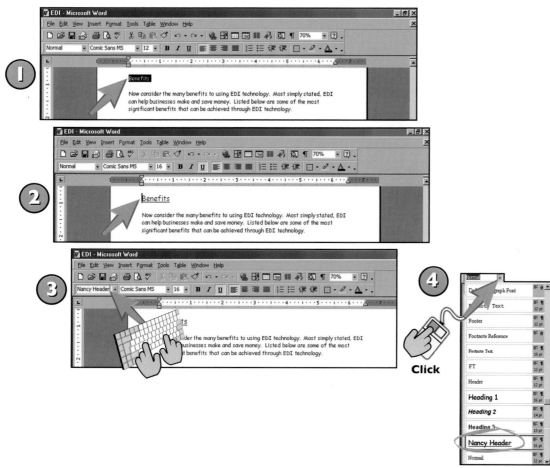

Click

Creating Your Own Formatting Style

Instead of assigning your text an existing Word 2000 style, you can create your own and apply it to text the same way you apply a default Word style. You begin by applying the specific formatting that you want the style to have, and then give the style a name.

1. Select the text you want to format and then use it as a basis for your new style.

2. Format the text as Comic Sans MS, 16-point size, underlined (refer to Part 3, "Working with Word Documents," for more information on how to alter text).

3. Type the new style name (for example, **Nancy Header**) in the **Style** list box and press the **Enter** key.

4. Click the **Style** drop-down arrow to see your style listed.

✓ **Saving the Style**
The next time you exit Word, you will be notified that you made a change to your global Word template and asked if you want to save the changes. If you want to keep the style you just created, click the **Yes** button; otherwise, click the **No** button.

Creating and Running a Macro

You can create a macro to accomplish just about any task. You don't even have to know anything about programming. With the macro recording option, you can record your actions, and these actions are performed each time you run the macro. For example, if you create a lot of formal memos, you might create a macro that opens a new blank document and adds the appropriate memo heading information automatically. You don't have to limit your macros; anything you do yourself, you can assign in a macro.

✓ Pausing Recording

When you click the Pause Recording button, the macro procedure is simply paused. When you click the Stop Recording button, the macro is stopped for good. You'll have to make any other changes to the macro manually in the Visual Basic for Applications code.

Task 3: Automating Repetitive Tasks with Macros

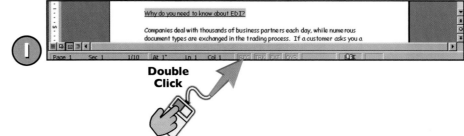

Double Click

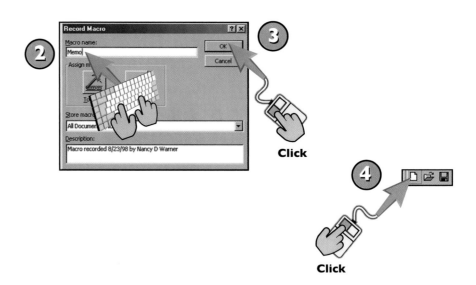

Click

Click

① Double-click **REC** in the status bar to open the Record Macro dialog box.

② Type a name for the macro. Make it something you can easily remember that has to do with what the macro accomplishes (for example, Memo).

③ Click the **OK** button. The Macro toolbar appears, with the Stop Recording and Pause Recording buttons.

④ Click the **New Blank Document** button on the Standard toolbar.

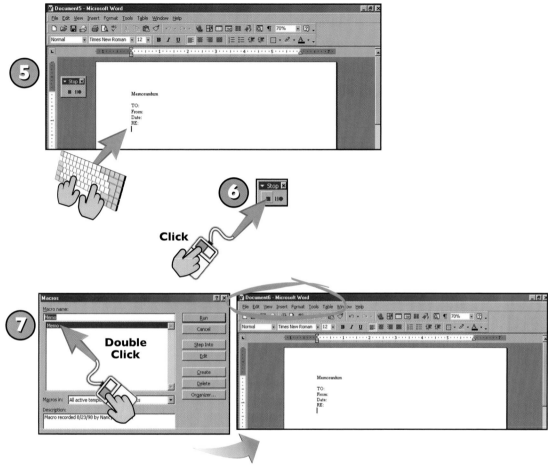

End
Task

Everything is Recorded

Keep in mind that when the macro is recording, everything you do is recorded. For example, if you page down through a document while recording a macro, that also happens when you run the macro. Click the **Pause Recording** button if you aren't sure of something you want to record.

Adding Macros to Your Toolbars

You learned how to add buttons to your toolbars in Part 1, Task 4, "Using Toolbars." Macros are also items that you can add to your toolbars to make them easy to launch. For example, follow the steps of adding a button to your toolbar, but choose **Macros** from the **Categories** list. Then choose the specific macro in the **Commands** list. It is as simple as that.

5. Type in the information you want to appear when you run the macro; you can add whatever you want and any formatting you like.

6. Click the **Stop Recording** button.

7. Press the **Alt+F8** shortcut key to open the Macros dialog box. Double-click on the macro name **Memo**, and the macro runs (opening a new document and adding the memo text).

Making a Table

Instead of creating long lists
of information and trying to
cross-reference these lists
(for example, a list of sales
representatives and a
separate, corresponding
sales region list), you can
simply add a table to your
document. You can use tables
to organize information and
create side-by-side columns
of text for organizing and
presenting data in an easy-
to-read manner.

WARNING
When you press **Enter** in
a Word table, you don't
move down a cell (as you
do in Excel); you simply
wrap to the next line
within the cell.

Altering Page Margins Before You Begin
You save a lot of time if you
set your page margins
before you insert a table.
See Part 3, Task 20, "Setting
Page Margins," for instructions on setting page
margins.

Task 4: Creating a New Table

Start Here

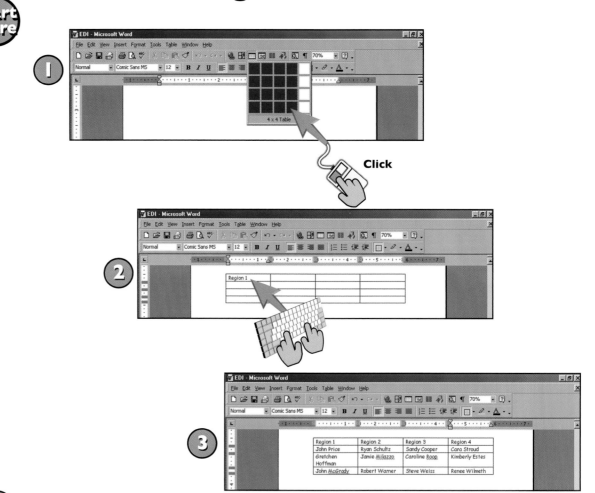

Click

1. Click the **Insert Table** button on the Standard toolbar and select the number of rows and columns you want the table to have (for example 4×4).

2. Type the text you would like to have in the first cell of the table (for example, **Region 1**).

3. Press the **Tab** and ↑ and ↓ keys to move through the table to add text. Notice that the rows automatically resize to fit the information you type.

Task 5: AutoFormatting a Table

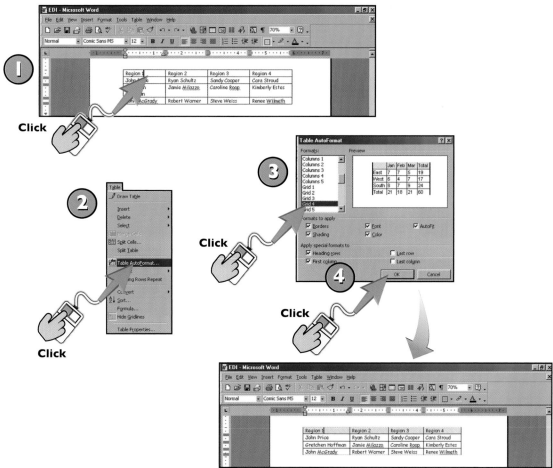

Click

Click

Click

Click

Click

Automatically Formatting a Table

Tables present information in a way that can be quite effective to understand and review. To make a table look even better, you can format it in all kinds of ways. If you don't want to take the time to format the table on your own, Word can quickly format it for you.

① Click in any cell of the table you want to format.

② Choose **Table**, **Table AutoFormat** to open the Table AutoFormat dialog box.

③ Click an option in the **Formats** list (for example, **Grid 4**) to view a format sample in the **Preview** area.

④ Click the **OK** button to automatically apply the format to your table.

✓ **No Table Formatting**
To quickly remove all formatting from a table, return to the Table AutoFormat dialog box, choose **(none)** from the **Formats** selection, and then click the **OK** button.

Working with Rows and Columns

When adding text to your table, you might notice either too much or too little space between the table's lines and the text. Word enables you to easily change the row height and column width to minimize or maximize space.

✓ **Print Layout View**
Notice that the ruler is visible on the left side of the screen in this task's figures. That's because Word is in Print Layout view. See Part 2, Task 8, "Changing the Document View," to learn how to change the document view.

Task 6: Altering Row Height and Column Width

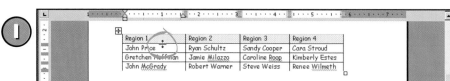

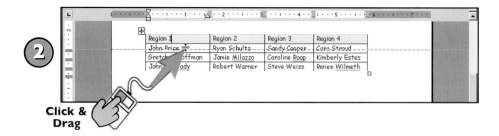

Click & Drag

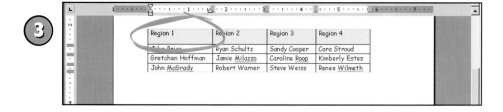

① Move the mouse pointer over the bottom edge of the row you want to alter. The mouse pointer changes shape to a two-headed arrow.

② Press and hold down the left mouse button and drag the row edge to the new size.

③ Release the mouse button to drop the line in the new location.

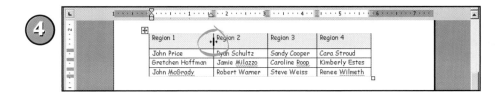

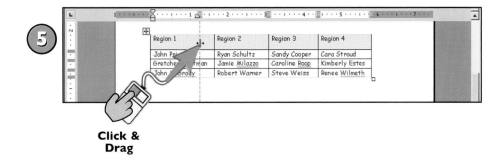

**Click &
Drag**

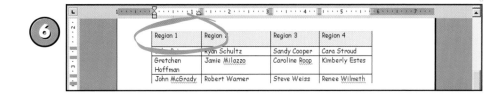

✅ **Distributing Evenly**
You might have noticed that when you released the mouse button in Step 6, the Region I column got smaller, but the Region 2 column got larger. If you want to distribute the columns (or rows) evenly, select the entire table, right-click, and choose **Distribute Columns Evenly** (or **Distribute Rows Evenly**).

✅ **Altering Multiple Items**
In addition to changing the height and width of a single row or column, you can select multiple items, and the formatting you apply is used for all the items.

④ Move the mouse pointer over the right edge of the column you want to alter. The mouse pointer changes shape to a two-headed arrow.

⑤ Press and hold down the left mouse button and drag the column edge to the new size.

⑥ Release the mouse button to drop the line in the new location.

Task 7: Adding and Deleting Rows

Inserting and Removing Rows

When working with Word tables, you might find that you need another row after you have already created a table. Word makes it easy to add rows while working in a table. Word always inserts a row above (and identical to) the row you select. In addition, after you have been working with a table, you might determine that some of the information is not necessary. Word enables you to delete rows quickly and easily.

✓ **Deleting Text Only**
Selecting a row and then pressing the **Delete** key removes the text within the cells, leaving the row empty but still there.

✓ **Adding a Row at the End**
To add a row to the bottom of the table, place the cursor at the end of any text in the bottom-right cell in the table and press the **Tab** key.

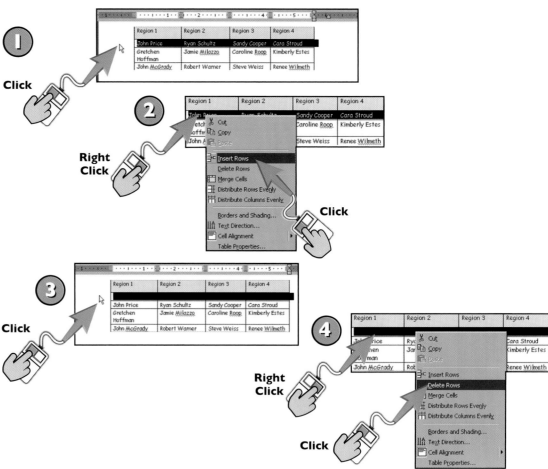

Click

Right Click

Click

Click

Right Click

Click

1. Click in the margin to the left of the row above which you would like to insert another row; the row becomes highlighted.

2. Right-click the row and choose **Insert Rows** from the shortcut menu; the new row appears.

3. Click in the margin to the left of the row above which you would like to delete another row; the row becomes highlighted.

4. Right-click the row and choose **Delete Rows** from the shortcut menu; the new row disappears.

Task 8: Adding and Deleting Columns

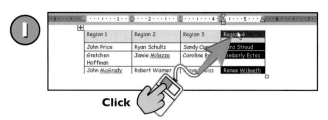

Click

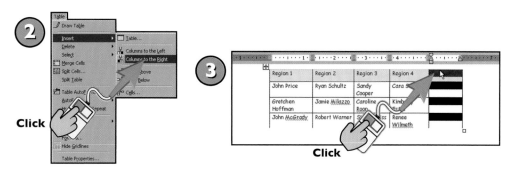

Click

Click

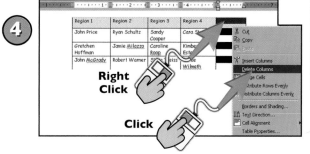

Right Click

Click

Inserting and Removing Columns

When working with Word tables, you might find that you need another column after you have already created the table. Word makes it easy to add columns while working in a table. Word lets you insert a column to the left or right of (and identical to) the column you select. In addition, after you have been working with a table, you might determine that some of the information is not necessary. Word enables you to delete columns quickly and easily.

① Click the column to the left or right of where you would like to insert a column; the column becomes highlighted.

② Choose **Table**, **Insert**, **Columns to the Right**; the new column appears.

③ Click the column you would like to delete; the column becomes highlighted.

④ Right-click the row and choose **Delete Columns** from the shortcut menu; the new column disappears.

⊘ Using a Right-click
Instead of using the Table menu, you can right-click on the table and manipulate the columns from the shortcut menu.

Task 9: Converting a Table to Text

Making Text from a Table

Sometimes you might want to use the information in a table without all the formatting. For example, you can convert the table to text and save it as a file you can import into a database. When you convert a table to text, you can specify several ways (such as commas, tab characters, or paragraph marks) to separate the table's cells.

✓ **Formatting the Text**
After you have converted a table to text, you usually have to work with and format the text to put it in the format you want. See Part 3, "Working with Word Documents," for more information.

✓ **Converting Text to a Table**
You can also convert text to a table. Select the text you want to convert, right-click on the selected text, and click **Convert Text to a Table** from the shortcut menu.

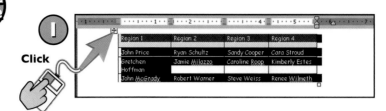

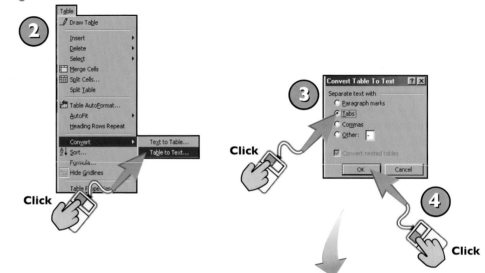

① Click the four-headed arrow at the upper-left corner of the table to select the entire table.

② Choose **Table**, **Convert**, **Table to Text** to open the Convert Table to Text dialog box.

③ Click the **Separate text with** option button (for example, **Tabs**).

④ Click the **OK** button; Word converts the selected table into tabbed columns.

Task 10: Deleting a Table

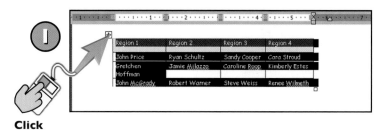

Click

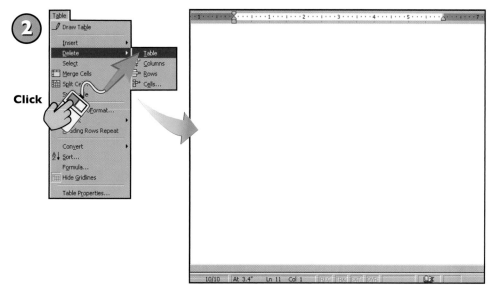

Click

Removing a Table

You might decide not to use a table in your document after all. In this case, you want to delete the entire table from your document. Deleting a table all at once is a new operation in Word 2000. It is available on the Table menu.

① Click the four-headed arrow at the upper-left corner of the table to select the entire table.

② Choose **Table**, **Delete**, **Table**; the table disappears.

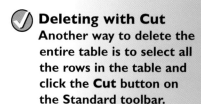 **Deleting with Cut**
Another way to delete the entire table is to select all the rows in the table and click the **Cut** button on the Standard toolbar.

Task 11: Saving a Document as a Web Page

Using Save As Web Page

To use your Word document as a Web page, you need to save it in the correct file format. Word 2000 has the capability of saving your files in HTML format and allows you to open your documents up in Word again and use the available Word features.

✓ **Other Office Applications**

Saving as a Web page is also simple in the other applications in Office 2000. Follow the same procedure when using Excel 2000 and PowerPoint 2000.

✓ **Alternate Save-In Locations**

If necessary, click the **Save-In** drop-down arrow and select the folder from the list. To move up a folder level, click the **Up One Level** button on the Save toolbar. If you double-click a subfolder, its contents appear in the list of files and folders.

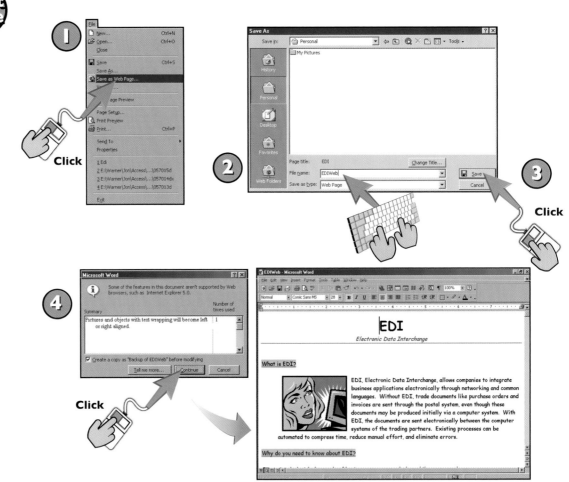

1. Choose **File**, **Save as Web Page** to open the Save As dialog box.

2. Type in the **File name** you would like the Web document saved as (for example, **EDIWeb**).

3. Click the **Save** button, and the document is saved with the file name you assigned in the title bar.

4. Click the **Continue** button to return to working in your document in Web Layout view if you are asked about the saving of particular features in your document.

Task 12: Applying Frames to Documents

Start Here

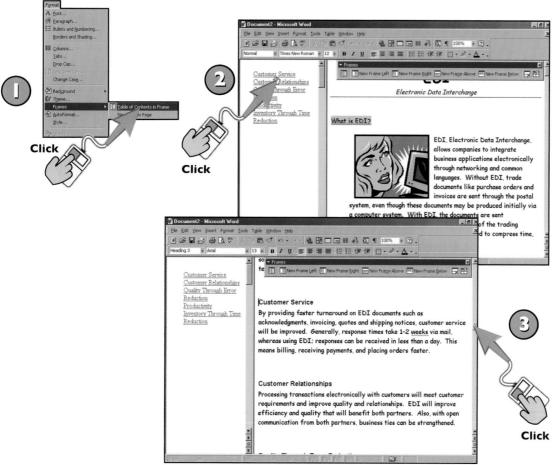

Click

Click

Click

Adding Sections to Your Documents

One way to make your documents easier to read and maneuver through is to add a *frame* with a table of contents. Word 2000 is a full HTML editor, giving you the tools to create and view **WYSIWYG** (which stands for "what you see is what you get") frame pages. You have probably seen frames on Web pages while browsing the Internet.

WARNING

When you add the first frame to your document, the document name changes to Document*n* (where *n* is the next new document number). You need to make sure you save your changes to your Web page document often and under a new name. Word saves many elements with each simple change you make to your document.

---

① Choose **Format**, **Frames**, **Table of Contents in Frame** to insert a document frame with a table of contents.

② Click on the section headers in the left frame to be taken immediately to the document link. Notice that, like a Web hyperlink, the link is a different color after you click it.

③ Click the scrollbars to move through the document in the right frame.

End Task

Task 13: Adding and Deleting Frames

Inserting and Removing Sections

Adding information to a page in a visually appealing format is a goal of many people who create Web pages. Multiple frames can give the user browsing a Web page many different ways to view and access information. For example, you might have a table of contents in one frame, a list of helpful information in another frame, and the main document in another frame.

✓ Saving Different Frames

You can save each frame in your Web page as a different document. This allows you to also open different documents in your Web pages. For example, choose **Insert**, **File**, and insert the document you want to add.

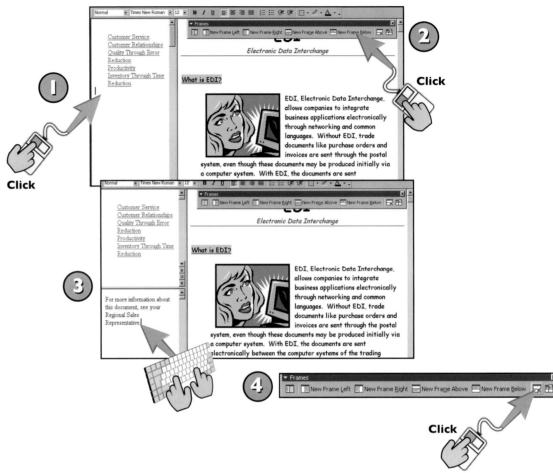

Start Here

Click

Click

Click

1. Click in the frame where you want to add another frame.

2. Click the appropriate frame button on the Frames toolbar (for example, **New Frame Below**).

3. Type the information you want in the new frame.

4. Click the **Delete Frame** button on the Frames toolbar if you decide not to add the informational frame.

End Task

Task 14: Applying a Background

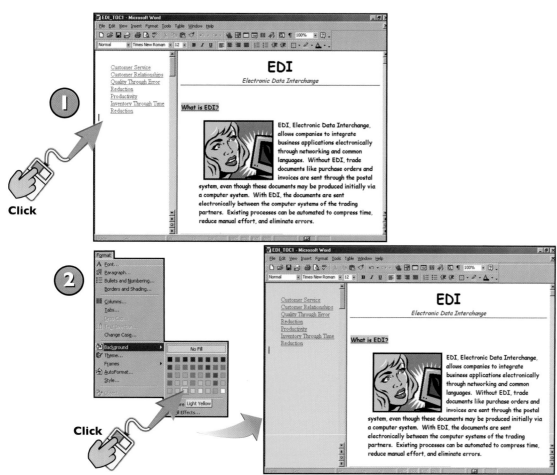

Click

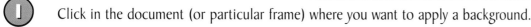

Click

1. Click in the document (or particular frame) where you want to apply a background.

2. Choose **Format**, **Background** and click the color you wish to apply (for example, **Light Yellow**).

Adding Color to Your Documents

When working in documents or creating Web pages, you can apply a background color to your documents to add visual interest. You don't want to add colors that take interest away from the information you are providing; you want to make sure that the colors are pleasing and coordinated. Have you ever browsed a Web page, and the colors were so bright it hurt your eyes? You probably didn't stay on that page long. Remember your audience when adding background colors to your documents.

✓ **Fill Effects**
You can add all kinds of fill effects to the colors you choose for backgrounds. Choose **Format, Background, Fill Effects**, and choose from among the different gradients, textures, patterns, and pictures available.

Adding Consistent Document Formatting

Instead of or in addition to adding background color, you can apply a document theme. Themes are a new feature in Word 2000 and have been created to be consistent with other Microsoft applications such as design templates in PowerPoint. Themes help create consistent-looking documents and Web pages.

✓ **Themes in Frames**
You can apply different themes to different frames in your Web document. Keep in mind that this might not be the most visually appealing option, but you can practice applying themes this way.

Task 15: Applying a Document Theme

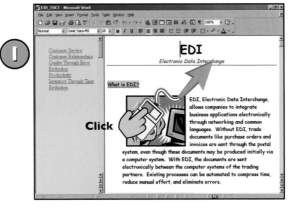

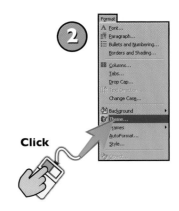

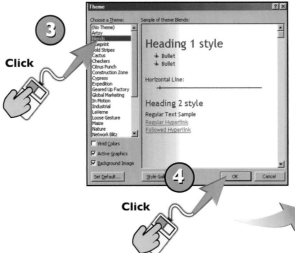

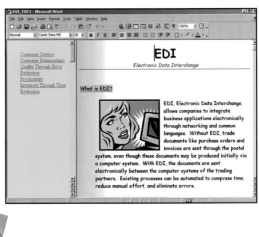

① Click in the document (or particular frame) where you want to apply a theme.

② Choose **Format**, **Theme** to open the Theme dialog box.

③ Click on a theme (for example, **Blends**) in the **Choose a Theme** list box.

④ Click the **OK** button, and see the theme applied to your document.

Task 16: Using Web Page Preview

Start
Here

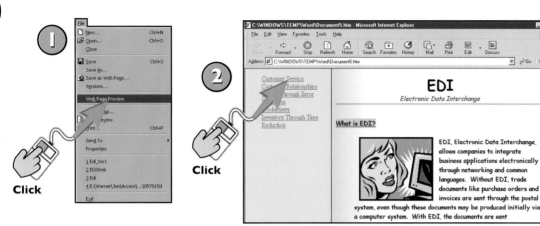

Click

Click

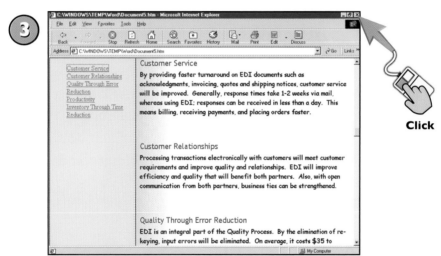

Click

Click

Viewing Your Document as a Web Page

Now that you have created a Web page document and added frames, backgrounds, and themes to it, you want to see what the document will look like to everyone else viewing your Web page document. You can view your documents in Web Page Preview even before you have saved the file. This makes it easy to see exactly what a color or theme looks like.

 Browser Buttons and Links
Notice that the Web browser acts just as if it were displaying an active Web page. The document name is in the menu bar, and the Explorer bar buttons are active.

 Other Office Applications
Previewing a Web page is also simple in the other applications in Office 2000. Follow the same procedure when using Excel 2000 and PowerPoint 2000.

---

1 Choose **File**, **Web Page Preview** to view your document in your default Web browser.

2 Click a table of contents link (for example, **Customer Service**) to move through the document.

3 Click the **Close** (×) button to close the browser and return to your document in Word's Normal view.

End
Task

Excel 2000 Basics

When you start the application, Excel displays a blank workbook. A *workbook* is a file in which you store your data, similar to a three-ring binder. Within a workbook are worksheets, chart sheets, and macro sheets. A new workbook contains three sheets, named Sheet I through Sheet 3. You can add sheets, up to 255 total per workbook, depending on your computer's available memory.

Multiple sheets help you organize, manage, and consolidate your data. For example, you might want to create a sales forecast for the first quarter of the year. SheetI, Sheet2, and Sheet3 could contain worksheet data for January, February, and March, Sheet4 a summary for the three months of sales data, and Sheet5 a chart showing sales over the three-month period.

A *worksheet* is a grid of columns and rows. The intersection of any column and row is called a *cell*. Each cell in a worksheet has a unique cell reference—the designation formed by combining the row and column headings. For example, A8 refers to the cell at the intersection of column A and row 8.

The cell pointer is a cross-shaped pointer that appears over cells in the worksheet. You use the cell pointer to select any cell in the worksheet. The selected cell is called the *active cell*. You always have at least one cell selected.

A *range* is a specified group of cells. A range can be a single cell, a column, a row, or any combination of cells, columns, and rows. Range coordinates identify a range. The first element in the range coordinates is the location of the upper-left cell in the range; the second element is the location of the lower-right cell. A colon (:) separates these two elements. The range AI:C3, for example, includes the cells AI, A2, A3, BI, B2, B3, CI, C2, and C3.

Tasks

Task 1: Entering Data

Typing Information into the Worksheet

The easiest way to enter data is to start typing when Excel opens a worksheet. Notice that when you type numbers, they align by default to the right; when you type text, it aligns by default to the left. Also notice that whatever you type appears in the Formula bar.

✓ **Accepting Entered Data**

When you have entered data into a cell, you can do one of two things to accept it: press the **Enter** key (which moves you to the next cell below) or press an arrow key (which moves you to a cell in that direction).

✓ **The Backspace Key**

If you make a mistake when typing an entry, use the **Backspace** key to correct it. Excel does not place the entry in the cell until you press **Enter**, press an arrow key, or click the green check mark in the Formula bar.

Start Here

Click

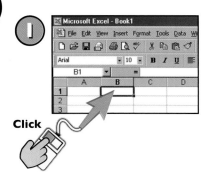

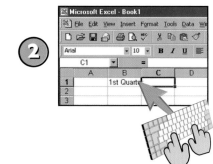

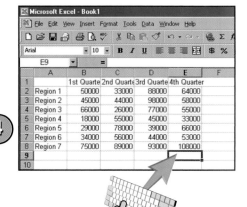

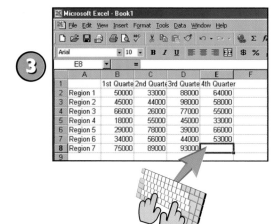

1. Click the mouse button when the pointer (notice that it is a plus sign) is in the cell you want (for example, cell **B1**).

2. Type text into a cell—in this case, **1st Quarter**—and press the → key to move one cell to the right.

3. Type data similar to that in the figure until you are familiar with how Excel displays the data in a worksheet.

4. Type your last cell of data and press the **Enter** key.

End Task

Task 2: Moving Around a Worksheet

Start Here

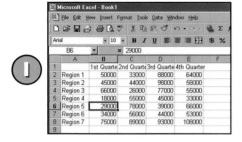

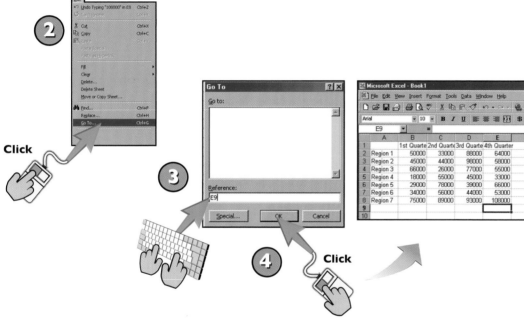

Click

Click

Getting Around in a Spreadsheet

Using a mouse is often the easiest way to move around a worksheet; you use the vertical or horizontal scrollbars to see other portions of the worksheet. However, you can also use the keyboard to move around, and with Excel's Go To command, you can quickly jump to cells that are out of view.

① Press the arrow keys (←, →, ↑, ↓) to get the feel of how you can move from cell to cell.

② Choose **Edit**, **Go To** to open the Go To dialog box.

③ Type the location of the cell you would like to go to in the Reference text box (for example, **E9**).

④ Click the **OK** button to move immediately to the cell reference.

✓ **The Beginning of the Worksheet**
Press the **Ctrl+Home** shortcut key to move immediately to cell A1 at the top left of the worksheet.

✓ **Quick Go To**
Press the **Ctrl+G** shortcut key to quickly open the Go To dialog box.

End Task

Task 3: Moving Around a Workbook

Getting Around in a Workbook

You can keep data stored on different worksheets pertinent to an entire workbook. Each tab in a workbook represents a worksheet. To view a sheet, click its tab. For example, you might want to keep sales data for the past two years. You can keep each year separately on its own worksheet but save everything in the same workbook file. You can also assign each worksheet a specific name and add more worksheets.

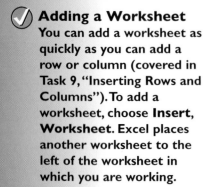

✓ Adding a Worksheet

You can add a worksheet as quickly as you can add a row or column (covered in Task 9, "Inserting Rows and Columns"). To add a worksheet, choose **Insert, Worksheet**. Excel places another worksheet to the left of the worksheet in which you are working.

Start Here

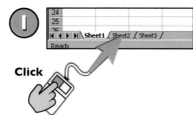

Click

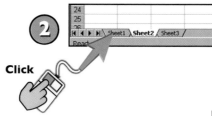

Click

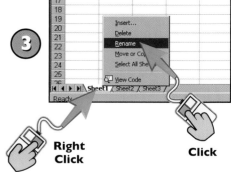

Right Click

Click

1. Click the **Sheet2** tab at the bottom left of the worksheet.

2. Click the **Sheet1** tab to return to the worksheet where you entered data.

3. Right-click the **Sheet1** tab and choose **Rename** from the shortcut menu.

Next Step

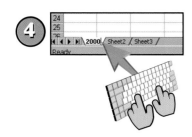

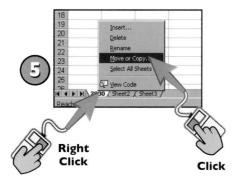

Right Click

Click

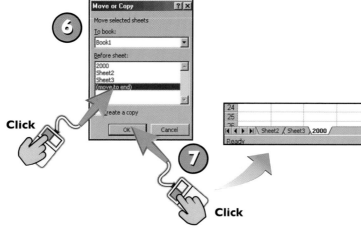

Click

Click

Deleting a Worksheet
To delete a worksheet quickly, right-click the sheet you want to delete and choose **Delete** from the shortcut menu.

Worksheet Charts
An option when creating a chart is to place the chart on a separate worksheet in a workbook. This can be a convenient way to view your data separately from the chart. See Part 6, Task 20, "Inserting Charts," for more information.

④ Type the name you would like for the worksheet (for example, **2000**) and press the **Enter** key.

⑤ Right-click the **2000** tab and choose **Move or Copy** from the shortcut menu to open the Move or Copy dialog box.

⑥ Click the location—for example, click **(move to end)**—you would like to move the worksheet to.

⑦ Click the **OK** button to move the worksheet.

Storing Your Work on Disk

Until you save the workbook you are working in, the data in the file is not stored on disk. It is good practice to regularly save your workbooks as you work in them. After you save a workbook, you can retrieve it later to work on.

✓ **Save In Options**
If you don't want to save your file in the **My Documents** directory, you can select the **Save In** drop-down list box and maneuver through your folders to save the file in a different location.

✓ **The Save Button**
If you have already named a file, you can click the **Save** button on the Standard toolbar to quickly save your recent changes.

Task 4: Saving a Workbook

Start Here

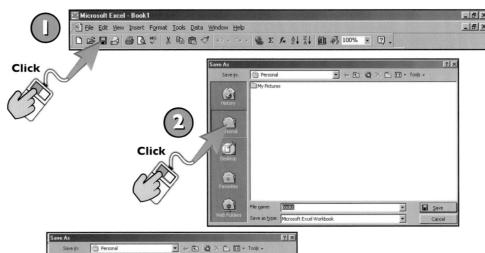

Click

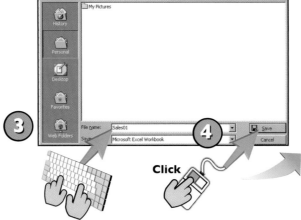

Click

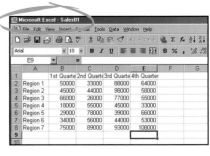

Click

① Click the **Save** button on the Standard toolbar.

② Click the **Personal** icon. (Your computer might show a **My Documents** icon instead.)

③ Type a different file name if you want (for example, **Sales01**) in the Save As dialog box.

④ Click the **Save** button in the Save As dialog box. The title bar now contains your workbook's name.

End Task

Task 5: Closing a Workbook

Start Here

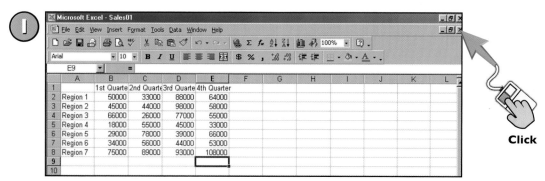

Click

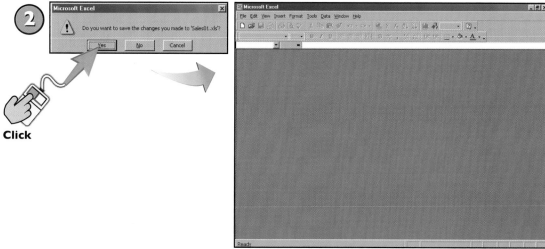

Click

Finishing with a Workbook

When you finish working on a workbook, you can close it and continue to work in the application. You can close a workbook with or without saving changes. If you have been working in a workbook and you try to close it, Excel asks you whether you want to save the workbook before it closes.

 **Available Buttons**
When Excel has no workbooks open, only a few buttons are available on the Standard toolbar. Notice that as soon as you create a new workbook (see Task 6, "Creating a New Workbook") or open a workbook (see Task 7, "Opening a Workbook"), the buttons are available again.

1. Click the **Close (×)** button. If you have made any changes to the workbook, Excel asks you to save the workbook.

2. Click the **Yes** button if you want to save changes; click the **No** button to close Excel without saving changes. Excel then closes the workbook.

End Task

Task 6: Creating a New Workbook

Adding a Workbook

Excel presents a new blank workbook each time you start the application. You can create another new workbook at any time, however. For example, when you save and close one workbook, you might want to begin a new one.

Start Here

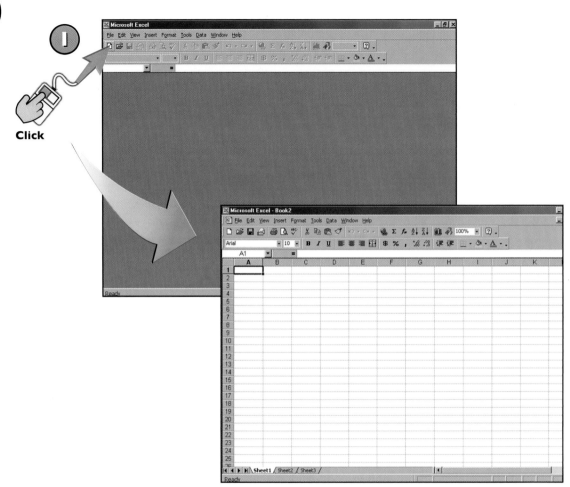

Click

✓ Default File Names

The default file name for each new workbook (Book1, Book2, Book3, and so on) automatically increases sequentially as you open new books. If you exit and start Excel again, the numbers begin at 1 again.

1 Click the **New** button on the Standard toolbar. Excel opens a new workbook with A1 as the active cell.

End Task

Task 7: Opening a Workbook

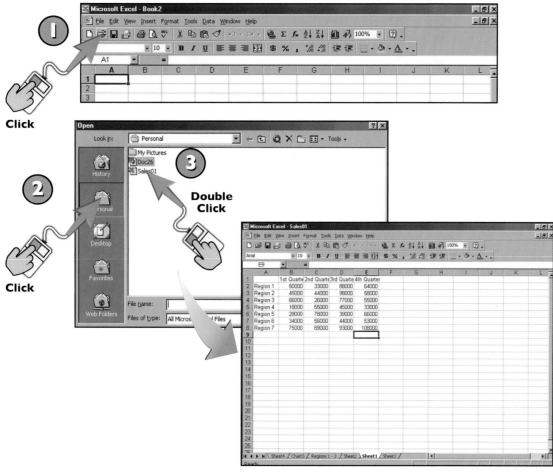

Click

Double Click

Click

Retrieving a Workbook from Disk

Each time you want to work with an Excel workbook, you need to open it. You have many options to choose from in the Open dialog box. If necessary, click the **Look In** drop-down arrow and choose a folder from the list. To move up a folder level, click the **Up One Level** button on the Open toolbar. If you double-click a subfolder, its contents appear in the **Files and Folders** list.

✅ Changing Dialog Box Views

You can view different information about the files in the Open dialog box (and the Save As dialog box, as shown in Task 4, "Saving a Workbook") by clicking the **Views** button on the dialog box's toolbar.

1. Click the **Open** button on the Standard toolbar.

2. Click the **Personal** icon on the **Places** bar (your icon might say **My Documents** instead).

3. Double-click the file you want to open in the Open dialog box (for example, **Sales01**), and Excel opens the workbook.

End Task

Task 8: Viewing Multiple Workbooks

Seeing Several Workbooks on the Screen

Instead of constantly switching between workbooks, you can view multiple workbooks on screen in Excel. This can be a convenient feature if you are comparing two workbooks or working on two workbooks at the same time. You can have more than two workbooks open at a time, and you can also resize their windows. The workbook displaying a darker title bar is the active workbook, and the active cell is visible in the active workbook.

✓ **Maximizing One Workbook**
To return to viewing only one workbook (maximizing the workbook), double-click the title bar of the workbook in which you want to work.

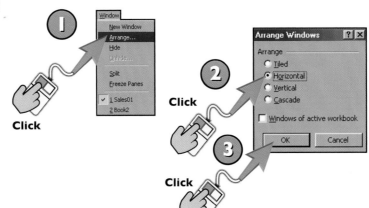

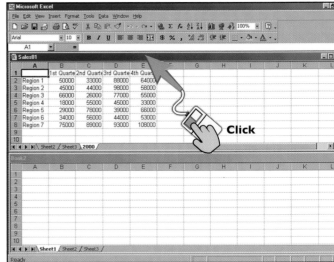

Click

Click

Click

Click

① Choose **Window, Arrange** to open the Arrange Windows dialog box.

② Click how you want the windows arranged (for example, **Horizontal**).

③ Click the **OK** button.

④ Click the title bar or in the body of the workbook you want to work in to make it the active worksheet.

Task 9: Inserting Rows and Columns

Start Here

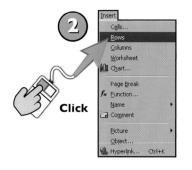

Click

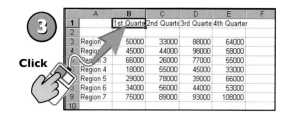

Click

Click

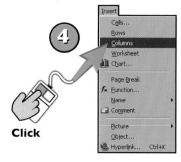

Click

End Task

Adding Rows and Columns

You can insert extra rows to make more room for additional data or formulas. Adding more rows, which gives the appearance of adding space between rows, can also make the worksheet easier to read. You can insert extra columns to make room for more data or formulas. Adding more space between columns also makes the worksheet easier to read.

 Automatic Formula Row Updates
When you insert a new row or column, Excel automatically updates any formulas affected by the insertion (see Part 6, "Working with Excel Worksheets," for more information).

① Click the cell above where you want to add a row (for example, **A2**).

② Choose **Insert, Rows** to insert a row above the column titles.

③ Click the cell to the left of which you want to add a column (for example, **B1**).

④ Choose **Insert, Columns** to insert a column to the left of the row titles.

Task 10: Deleting Rows and Columns

Removing Rows and Columns

You can delete rows or columns from a worksheet to close up some empty space or remove unwanted information.

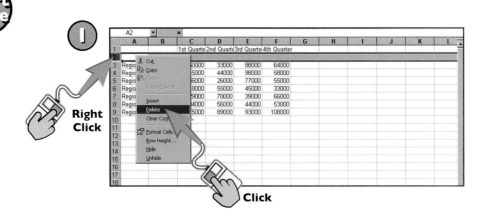

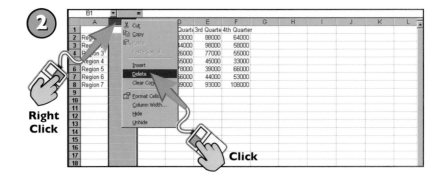

✅ #REF! Error

If the #REF! error appears in a cell after you delete a row, it means you deleted a cell or cells that contained data your worksheet needs to calculate a formula. Undo the change; Task 17, "Undoing and Redoing Changes," tells you how.

1 Right-click the heading of the row you want to delete (for example, **2**) and choose **Delete** from the shortcut menu.

2 Right-click the column heading of the column you want to delete (for example, **B**) and choose **Delete** from the shortcut menu.

Task 11: Selecting Cells

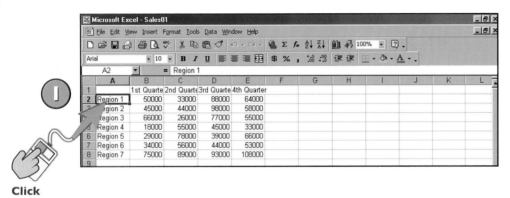

Click

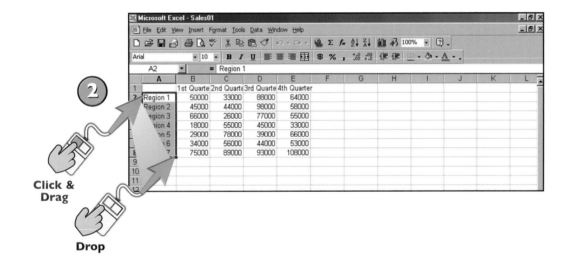

Click & Drag

Drop

Choosing Cells to Work With

You commonly need to select cells—it's the first step in doing anything with them, such as copying and pasting, formatting, and even deleting.

✓ **Using the Keyboard to Select Cells**
You can also select cells with the keyboard by pressing the **Shift** key and using the arrow keys (←, →, ↑, ↓) to select the cells. In addition, you can press and hold the **Ctrl** key while you click specific cells.

✓ **Selecting All Cells**
If you want to select the entire worksheet, click the gray box above row 1 and to the left of column A. In addition, you can use the **Ctrl+A** shortcut key to select the entire worksheet.

1 Click the first cell in the range of cells you want to select (for example, **A2**).

2 Click and drag to the opposite corner of the range of cells you want to select (for example, **A8**).

Task 12: Inserting Cells

Adding Cells

There are times when you are entering data into your worksheet and notice that you typed the wrong information so that you are off by one cell in a column or row. To avoid retyping all the data again, you can insert cells and shift the current cells to their correct locations.

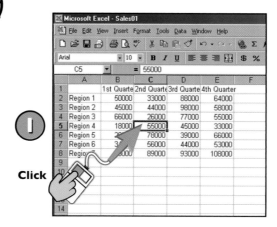

Click

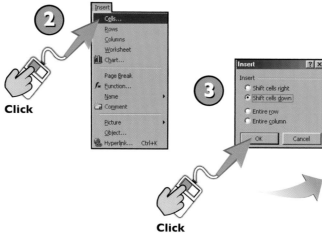

Click

Click

Click

✓ **Using the Shortcut Menu**
Another way to insert a cell is to right-click a cell and choose **Insert** from the shortcut menu to open the Insert dialog box.

1 Select the cells where you want to insert a cell (for example, **C5**).

2 Choose **Insert, Cells** to open the Insert dialog box.

3 Click the **OK** button to accept the **Shift Cells Down** default option when you insert the cells.

End Task

Task 13: Deleting Cells

Start Here

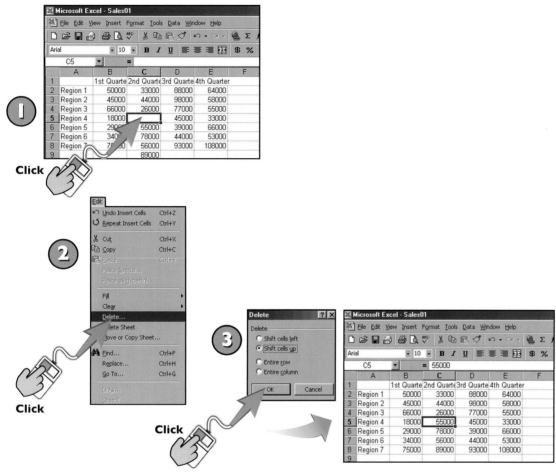

Click

Click

Click

Removing Cells

Sometimes when you're working with worksheets, you find that data needs to be eliminated to keep the worksheet up-to-date. Or perhaps you added an extraneous cell of data in a row or column. To avoid retyping all the data again, you can delete cells and shift the current cells to their correct locations.

 #REF! Error
If the #REF! error appears in a cell after you delete, it means you deleted data your worksheet needs to calculate a formula. Undo the change; Task 17, "Undoing and Redoing Changes," tells you how. For more on formulas, see Part 6, "Working with Excel Worksheets."

① Select the cells you want to delete (for example, cell **C5**).

② Choose **Edit**, **Delete** to open the Delete dialog box.

③ Click the **OK** button to accept the **Shift Cells Up** default option when you delete the cells.

End Task

Task 14: Cutting, Copying, and Pasting Data

Reusing Information

You can save the time and trouble of retyping information in the worksheet by copying cells and pasting them over and over again. A great new feature in Office 2000 is the ability to cut, copy, and paste up to 12 different items at a time. For example, if you need to copy two different selections of data from the beginning of a worksheet to two different locations toward the end of a worksheet, you can do the procedure in fewer steps, by using the Clipboard, than if you copy and paste each separately.

✓ **Cut Versus Copy**

When you want to move data from its current location and place it in a new location (rather than copying it), click the **Cut** button on the Standard toolbar instead of the **Copy** button. The Cut option removes the selected value from the old location.

Start Here

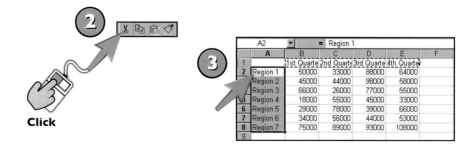

Click

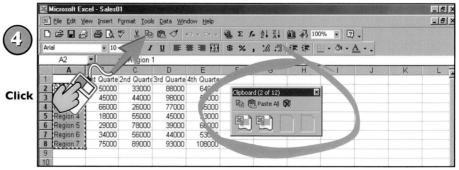

Click

(1) Select the cells you want to cut and paste, using the instructions in Task 11, "Selecting Cells."

(2) Click the **Cut** button on the Standard toolbar.

(3) Select the cells you want to copy and paste.

(4) Click the **Copy** button on the Standard toolbar. Notice that the Clipboard toolbar appears.

Next Step

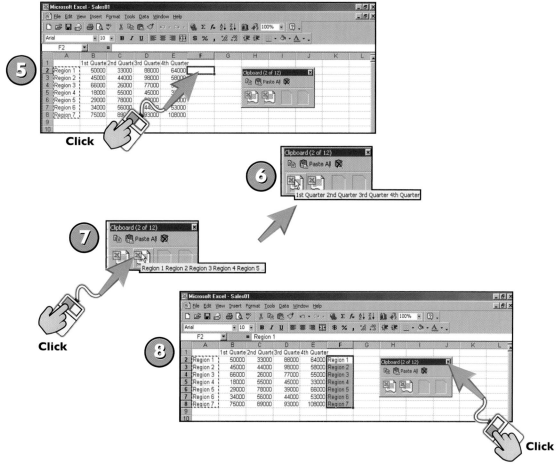

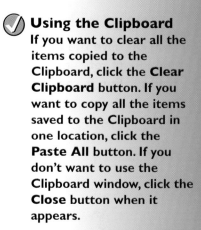

✓ Using the Clipboard

If you want to clear all the items copied to the Clipboard, click the **Clear Clipboard** button. If you want to copy all the items saved to the Clipboard in one location, click the **Paste All** button. If you don't want to use the Clipboard window, click the **Close** button when it appears.

✓ Keeping the Clipboard Open

You can keep the Clipboard window open and use the buttons while you work. It might be easier to move the Clipboard window out of the way by dragging and dropping it as you would a toolbar or docking it with your other toolbars (see Part 1, Task 4, "Using Toolbars," for more information).

✓ Pasting Formulas

If you paste cells using **Ctrl+V**, you can paste cell *formulas*. If you paste cells with formulas from the multi-element Clipboard, you paste the *values*, not the formulas.

5 Click to place the cursor in the worksheet where you want to paste the data.

6 Move the mouse pointer over the Clipboard items, and a ScreenTip displays what is contained in each copied clip.

7 Click the Clipboard toolbar clip button of the item you want to copy.

8 Click the **Close (×)** button to return to the worksheet.

Task 15: Moving Data

Putting Data Somewhere Else

Excel lets you move information from one cell and place it into another cell. You do not have to go to the new cell and enter the same data and then erase the data in the old location. For example, you might want to move data in a worksheet because the layout of the worksheet has changed.

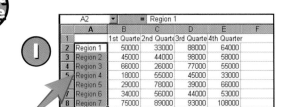

Start Here

Click & Drag

A10:A16

Drop

✓ Undoing a Move

If you move the wrong data or move the data to the wrong location, click the **Undo** button on the Standard toolbar to undo the most recent move. Then start over. See Task 17, "Undoing and Redoing Changes," for more information.

1 Select the cells you want to move (for example, **A2:A8**). See Task II, "Selecting Cells," for instructions.

2 Click the border of the selected cells and drag the cells to the location where you want to paste the cell data (for example **A10:A16**).

3 Drop the data you are moving, and it remains in the new location.

End Task

Task 16: Overwriting and Deleting Data

Start Here

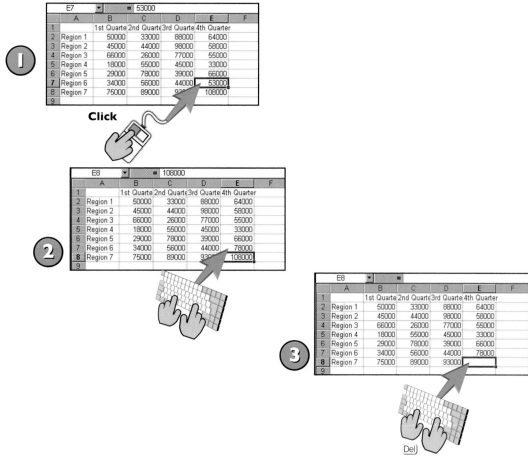

Click

Del

End Task

Getting Rid of Data

Overwriting a cell means replacing the cell's contents with new data. Overwriting is handy when you want to correct typing errors or when a cell contains the wrong data. You can also easily erase the contents of a cell by using the Delete key. Erasing a cell is useful when you change your mind about the contents after you enter the data in the cell. You might find that a piece of data you initially typed into a cell is incorrect and needs to be changed.

! WARNING

Be careful not to overwrite formulas if that is not what you intended. If you overwrite a formula with a constant value, Excel no longer updates the formula. If you accidentally overwrite a formula but you've saved your spreadsheet recently, use the **Undo** button or reopen the spreadsheet to a version saved before you overwrote the formula.

---

1 Click the cell you want to overwrite, making it the active cell (for example, **E7**).

2 Type the correct data into the cell (for example, **78000**) and press the **Enter** key.

3 Press the **Delete** key to delete data in a cell, such as the contents of cell **E8**.

Task 17: Undoing and Redoing Changes

Using Undo and Redo

Many times you when you are making numerous changes to your worksheets, you need to undo some of the changes. Excel enables you to undo changes and redo them so you can quickly see the differences between the two.

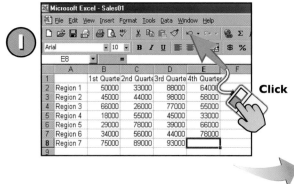

Click

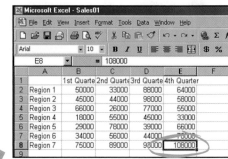

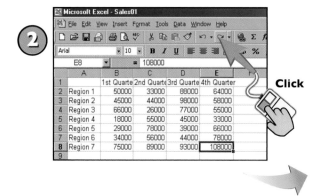

Click

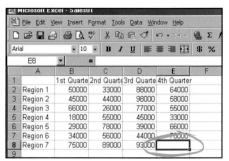

✓ **Multiple Undo and Redo**
Instead of repeatedly clicking the **Undo** and **Redo** buttons to get your worksheet back to the way you want it, you can click the drop-down arrow next to either button and select all the actions you want to undo or redo all at once.

① Click the **Undo** button on the Standard toolbar to undo each change you recently made.

② Click the **Redo** button on the Standard toolbar to redo each change you recently made.

✓ **Keyboard Undo**
A quick and easy way to undo an action is to use the **Ctrl+Z** shortcut key.

Task 18: Finding Data

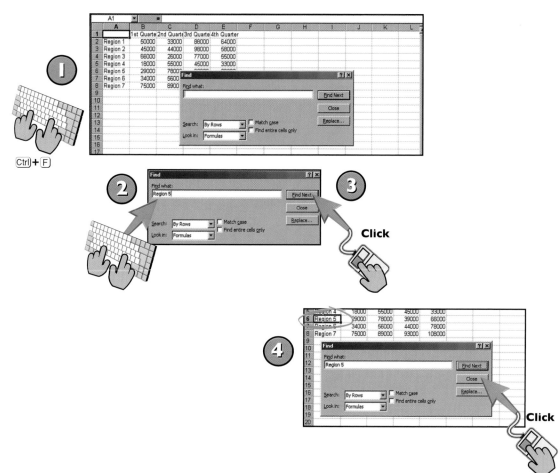

Ctrl + F

Click

2

3

Click

4

Using Find

You'll sometimes need to find specific information in a large spreadsheet. For example, suppose you want to quickly find the row that deals with sales data in Region 5. The worksheet in this task is small, so it's not hard to find the information, but it serves as a simple example.

✓ **Doesn't Exist**
If the data you are searching for doesn't exist in the worksheet, Excel will alert you in a message box.

✓ **Finding Other Instances of Data**
Another way to search for data is to choose **Edit, Find**. To continue searching for more occurrences of a Find criterion, click the **Find Next** button.

1. Press **Ctrl+F** to open the Find dialog box.

2. Type the data you would like to find (for example, **Region 5**) in the **Find What** text box.

3. Click the **Find Next** button. Excel immediately finds the first instance of the information (if it exists in the worksheet) and makes it the active cell.

4. Choose the **Close** button to end the search.

Task 19: Replacing Data

Using Find and Replace

You may be working in a workbook and notice that you need to alter multiple cells of data. Perhaps you spelled a company name incorrectly throughout the workbook, or maybe you just want to enhance the data (for example, capitalizing a particular word throughout).

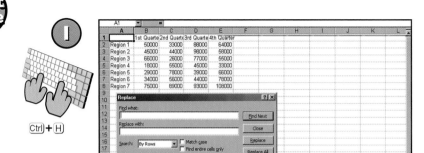

Ctrl + H

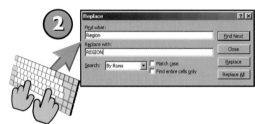

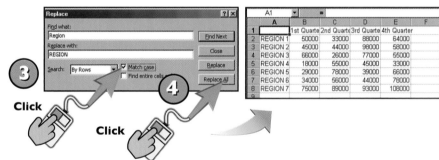

Click

Click

Start
Here

✓ **Searching and Replacing One at a Time**
You can search the workbook and replace each occurrence one at a time by clicking Replace instead of Replace All.

1 Press **Ctrl+H** to open the Replace dialog box.

2 Type the data to find (for example, **Region**) in the **Find What** text box. Then, type the data to replace it with (for example, **REGION**) in the **Replace With** text box.

3 Click the **Match Case** check box. With this box checked, *Region* doesn't match *REGION*. With this box unchecked, *Region* matches *REGION*.

4 Click the **Replace All** button. Excel replaces all the occurrences, and closes the Replace dialog box.

Task 20: Protecting and Sharing Workbooks

Start Here

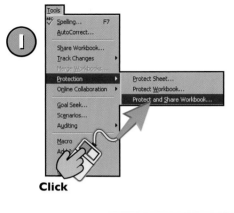

Click

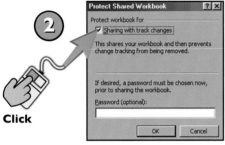

Click

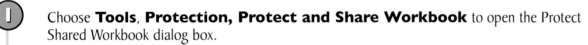

End Task

Assigning File Sharing Options

When you share files with other users, you might find it useful to protect your workbooks. You can protect your workbooks by restricting access to the workbook and preventing changes being made within each particular workbook. You can unprotect your worksheet by choosing **Tools, Protection, Unprotect Shared Workbook**.

① WARNING
Don't forget the password you assign to your workbooks. If you forget the password, you are not able to access the workbook. Choose a password you can remember but that others can't guess. Avoid names of pets or family members. The most difficult passwords to guess are at least five characters long and contain at least one symbol character, such as $, %, &, or @.

① Choose **Tools, Protection, Protect and Share Workbook** to open the Protect Shared Workbook dialog box.

② Click the **Sharing with Track Changes** option (this activates the optional password text box), and then press the **Tab** key (see Task 21, "Tracking Changes").

③ Type a password in the **Password (optional)** text box, and press the **Enter** key. This means that any other user needs to enter the same password to open this workbook.

④ Type the same password in the Confirm Password dialog box, and press the **Enter** key. Have someone else try to open the file with and without the password.

Task 21: Tracking Changes

Keeping Track of Revision Marks

Excel lets you track changes that have been made to your worksheets. This is convenient when you are working on a team project, such as when multiple people are writing a report. For example, each person who adds data to the workbook can turn revision marks on so any changes they make show up in a different color from changes other team members make. The only time the colors won't be different is when two people use the same computer or user information (such as login or password).

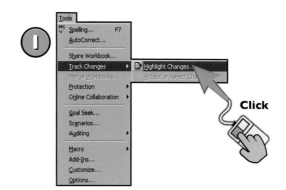

Click

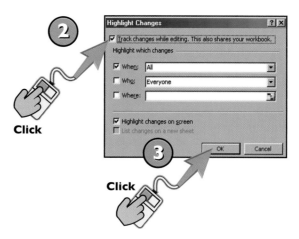

Click

Click

Start Here

✓ **Shared Workbooks**
If you performed the tasks in Task 20, "Protecting and Sharing Workbooks," the option in Step 2 is not available. This is because you are automatically tracking changes if your workbook is shared.

1. Choose **Tools**, **Track Changes**, **Highlight Changes** to open the Highlight Changes dialog box.

2. Click **Track Changes While Editing. This Also Shares Your Workbook**.

3. Click the **OK** button. A message box appears, telling you that this action will save the workbook and asking if you want to continue.

Next Step

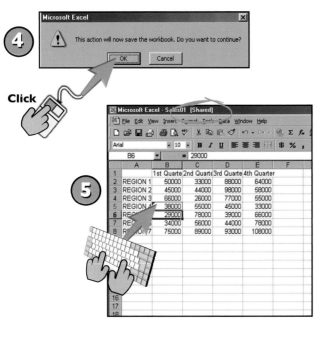

Click

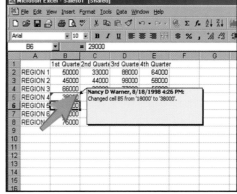

Tracked Changes
Excel remembers the previous value for a tracked change in case you want to go back; Task 22 explains how.

Shared Workbooks
Notice the word [Shared] in the title bar. This means that other people can use the workbook. This is mostly useful in a network setting, where others can easily access your worksheet via the network. When you turn on tracking marks, you automatically share the workbook. In the Highlight dialog box, deselect the check box next to **Track Changes While Editing. This Also Shares Your Workbook.** This turns off track marks and stops sharing your workbook.

④ Click the **OK** button, and the workbook title bar states that the workbook is now **[Shared]** next to the filename.

⑤ Type a change in a cell (for example, cell **B5**), and press the **Enter** key. Notice that the cell now has a comment marker in the upper-left corner and colored border.

⑥ Move the mouse pointer over the revised cell, and a ScreenTip appears, showing the change that was made, who made the change, and when.

Task 22: Accepting or Rejecting Tracked Changes

Keeping or Discarding Revision Marks

When you are ready to finalize any tracked changes that have been made to a worksheet, you need to determine which changes you want to accept or reject. If you accept a change, Excel keeps it. If you reject a change, Excel restores the previous value and deletes the tracked change.

(✓) **Accepting and Rejecting**

In the Select Changes to Accept or Reject dialog box, click the **Reject** button to return the tracked mark to the original text; click the **Accept** button to accept a tracked change as you review the workbook changes; or click the **Reject All** button to reject all changes that have been made to the workbook.

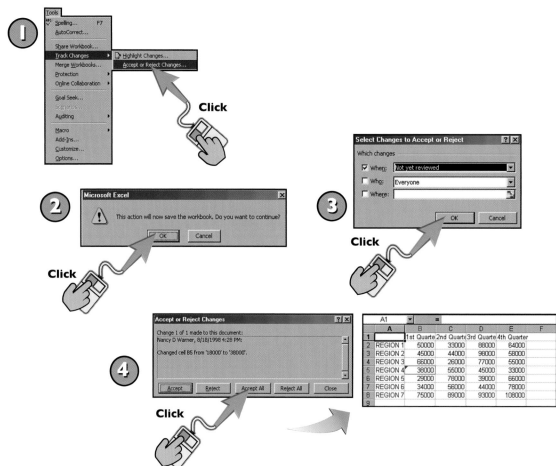

Click

Click

Click

Click

Click

1 Choose **Tools**, **Track Changes**, **Accept or Reject Changes**.

2 Click the **OK** button in the message box that appears, telling you that this action saves the workbook, unless you just recently saved the workbook.

3 Click the **OK** button to accept the default options in the list boxes for **When**, **Who**, and **Where** you want to accept or reject a change.

4 Click the **Accept All** button to accept all changes in the workbook. Notice that the comment marker remains for your reference.

Task 23: Checking Spelling

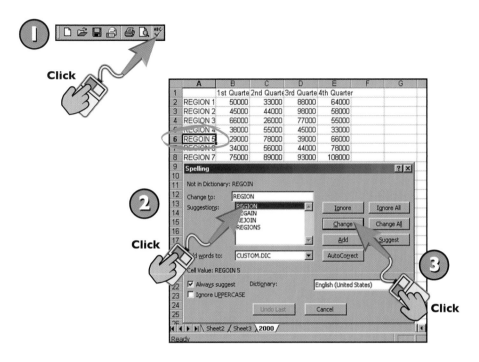

Click

Click

Click

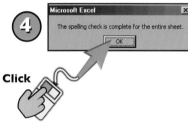

Click

Making Sure Your Data Is Spelled Correctly

Many people take spelling in workbooks for granted. But if you turn in a report to your manager, he or she might not like seeing spelling errors and mistakes. You can check spelling in Excel 2000 quickly and easily. Of course, you should always review your workbooks, but it never hurts to have a little help.

✓ Checking from the Beginning
You don't have to be at the beginning of a workbook when you check for spelling errors. If you start in the middle of a workbook, Excel checks until it reaches the end and then asks you whether you want to continue checking from the beginning of your workbook.

---

1 Click the **Spelling** button on the Standard toolbar. The Spelling dialog box opens, displaying the first spelling or grammar error it finds.

2 Click the appropriate spelling option in the **Suggestions** list box (in this case, **REGION**).

3 Click the **Change** button. Excel makes the change in the workbook and moves to the next error it finds.

4 Click the **OK** button when Excel displays a message telling you the spelling check is complete. This means all inaccuracies have been reviewed.

Working with Excel Worksheets

In Excel, a *formula* calculates a value based on the values in other cells of the workbook. Excel displays the result of a formula in a cell as a numeric value.

Functions are abbreviated formulas that perform a specific operation on a group of values. Excel provides more than 250 functions that can help with tasks ranging from determining loan payments to calculating investment returns. For example, the SUM function is a shortcut for entering an addition formula. SUM is the name of the function that automatically adds entries in a range. First you type **=SUM(** in either lower- or uppercase letters. Then you select the range. You end the function by typing **)**, which also tells Excel you are finished selecting the range.

The way you refer to a cell in a formula determines how the formula is affected when you copy it into a different cell. You can use three types of cell references—relative, absolute, and mixed. The formulas you create in this part contain *relative cell references*. When you copy a formula from one cell to another, the relative cell references in the formula change to reflect the new location of the formula.

An *absolute cell reference* does not change when you copy the formula to a new cell. In certain formulas, you might want an entry to always refer to one specific cell value. For example, you might want to calculate the interest on several different principal amounts. The interest percentage remains unchanged, or absolute, so you designate the entry in the formula that refers to the interest percentage as an absolute cell reference. The principal amounts do change, so they have relative cell reference entries in the formula. When you copy this absolute formula, the interest cell reference always refers to the one cell that contains the interest percentage.

A *mixed cell reference* is a single cell entry in a formula that contains both a relative and an absolute cell reference. A mixed cell reference is helpful when you need a formula that always refers to the values in a specific column but the values in the rows must change, and vice versa.

Tasks

Task 1: Using AutoSum

Automatically Summing Cells

In a worksheet, if you want to show a sum of values from some cells, you could add them yourself and type the total. But if you then change any of the values, the sum becomes inaccurate. Excel can use formulas to perform calculations for you. Because a formula refers to the cells rather than to the values, Excel updates the sum whenever you change the values in the cells.

✓ Selecting Specific AutoSum Cells

If you don't want to use AutoSum on the cells Excel selects for you, you can click the first cell you want, hold down the **Shift** key, and click each additional cell you would like to include in the calculation. When you finish selecting the cells you want to calculate, press **Enter** to see the result.

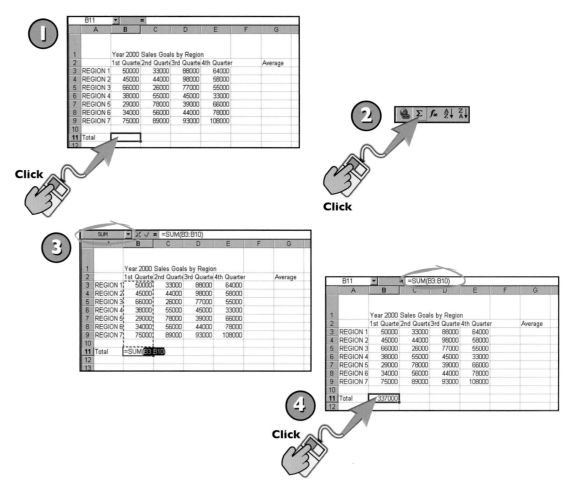

Start Here

Click

Click

Click

① Click cell **B11**. The result of the formula will appear in this cell.

② Click the **AutoSum** button on the Standard toolbar. Excel selects the most obvious range of numbers to calculate and indicates this with a dotted line around the cells.

③ Press the **Enter** key; the Function box displays the type of function (SUM).

④ Click cell **B11** to make it the active cell. Notice that the formula is displayed in the Formula bar.

End Task

Task 2: Entering a Formula

Start Here

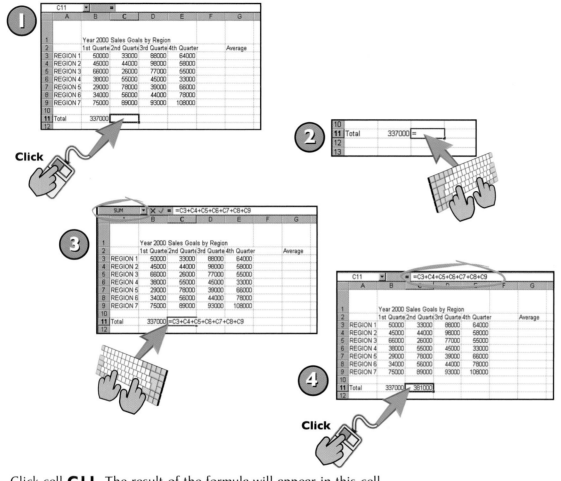

Typing Formulas

Sometimes you don't want to use **AutoSum** because you have specific cell references on which you want to perform calculations. In this instance, you can simply type the desired formula directly into the cell.

✓ **Altering Values**

After you enter a formula, you can change the values in the referenced cells, and Excel automatically recalculates the value of the formula based on the cell changes. You can include any cells in your formula; they do not have to be next to each other. Also, you can combine mathematic operations—for example, **C3+C4-D5**.

① Click cell **C11**. The result of the formula will appear in this cell.

② Type = (an equals sign).

③ Type **C3+C4+C5+C6+C7+C8+C9** and press the **Enter** key. Notice that the Function box displays the type of function (SUM), and the results appear in the cell.

④ Click cell **C11** to make it the active cell. Notice that the formula is displayed in the Formula bar.

✓ **Canceling a Formula**

If you start to enter a formula and then decide you don't want to use it, you can skip entering the formula by pressing the Esc key.

End Task

Task 3: Entering a Function

Working with Functions

A function is one of Excel's many built-in formulas for performing a specialized calculation on the data in your worksheet. For example, instead of totaling your sales data, maybe you want to know the average of each quarter per region (the Average function). Or maybe you want to know in which quarter you had the largest sales (the Max function) and smallest sales (the Min function).

✓ **The Paste Function Dialog Box**

The Paste Function dialog box offers many functions. Practice using different functions and see the results you get from your calculations. As you experiment, you can move the Paste Function dialog box around or collapse it to see your cells.

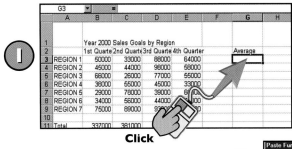

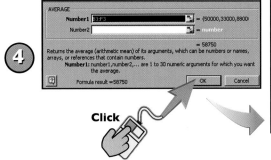
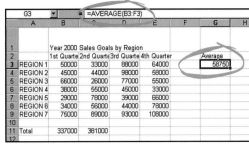

Start Here

1 Click cell **G3**. The result of the function will appear in this cell.

2 Click the **Paste Function** button on the Standard toolbar to open the Paste Function dialog box.

3 Double-click the **AVERAGE** option in the **Function Name** list box. Excel selects the range of cells that it determines you want to average.

4 Click the **OK** button. The result appears in the active cell, and the function is displayed in the Formula bar.

Task 4: Copying a Formula

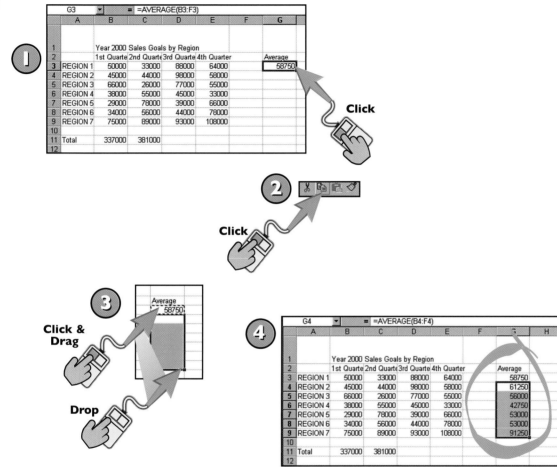

Click

Click

Click & Drag

Drop

Reusing a Formula

When you build your worksheet, you probably use the same data and formulas in more than one cell. With Excel's Copy command, you can create the initial data or formula once and then place copies of this information in the appropriate cells. You do not have to go to each cell and enter the same formula. You create the formula for the first cell and copy it to the other cells where you want the formula.

List AutoFill

A new feature in Excel 2000 is List AutoFill, which automatically extends formatting and formulas in lists. For example, create a list with different fields in each column and totals in the bottom row; format the list in a consistent way (font size and color). If you add a new column to the right, Excel fills in the formatting and total formula for you.

---

1. Click the cell that contains the formula you want to copy (here, **G3**).

2. Click the **Copy** button on the Standard toolbar.

3. Click and drag the mouse pointer over all the cells where you want to paste the function. A dotted line surrounds the cell you are copying.

4. Press the **Enter** key to paste the function into each of the specified cells.

Task 5: Using AutoCalculate

Automatically Calculating Results

Perhaps you want to see a function performed on some of your data, such as finding out which region has the highest fourth quarter sales goal in the year 2000. But you don't want to add the function directly into the worksheet. Excel's AutoCalculate feature can help.

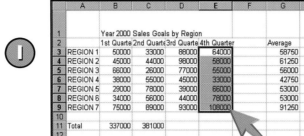

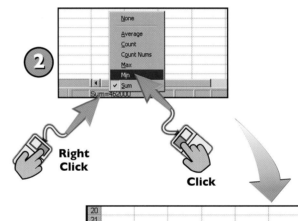

Right Click

Click

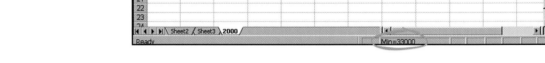

✓ **Order of Operation**

Excel first performs any calculations within parentheses: (1+2)=3. Then it performs multiplication or division calculations, from left to right: (12+24)/(3*2)=6. Finally, it performs any addition or subtraction, from left to right: (12+24)/(3*2)-5=1.

✓ **Turning Off AutoCalculate**

You can turn off the AutoCalculate feature by choosing **None** from the AutoCalculate shortcut menu.

Select the cells that you want to automatically calculate the average, count, count numbers, maximum, minimum, or sum.

Right-click the status bar and choose **Min** (to choose the minimum number in the selection) from the shortcut menu. Notice that the default AutoCalculate feature is to sum the numbers.

Task 6: Applying Styles to Numeric Data

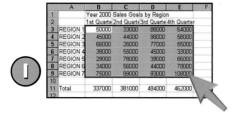

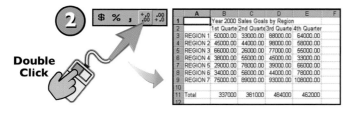

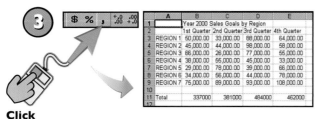

Working with Styles

You can apply different styles to cells, depending on the type of data the cells contain. Using styles affects the way cells display data but does not limit the type of data you can enter. By placing data into a style, you can display it in a familiar format that makes it easier to read. For example, sales numbers tend to be styled in a currency format, and scientific data is usually styled with commas and decimal points.

1. Select the cells you want to format.

2. Double-click on the **Increase Decimal** button on the Formatting toolbar.

3. Click the **Comma Style** button on the Formatting toolbar.

4. Click the **Currency Style** button on the Formatting toolbar.

✔ **Choosing Other Styles**
You can choose from numerous other styles that you can apply to data. To see the selection of other styles, choose **Format, Cells**, and click through the many **Category** options.

Formatting Data

You can format the data contained in one or more cells to draw attention to it or make it easier to find. Numbers attract attention when formatted with bold, italic, or underline. Indicating summary values, questionable data, or any other cells is easy with formatting.

✓ **Combination Formatting**

You can use several formatting techniques in combination, such as bold and italic or italic and underline.

Task 7: Applying Bold, Italics, and Underline

Start Here

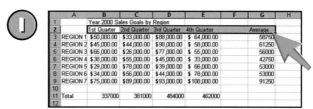

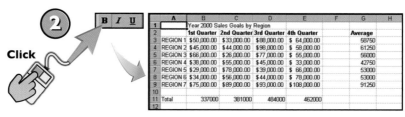
Click

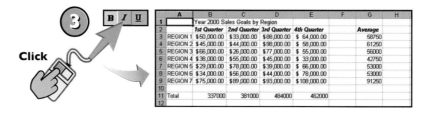
Click

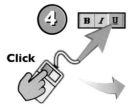
Click

End Task

① Select the cells you want to format.

② Click the **Bold** button on the Formatting toolbar.

③ Click the **Italic** button on the Formatting toolbar.

④ Click the **Underline** button on the Formatting toolbar.

Task 8: Changing Alignment

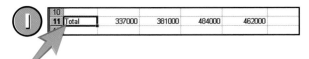

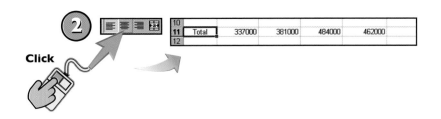

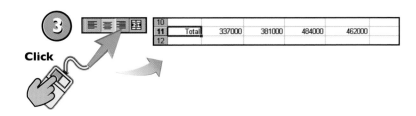

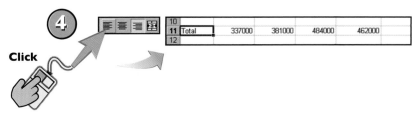

Aligning Data in a Cell

Excel provides several ways to format data. One way is to align data. The most common alignment changes you make are probably to center data in a cell, align data with a cell's right edge (right-aligned), or align data with a cell's left edge (left-aligned). The default alignment for numbers is right-aligned; the default alignment for text is left-aligned.

(1) Select the cells you want to align.

(2) Click the **Center** button on the Formatting toolbar.

(3) Click the **Align Right** button on the Formatting toolbar.

(4) Click the **Align Left** button on the Formatting toolbar.

✓ Default Alignment
After you select text to align, if you click the same alignment button a second time, the cell returns to its default alignment.

Task 9: Wrapping Text in a Cell

Using the Wrap Text Feature

Excel provides several ways to format data. One way is to allow text to wrap in a cell. Many times a heading (row or column, for example) is longer than the width of the cell holding the data. If you are trying to make your worksheet organized and readable, it is a good idea to wrap text so it is completely visible in a cell.

Start Here

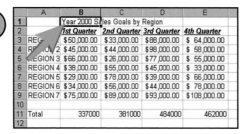

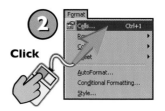

2 Click

3 Click

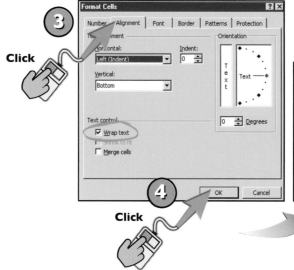

4 Click

✓ **Aligning Wrapped Text**
You can align text that has been wrapped. Sometimes this gives a cleaner look to your text. See Task 8, "Changing Alignment," to learn how to align text in a cell.

1 Select the cells in which you want text to wrap.

2 Choose **Format, Cells** to open the Format Cells dialog box.

3 Click the **Alignment** tab and select **Wrap Text** in the **Text Control** area of the Format Cells dialog box.

4 Click the **OK** button.

End Task

Task 10: Using Merge and Center on a Cell

	A	B	C	D	E
1		Year 2000 Sales Goals by Region			
2		*1st Quarter*	*2nd Quarter*	*3rd Quarter*	*4th Quarter*
3	REGION 1	$50,000.00	$33,000.00	$88,000.00	$ 64,000.00
4	REGION 2	$45,000.00	$44,000.00	$98,000.00	$ 58,000.00
5	REGION 3	$66,000.00	$26,000.00	$77,000.00	$ 55,000.00
6	REGION 4	$38,000.00	$55,000.00	$45,000.00	$ 33,000.00
7	REGION 5	$29,000.00	$78,000.00	$39,000.00	$ 66,000.00
8	REGION 6	$34,000.00	$56,000.00	$44,000.00	$ 78,000.00
9	REGION 7	$75,000.00	$89,000.00	$93,000.00	$108,000.00
10					
11	Total	337000	381000	484000	462000
12					

Merging Cells

Excel provides several ways to format data. One way is to use the **Merge and Center feature. Columns of data usually have column headers, but they can also have group header information within a set of columns. For example, you might have four quarters' worth of sales data for the past two years, but want to have a header that distinguishes each set of quarters by year.

Click

	A	B	C	D	E	F	G	H
1								
2		Year 2000 Sales Goals by Region						
2		*1st Quarter*	*2nd Quarter*	*3rd Quarter*	*4th Quarter*		*Average*	
3	REGION 1	$50,000.00	$33,000.00	$88,000.00	$ 64,000.00		58750	
4	REGION 2	$45,000.00	$44,000.00	$98,000.00	$ 58,000.00		61250	
5	REGION 3	$66,000.00	$26,000.00	$77,000.00	$ 55,000.00		56000	
6	REGION 4	$38,000.00	$55,000.00	$45,000.00	$ 33,000.00		42750	
7	REGION 5	$29,000.00	$78,000.00	$39,000.00	$ 66,000.00		53000	
8	REGION 6	$34,000.00	$56,000.00	$44,000.00	$ 78,000.00		53000	
9	REGION 7	$75,000.00	$89,000.00	$93,000.00	$108,000.00		91250	
10								
11	Total	337000	381000	484000	462000			
12								

 Select the cells you want to merge and center.

 Click the **Merge and Center** button on the Formatting toolbar.

 Undoing Merged and Centered Cells
You can undo a set of merged and centered cells by first selecting the set of cells that are merged together. Choose **Format, Cells.** Then click the **Alignment** tab and click the **Merge Cells** check box to deselect this option.

Task 11: Changing Borders

Working with Cell Borders

Each side of a cell is considered a border. These borders provide a visual cue as to where a cell begins and ends. You can customize borders to indicate other beginnings and endings, such as grouping similar data or separating headings from data. For example, a double line is often used to separate a summary value from the data being totaled. Changing the bottom of the border for the last number before the total accomplishes this effect.

	A	B	C	D	E	F	G
1			Year 2000 Sales Goals by Region				
2		*1st Quarter*	*2nd Quarter*	*3rd Quarter*	*4th Quarter*		*Average*
3	REGION 1	$50,000.00	$33,000.00	$88,000.00	$ 64,000.00		58750
4	REGION 2	$45,000.00	$44,000.00	$98,000.00	$ 58,000.00		61250
5	REGION 3	$66,000.00	$26,000.00	$77,000.00	$ 55,000.00		56000
6	REGION 4	$38,000.00	$55,000.00	$45,000.00	$ 33,000.00		42750
7	REGION 5	$29,000.00	$78,000.00	$39,000.00	$ 66,000.00		53000
8	REGION 6	$34,000.00	$56,000.00	$44,000.00	$ 78,000.00		53000
9	REGION 7	$75,000.00	$89,000.00	$93,000.00	$108,000.00		91250
10							
11	Total	337000	381000	484000	462000		
12							

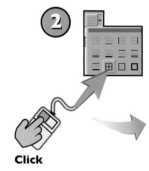

Click

	A	B	C	D	E	F	G
1			Year 2000 Sales Goals by Region				
2		*1st Quarter*	*2nd Quarter*	*3rd Quarter*	*4th Quarter*		*Average*
3	REGION 1	$50,000.00	$33,000.00	$88,000.00	$ 64,000.00		58750
4	REGION 2	$45,000.00	$44,000.00	$98,000.00	$ 58,000.00		61250
5	REGION 3	$66,000.00	$26,000.00	$77,000.00	$ 55,000.00		56000
6	REGION 4	$38,000.00	$55,000.00	$45,000.00	$ 33,000.00		42750
7	REGION 5	$29,000.00	$78,000.00	$39,000.00	$ 66,000.00		53000
8	REGION 6	$34,000.00	$56,000.00	$44,000.00	$ 78,000.00		53000
9	REGION 7	$75,000.00	$89,000.00	$93,000.00	$108,000.00		91250
10							
11	Total	337000	381000	484000	462000		
12							
13							

✓ **Removing Borders**
To remove a border, click the **No Border** option from the **Borders** drop-down menu.

✓ **Floating Toolbars**
You can click the top of the **Borders** drop-down menu and drag the menu to make it a floating toolbar.

1 Select the cells to which you want to add some type of border.

2 Click the Borders option (for example, **All Borders**) on the drop-down menu.

End Task

Task 12: Choosing Font Settings

Start Here

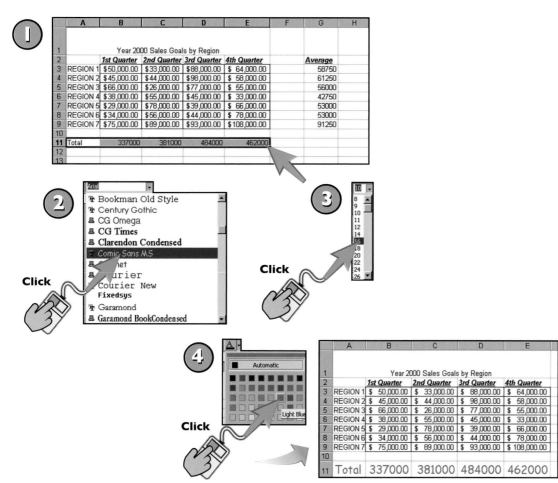

Changing Typefaces

You can format data by changing the font used to display it. Changing the font gives data a different look and feel, which can help differentiate the type of data a cell contains. You can also change the font's size and color for added emphasis. For example, you can display subheadings as a different size font than main headings, or display different columns of data in different colors to differentiate them.

✓ Fonts Sample
New in Office 2000 is the ability to see a sample of a font in the Font drop-down list box. You can see what the font looks like before you apply it to your cells. This helps you choose the right font faster.

✓ Formatting Options
To format only a portion of a cell's data, select only that portion and then change the font.

1 Select the cells you want to format.

2 Click the **Font** drop-down list and choose the font you would like to apply to the cells (for example, **Comic Sans MS**).

3 Click the **Font Size** drop-down list and choose the font size you would like to apply to the cells (for example, **16**).

4 Click the **Font Color** drop-down menu and click the font color you would like to apply to the cells (for example, **Light Blue**).

End Task

Task 13: Filling Cell Color

Coloring Cells

Generally, cells present a white background for displaying data. However, you can apply other colors or shading to the background. In addition, you can combine these colors with various patterns for a more attractive effect. As with most formatting options, this can help emphasize more important data.

⚠ WARNING

Be sure a shading or color pattern doesn't interfere with the readability of data. The data still needs to be clear; you might need to make the text bold or choose a complementary text color. If you print the worksheet to a noncolor printer, the color you choose prints gray. The darker the gray, the less readable the data. Yellow generally prints to a pleasing light gray that doesn't compete with the data.

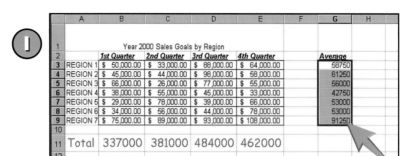

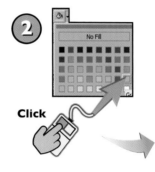

Click

1 Select the cells you want to color.

2 Click the shading or color you would like to apply on the **Fill Color** drop-down menu.

End Task

Task 14: Changing Cell Orientation

Start Here

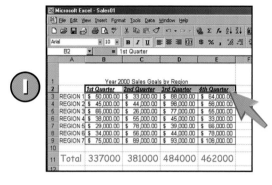

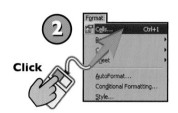

Click

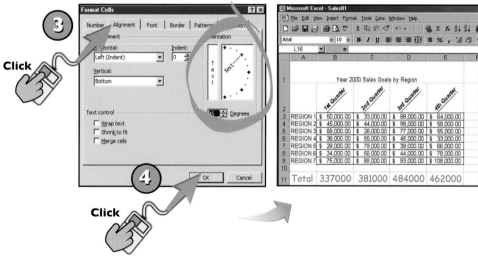

Click

Click

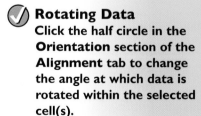

Running Text at an Angle

Excel lets you alter the orientation of cells—that is, the angle at which it displays information. The main reason for doing this is to help draw attention to important or special text. This feature can be convenient when you have a lot of columns in a worksheet and you don't want your column headers to take up much horizontal space or if you simply want the information to stand out.

① Select the cells that you want to alter the orientation.

② Choose **Format, Cells** to open the Format Cells dialog box.

③ Click the **Alignment** tab and select orientation options in the **Orientation** area (for example, **45 Degrees**).

④ Click the **OK** button.

✓ **Rotating Data**
Click the half circle in the **Orientation** section of the **Alignment** tab to change the angle at which data is rotated within the selected cell(s).

End Task

Task 15: Changing Row Height

Sizing Rows

Depending on the other formatting changes you make to a cell, data might not display properly. Increasing the font size or forcing data to wrap within a cell might prevent data from being entirely displayed or cause it to run over into other cells. You can frequently avoid these problems by resizing rows.

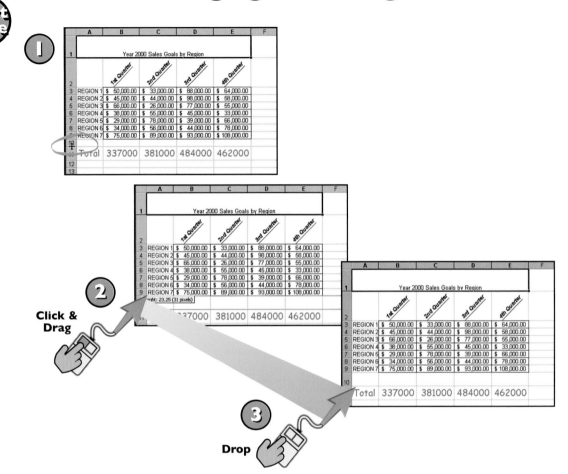

Click & Drag

Drop

✓ **Multiple Rows, Same Height**

To make multiple rows the same height, click the mouse and drag over all the row headers you want resized. Then resize one of the rows. Each row becomes that size.

✓ **AutoFit Rows**

To automatically make a row fit the height of the tallest cell, choose **Format, Row, AutoFit Selection.**

1. Move the mouse pointer over the bottom edge of the row header you want to alter. The pointer changes to a two-headed arrow.

2. Click and drag the row edge to the new size.

3. Release the mouse button to drop the line in the new location.

Task 16: Changing Column Width

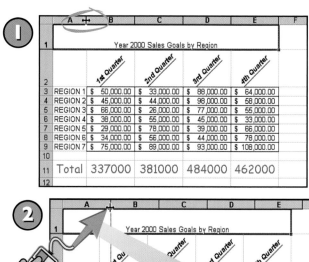

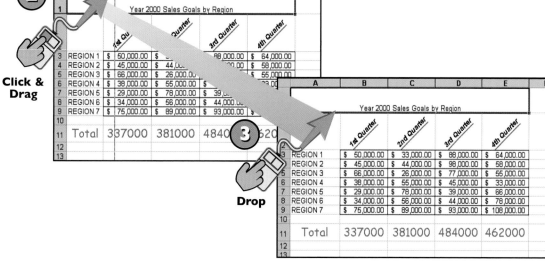

Click & Drag

Drop

Resizing Columns

Many times data is too wide to be displayed within a cell. Excel provides several alternatives for remedying this problem. You can select columns and either specify a width or force Excel to automatically adjust the width of a cell to exactly fit its contents.

✓ **Multiple Columns, Same Width**
To make multiple columns the same width, click the mouse and drag over all the column headers you want resized. Then resize one of the columns. Each column becomes that size.

✓ **AutoFit Columns**
To automatically make a column fit the width of the widest cell, choose **Format, Column, AutoFit Selection.**

1. Move the mouse pointer over the side of the column header you want to alter (the pointer changes to a two-headed arrow).

2. Click and drag the column edge to the new size.

3. Release the mouse button to drop the line in the new location.

Task 17: Freezing Rows and Columns

Creating a Nonscrolling Region

Many times your worksheet is large enough that you cannot view all the data on screen at the same time. In addition, if you have added row or column titles, and you scroll down or to the right, some of the titles are too far to the top or left of the worksheet for you to see. For example, if you are reviewing data in column FF, it would be nice to see the row title of the cell you are referencing. To help, you can freeze the heading rows and columns so they're always visible.

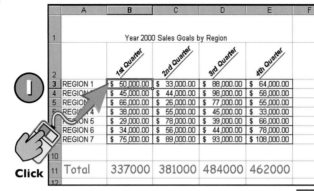

✓ Removing Frozen Panes

To remove the freezing of columns and rows, choose **Window, Unfreeze Panes.**

1 Click in the cell to the right of and below the area you want to freeze.

2 Choose **Window, Freeze Panes.**

3 Move through the worksheet, using the arrow keys (→, ←, ↑, ↓), and notice that the rows and columns you selected are frozen so you can reference data with the appropriate titles.

Task 18: Using AutoFormat

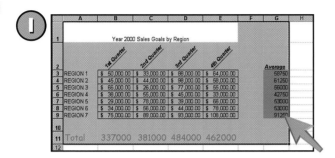

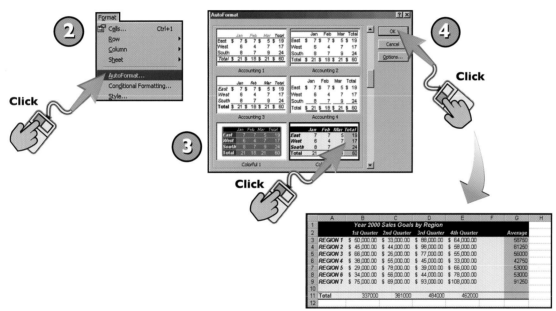

Automatically Formatting Worksheets

Using all the formatting capabilities discussed to this point, you could format your worksheets in a very effective and professional manner, but it might take a while to get good at it. In the meantime, you can use Excel's AutoFormat feature, which can format selected cells using predefined formats. This feature is a quick way to format large amounts of data and provides ideas on how to format data.

Click

Click

Click

① Select the cells you want to AutoFormat.

② Choose **Format, AutoFormat** to open the AutoFormat dialog box.

③ Click the AutoFormat you want (for example, **Colorful 2**) in the sample preview area.

④ Click the **OK** button to apply the AutoFormat to your data.

✓ **Modifying AutoFormat**
If you find a format in the AutoFormat dialog box that doesn't quite meet your requirements, you can use that format but then make any necessary changes directly in the worksheet.

Task 19: Using Conditional Formatting

Formatting Cells Based on Content

At times, you might want the formatting of a cell to depend on the value it contains. For this, use conditional formatting, which lets you specify up to three conditions that, when met, cause the cell to be formatted in the manner defined for that condition. If none of the conditions are met, the cell keeps its original formatting. For example, you can set a conditional format such that if sales for a particular quarter exceed $100,000, the data in the cell is red.

✓ **Painting a Format onto Other Cells**
You can copy the conditional formatting from one cell to another, click the cell whose formatting you want to copy. Then click the **Format Painter** button. Finally, drag over the cells to which you want to copy the formatting.

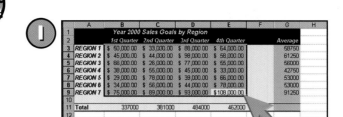

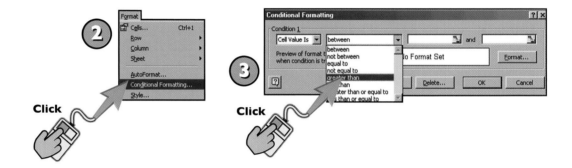

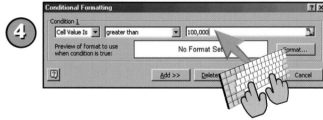

1. Select the cells to which you want to apply conditional formatting.

2. Choose **Format, Conditional Formatting** to open the Conditional Formatting dialog box.

3. Click the drop-down list to select the type of condition (for example, **greater than**).

4. Type the value of the condition (for example, **100,000**).

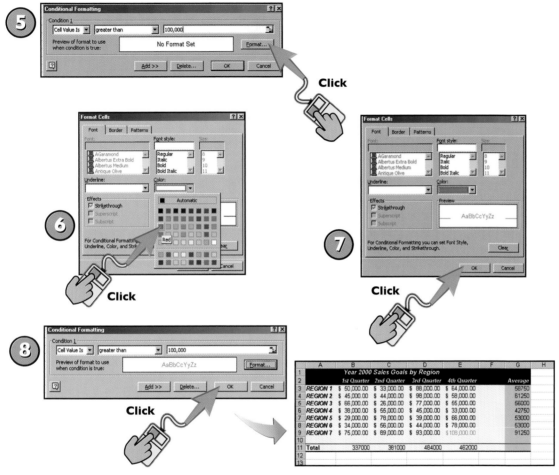

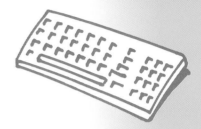

Click

Click

Click

Click

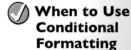

End Task

(5) Click the **Format** button to set the format to use when the condition is met.

(6) Click the options you want to set in the Format Cells dialog box (for example, the color **Red**).

(7) Click the **OK** button to accept your formatting changes.

(8) Click the **OK** button in the Conditional Formatting dialog box. Excel applies your formatting to any cells that meet the condition you specified.

✓ When to Use Conditional Formatting

Use conditional formatting to draw attention to values that have different meanings, depending on whether they are positive or negative, such as profit and loss values.

Task 20: Inserting Charts

Graphing Your Data

Numeric data can sometimes be difficult to interpret. Using data to create charts helps visualize the data's significance. For example, you might not have noticed that the same month of every year has low sales figures, but it becomes obvious when you make a chart from the data. The chart's visual nature also helps others review your data without poring over every single number.

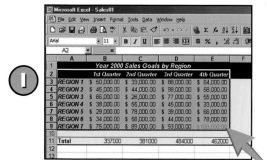

Start Here

Click

Click

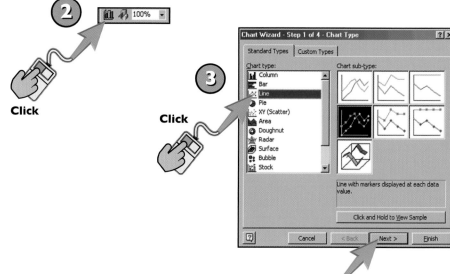

✓ **Clicking and Holding to View a Sample**
The first step of the Chart Wizard enables you to select how your data looks with a particular chart type and sub-type. You can see how it looks by clicking the **Click and Hold to View Sample** button.

1. Select the cells you want to have in your chart.

2. Click the **Chart Wizard** button on the Standard toolbar.

3. Click the **Chart type** (for example, **Line**) and **Chart sub-type** in the Chart Wizard dialog box; then click **Next**.

Next Step

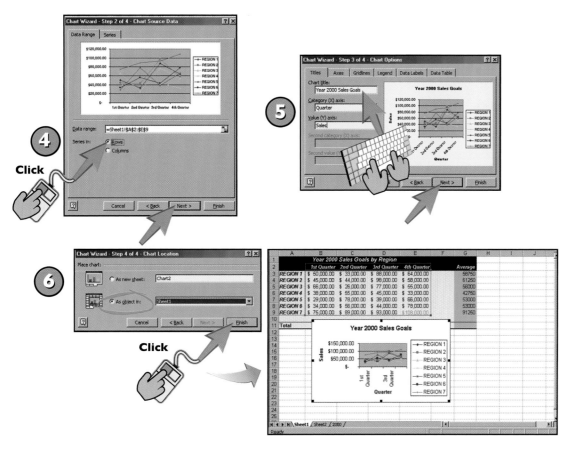

Click the option button for **Rows** (or **Columns**) to choose which data to base the chart on; then click **Next**.

5

Type the various titles for the chart (for example, `Year 2000 Sales Goals`); then click **Next**.

Select the option for where you want to place the chart (for example, choose **As Object In,** titled **Sheet1**); then click **Finish**.

✅ Chart Titles

You can place your charts on a separate worksheet and give them meaningful titles. This way, a single worksheet can be used to visually summarize an entire workbook.

✅ Back and Cancel Buttons

At any time while using the Chart Wizard, you can click the **Back** button to return to previous choices or the **Cancel** button to start over. In addition, you can click the **Finish** button early and add information to your chart afterward.

End Task

Task 21: Editing Chart Information

Changing Your Charts

Charts are useful for interpreting data; however, different people look at data in different ways. To accommodate different users, you can change titles, legend information, axis points, category names, and more.

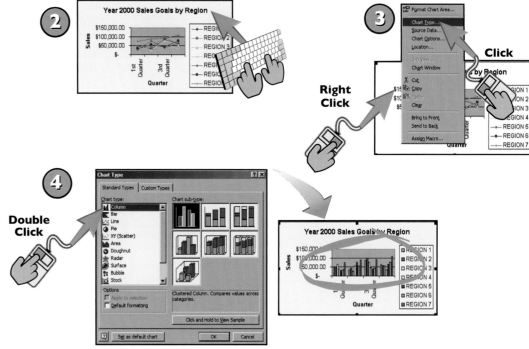

✓ **Double-clicking the Chart**

One of the fastest ways to edit charting options is to double-click the element in the chart you want to alter. The appropriate dialog box opens, and you can alter the chart options in that dialog box.

(1) Select the **Chart Title** text object in the chart you want to alter.

(2) Type any changes (for example, adding **by Region**).

(3) Right-click the chart and choose **Chart Type** from the shortcut menu to alter the type of chart.

(4) Double-click the chart type you want (for example, **Column**) to change the chart type.

Task 22: Editing Chart Data

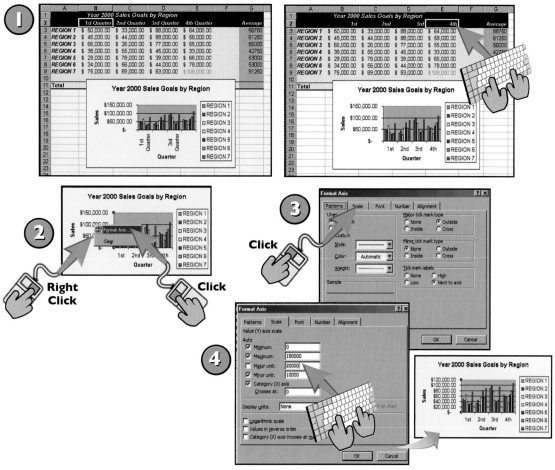

Changing Your Data

Perhaps you have entered data in your worksheet and created a chart, but now you need to go back and alter some of the data in the worksheet, which in turn alters the chart. This can be done easily by simply making corrections in your worksheet with which the chart data is created.

① Select data in the worksheet you want to alter (for example, remove the word **Quarter** from each of the **Category** axes). Notice that the **Category** axis information now fits horizontally in the chart.

② Right-click the **Value axis** and choose **Format Axis** from the shortcut menu.

③ Click the **Scale** tab.

④ Type a new **Major unit** scale amount (for example, **20000**) and press the **Enter** key. This makes the scale of the chart increase by smaller units.

⚠ WARNING
If you notice that one of the data points in your chart is way off scale, this is a good sign that you might have incorrectly entered data into your worksheet. If this is the case, simply edit the worksheet data, and the chart updates automatically.

End Task

Task 23: Moving a Chart

Changing Where You Keep Your Chart

When you first created your chart, you probably placed it in the same worksheet as your data. After your worksheet begins to grow and contain more data, you find that the chart is way off to the right or down below your data, out of view. If this is the case, you might find that it is more convenient to keep your chart on a different worksheet than the one on which you keep your data. Excel lets you move the chart to a different location.

✓ **Chart Sheet Versus Worksheet**

If you move your chart to a different sheet, it doesn't have to be a chart sheet. You can simply add a new worksheet (see Part 5, Task 2, "Moving Around a Worksheet") and move the chart to the new location.

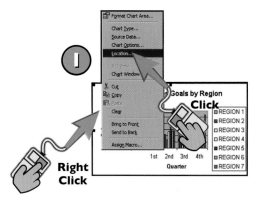

Right Click

Click

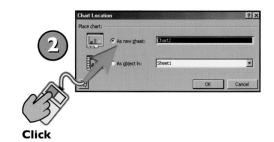

Click

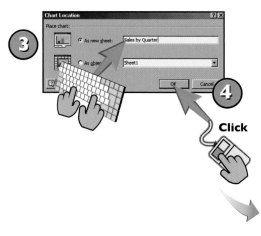

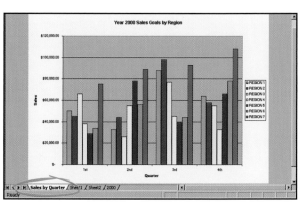

Click

① Right-click a blank area in the chart and choose **Location** from the shortcut menu.

② Click the **As New Sheet** option in the Chart Location dialog box.

③ Type in a new worksheet name (for example, `Sales by Quarter`).

④ Click the **OK** button, and Excel places the chart on a new worksheet named Sales by Quarter.

End Task

Task 24: Adding Cell Comments

Start Here

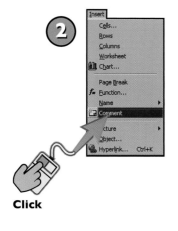

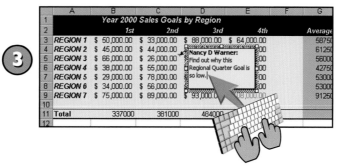

Adding Notes to a Cell

Some cells contain data or formulas that require an explanation or special attention. Comments provide a way to attach this type of information to individual cells without cluttering the cells with extraneous information. A red triangle indicates that a cell contains a comment, which you can view in several different ways.

① Click the cell to which you want to add a comment.

② Choose **Insert, Comment**.

③ Type the text into the comment area and click in the worksheet area to accept the comment. Notice that the cell's upper-right corner is now red to indicate the comment.

④ Move the mouse pointer over the comment marker in the cell to view the comment in a ScreenTip.

✓ Working with Comments

You can quickly edit or delete a comment by right-clicking the mouse on the cell that contains the comment marker and choosing either **Edit Comment** or **Delete Comment** from the shortcut menu.

Task 25: Inserting Clip Art

Adding Graphics to Worksheets

When you use Excel to generate reports or create presentation material, you might want to add some clip art graphics to improve the report's appearance or draw attention to a particular part of a worksheet. Office provides many pictures from which you can choose.

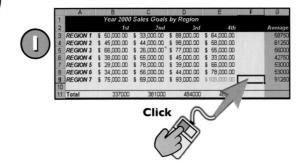

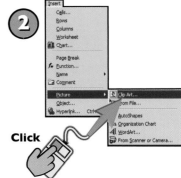

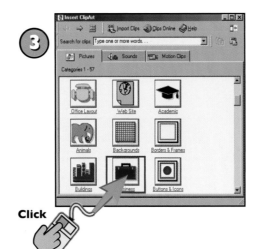

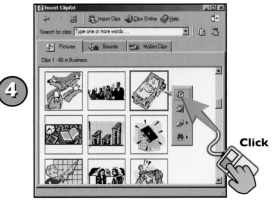

✓ **The Insert ClipArt Dialog Box**
You can leave the Insert ClipArt dialog box open if you need to insert more than one piece of clip art. In addition, you can use this dialog box to add sounds and movie clips.

1. Click the cursor in the document near where you want the clip art to appear.

2. Choose **Insert, Picture, Clip Art** to open the Insert ClipArt dialog box.

3. Click the category of clip art in the Pictures tab (for example, **Business**) and scroll through the options.

4. Click the piece of clip art and choose **Insert Clip** from the shortcut menu, which inserts the clip art into your document.

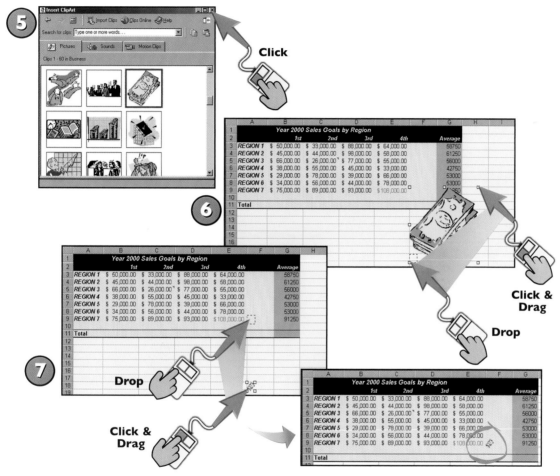

Click

Click &
Drag

Drop

Drop

Click &
Drag

Picture Toolbar
When you select a picture,
the Picture toolbar
appears, with tools you can
use to crop the picture,
add a border to it, and
adjust its brightness and
contrast.

Format Picture
You can double-click a
picture to open the
Format Picture dialog box.
This allows you to alter the
size, layout, colors and
lines, and more.

⑤ Click the **Close (×)** button to close the Insert ClipArt dialog box.

⑥ Click an object-sizing handle and drag the clip art to the size you want.

⑦ Click the clip art and drag it to the desired location in the worksheet.

End
Task

Task 26: Adding a Header and Footer

Adding Information That Prints on Every Page

Headers and footers appear at the top and bottom of printed pages of Excel worksheets. Headers and footers can display the file name, date and time printed, worksheet name, page number, and more. Excel offers many standard headers and footers to choose from, or you can create custom headers and footers.

✅ **Page Number and Count**

You can add page numbers and the total page count to the header or footer so that it reads, for example, "Page 2 of 7." Adding page numbers and page count makes it easier to reorganize papers if they are dropped and alerts the reader if some of the pages are missing.

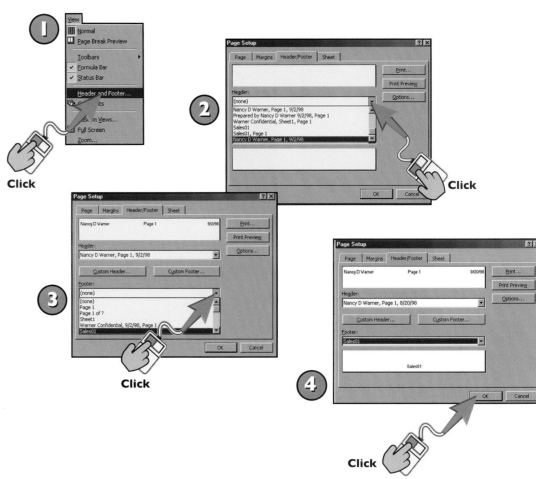

Click

Click

Click

Click

① Choose **View**, **Header and Footer** to open the Page Setup dialog box.

② Click the **Header** drop-down list to choose from standard header options (for example, **your name**, **page number**, **and date**).

③ Click the **Footer** drop-down list to choose from standard footer options (for example, the file name **Sales01**).

④ Click the **OK** button to accept the changes. To view these changes, you need to be in Print Preview (see Task 30, "Using Print Preview").

Task 27: Changing Margins

Start Here

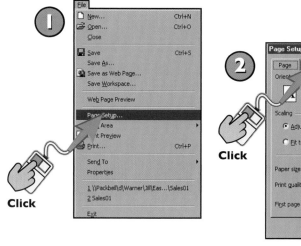

Click

Click

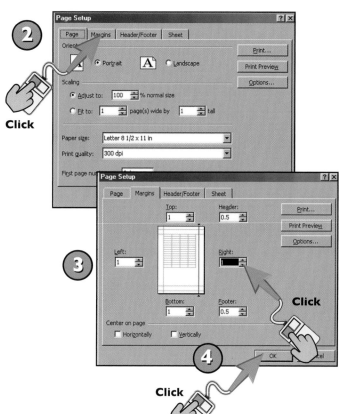

Click

Click

Working with Margins

Margins affect where data is printed on a page. They also determine where headers and footers are printed. Margins might be changed to conform to company standards or to make room for a logo on preprinted stationery.

✓ Setting Margins
It is a good idea to set your margins before you begin working in a worksheet. After you do, Excel displays dotted lines along the row and column that border the right and bottom sides of a worksheet's area within the page margins to let you know what data can print on each page.

1. Choose **File, Page Setup** to open the Page Setup dialog box.

2. Click the **Margins** tab.

3. Click the spin boxes to set the **Top**, **Left**, **Right**, and **Bottom** margins to **1** inch and the **Header** and **Footer** to **0.5** inch).

4. Click the **OK** button to accept the changes. To view these changes, you need to be in Print Preview (see Task 30, "Using Print Preview").

End Task

Task 28: Setting the Print Area

Choosing What to Print

Worksheets can include a large number of rows and columns. Setting the print area enables you to specify which rows and columns to print. If you don't have a print area set, when you print, all cells that have any data in them print. Sometimes this prints cells way off to the right or down the worksheet that you didn't intend to print.

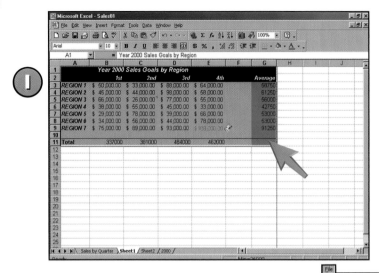

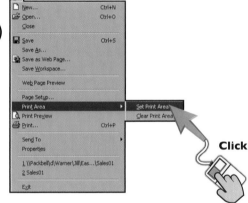

Click

✔ **Printing All on a Single Page**

Setting the print area does not cause all information to be printed on a single page. To do that, use the **Scaling** option in the Page Setup dialog box.

① Select the cells you want to print.

② Choose **File, Print Area, Set Print Area**.

Task 29: Printing Worksheet Gridlines

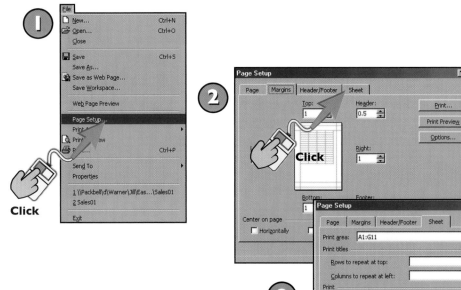

Start Here

Showing the Worksheet Gridlines

By default, Excel doesn't print worksheet gridlines unless you select to print them. Gridlines help you read information in a printed worksheet. Instead of using a ruler or running your finger across a page, you can use gridlines to keep rows and columns of data visually organized.

 Worksheet Borders
If you added borders throughout your worksheet or chose to autoformat your worksheet, you might not need to print your worksheet gridlines. See Task 11, "Changing Borders," for more information.

 Displaying Chart Gridlines
Besides using gridlines in a worksheet, you can apply gridlines to a chart. Choose **Chart, Chart Options,** and click the **Gridlines** tab.

① Choose **File, Page Setup** to open the Page Setup dialog box.

② Click the **Sheet** tab.

③ Click the **Gridlines** print checkbox.

④ Click the **OK** button.

Task 30: Using Print Preview

Seeing What Your Printout Will Look Like

Workbooks with lots of data can generate large print jobs, possibly containing hundreds of pages. Waiting until all these pages are printed to verify that the information is printed correctly can cost a lot in both time and printing supplies. To help prevent printing mistakes, use Print Preview to ensure that all the necessary elements appear on the pages being printed.

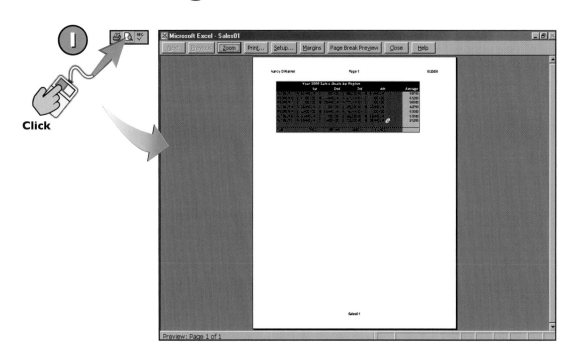

✔ **Margins**
If you're using Print Preview and you decide you want to alter the margins, you can click the **Margins** button. The margin guides become visible. Click and drag any of the margin or column guides to see how you can alter your worksheet.

① Click the **Print Preview** button on the Standard toolbar.

② Click the **Print** button to print the worksheet or the **Close** button to return to the worksheet.

Task 31: Printing Workbooks

Start Here

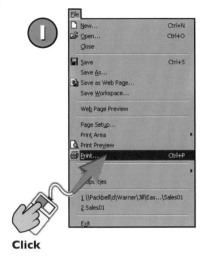

Click

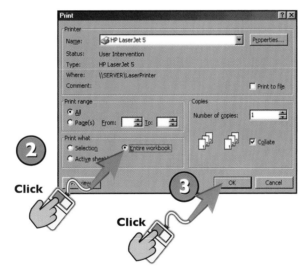

Click

Click

Getting Hard Copy

Printing a workbook is simple, but setting the option for printing a workbook can be complex. The number of options that must be set before printing a workbook depends on the amount of data stored in the workbook, how it is arranged, and how much of it needs to be printed.

① Choose File, Print to open the Print dialog box.

② Select printing options (for example, click **Entire Workbook**) in the **Print What** section. This prints all the worksheets you have in your workbook.

③ Click the **OK** button to print what you have selected.

✔ **Quick Printing**
Clicking the **Print** button on the Standard toolbar prints your worksheet based on Excel's default options. Use **Print Preview** to see what is to be printed. Then make any necessary changes before printing the workbook.

End Task

PART

PowerPoint 2000 Basics

You can use PowerPoint to plan every aspect of a winning presentation. PowerPoint even helps you organize the ideas in your presentation through its AutoContent Wizard, which quickly creates your presentation, including a title slide and several slides that help you come up with information.

You can get creative in your slide presentations. For example, you can apply bulleted and numbered lists, change your slide layout, or even apply a design template. In addition, you can add, delete, or duplicate a slide at any time.

Tasks

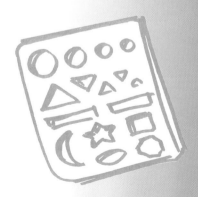

Using the AutoContent Wizard

Sometimes it just seems impossible to get started on a presentation. You don't even know where to start. In these situations, you can use the AutoContent Wizard, which asks you a series of questions and uses your answers to start a presentation for you. Then you fill in the details.

✓ Starting the AutoContent Wizard

You can start a new AutoContent Wizard presentation if you are already working in PowerPoint. Choose **File, New,** and click the **General** tab. Double-click **AutoContent Wizard,** and the process begins automatically.

Task 1: Starting a Presentation with the AutoContent Wizard

Start Here

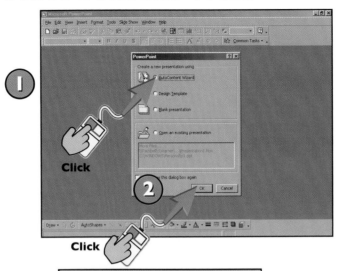

Click

Click

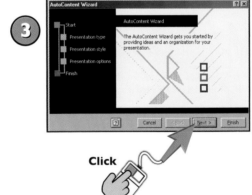

Click

Click

① Start PowerPoint and click the **AutoContent Wizard** option in the PowerPoint opening dialog box.

② Click the **OK** button.

③ Read the welcome information in the AutoContent Wizard dialog box; then click **Next**.

④ Click the kind of presentation you want to create (for example, **Recommending a Strategy**), and then click **Next**.

Next Step

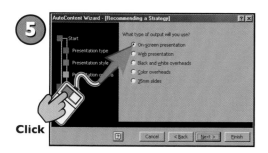

Click

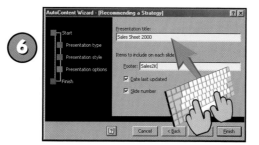

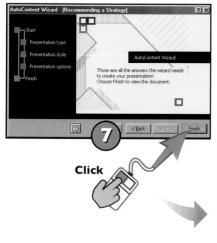

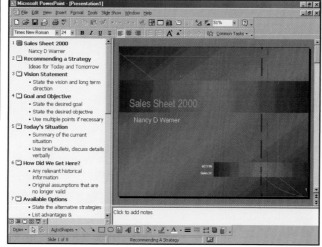

Click

✅ **Using the Back and Cancel Buttons**
You can click the **Back** button on the AutoContent Wizard dialog box at any time to alter previously entered information. Keep in mind that you must click the particular option you want to alter before you retype any changes. You can stop the AutoContent Wizard's progress at any time by clicking the **Cancel** button.

✅ **Creating Complex Presentations**
If you like the way the AutoContent Wizard gets a presentation off to a quick start, but you need more complex presentations, use the wizard to begin creating a presentation. Then add to the presentation by using templates or creating new slides from scratch.

⑤ Click the output option you would like to use (for example, **On-screen presentation**), and then click **Next**.

⑥ Type the title of the presentation (for example, **Sales Sheet 2000**) and any items you want included on each slide, and then click **Next**.

⑦ Click the **Finish** button to view the document PowerPoint creates.

Creating a Presentation from a Template

PowerPoint comes with several presentation templates that were created for various types of presentations and situations. These templates have basic artistic features and usually a skeleton outline you can fill in or expand on. You can take advantage of these to quickly create presentations.

✓ Starting with a Design Template

You can start a new presentation with a design template if you are already working in PowerPoint. Choose **File**, **New**, and click the **Design Templates** tab. Double-click the particular design template you want PowerPoint to apply automatically.

Task 2: Starting a Design Template Presentation

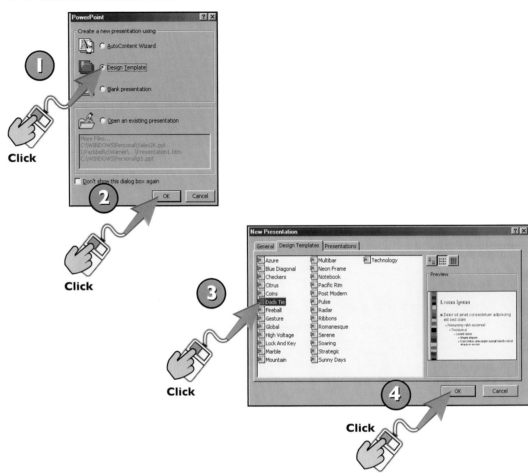

Start Here

Click

Click

Click

Click

1	Start PowerPoint and click the **Design Template** option on the PowerPoint opening dialog box.
2	Click the **OK** button.
3	Click a design template (for example, **Dads Tie**), and the Preview area gives you an idea of what it will look like.
4	Click the **OK** button.

Next Step

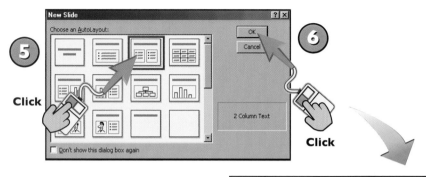

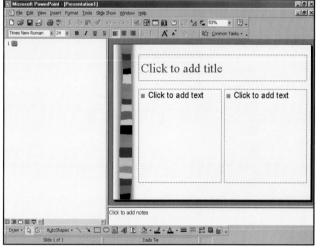

⑤ Click the type of slide you would like to begin with (for example, **2 Column Text**) in the **Choose an AutoLayout** area.

⑥ Click the **OK** button.

✓ Choosing an AutoLayout
Numerous options are available in the **Choose an AutoLayout** area. Practice selecting different options and adding text and graphics to the presentations. See Task 10, "Adding Slide Text," for more information.

✓ Applying a Design Template
You can apply a design template at any time by selecting **Apply Design Template** from the **Common Tasks** drop-down list on the Formatting toolbar. See Task 16, "Changing the Slide Design," for information on how to do this.

Making a Presentation from Scratch

For the most control over your PowerPoint presentations, start with a blank presentation and add only the items you want. This gives you the opportunity to use your creativity. It also allows you to use PowerPoint for creating files beyond basic business presentations. Your imagination is the only limitation.

✓ **Creating a New Presentation**
You can start a new presentation if you are already working in PowerPoint. See Task 8, "Creating a New Presentation Template," for more information.

✓ **Changing the Slide Design**
You can apply a template to your presentation at any time. See Task 16, "Changing the Slide Design," for more information.

Task 3: Starting a Blank Presentation

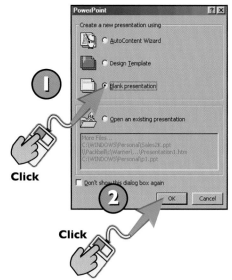

Click

Click

Click

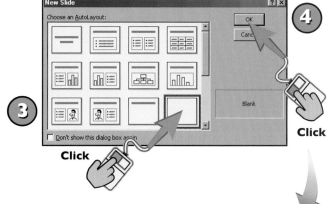

Click

Click

① Start PowerPoint and click the **Blank Presentation** option on the PowerPoint opening dialog box.

② Click the **OK** button.

③ Click the **Blank** slide in the **Choose an AutoLayout** area.

④ Click the **OK** button.

Task 4: Using Normal View

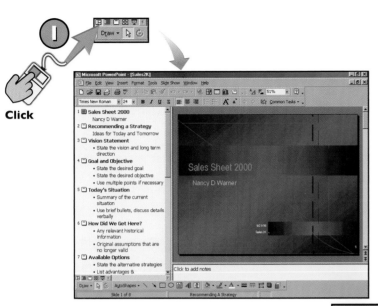

Click

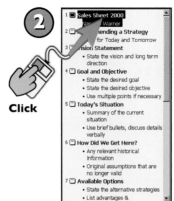

Click

Working with Your Presentation

Normal view is a new feature in PowerPoint 2000. It contains separate Outline, Slide Notes, and Slide panes. This default view shows an outline of your presentation, what the current slide looks like, and the speaker's notes for the current slide. You can edit text, navigate, format, and enter notes while working with your slides to create a presentation.

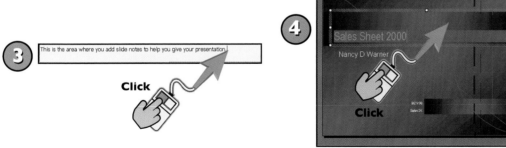

This is the area where you add slide notes to help you give your presentation.

Click

Click

✓ Showing Rulers and Guides

When creating slides and positioning information, you might want to use the ruler and guides that PowerPoint provides. To select these options, right-click a blank portion of the slide and choose **Ruler or Guides** from the shortcut menu.

① Click the **Normal View** button in the lower-left corner of the presentation area.

② Click in the **Outline** pane to edit the text throughout the presentation.

③ Click in the **Slide Notes** pane to add textual slide notes.

④ Click in the **Slide** pane to edit the slides directly.

End
Task

Task 5: Working in Different Views

Using Views

PowerPoint provides several different ways to view presentations while creating or modifying them. Each view provides a different perspective on a presentation, and switching between these views is simple.

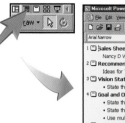

Click

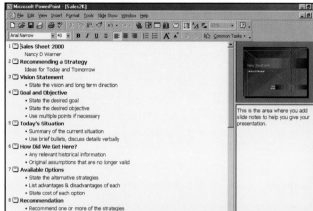

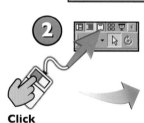

Click

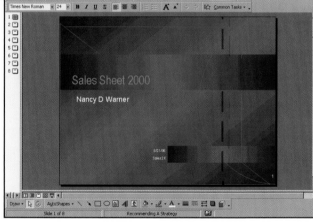

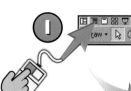

✓ Common Tasks

The common tasks you perform on slides are consolidated on a Common Tasks drop-down list. These tasks are creating a new slide, altering the slide layout, and applying a design template. This Common Tasks drop-down list is also a tear-off palette; you can click the drop-down menu bar and drag it onto your workspace, where it floats.

 Click the **Outline View** button. You can add text, and both the Slide and Slide Notes panes are still visible.

 Click the **Slide View** button. You can add both text and art on a slide-by-slide basis and move through the presentation with the slide numbers on the left side.

Next Step

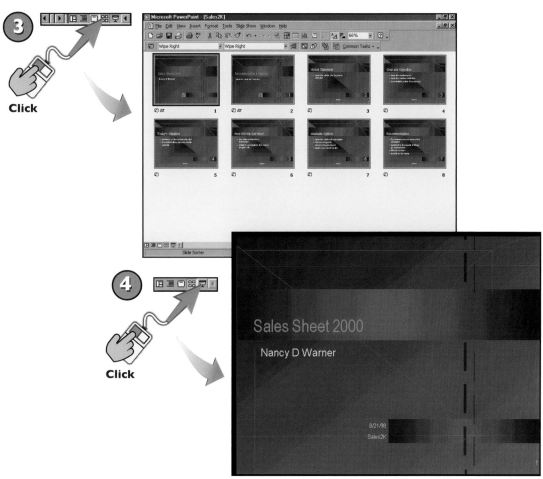

3 Click

4 Click

Slide Sorter Options
Slide Sorter view is a great place to add slide transitions and animation effects. To learn how to add slide transitions, see **Part 8, Task 8, "Adding Slide Transitions."** To learn how to add animation effects, see **Part 8, Task 9, "Adding Animation Effects."**

Using a Slide Master
You can make global changes to your slides using a slide master instead of changing each slide individually. You can create a slide master to control text characteristics (master text), background effects, styles, placeholder text, and even footer text. Make any changes on the slide master, and PowerPoint automatically updates the rest of the slides and any new slides you add. To work with a slide master, choose **View, Master, Slide Master.** You work with a slide master just as you work with any other slide.

3 Click the **Slide Sorter View** button. This enables you to rearrange your slides and view slide details such as action buttons.

4 Click the **Slide Show View** button. This enables you to view your slides as they would appear in a slide show. (Press the **Esc** key to exit the Slide Show view.)

End Task

Storing a Presentation on Disk

PowerPoint provides more than one method for saving presentations. You should take advantage of at least one of these often. Unsaved presentations are lost if anything happens to your application or computer.

Save In Options

If you don't want to save your file in the **Personal** directory, click the arrow in the **Save In** drop-down list box and maneuver through the directories to save the file in a different location.

Task 6: Saving a Presentation

Start Here

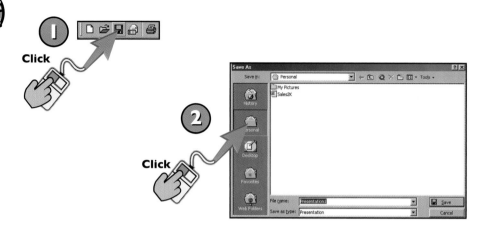

Click

Click

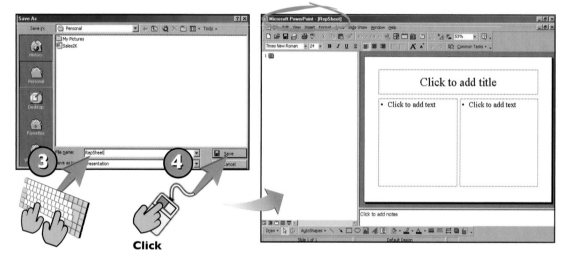

Click

(1) Click the **Save** button on the Standard toolbar; the Save As dialog box appears, with a default file name for your presentation.

(2) Click the **Personal** icon on the Places bar (you might have a **My Documents** icon instead).

(3) Type a different presentation name in the **File Name** list box if you like (for example, RepSheet).

(4) Click the **Save** button, and the presentation saves, with the file name you assigned in the title bar.

End Task

Task 7: Closing a Presentation

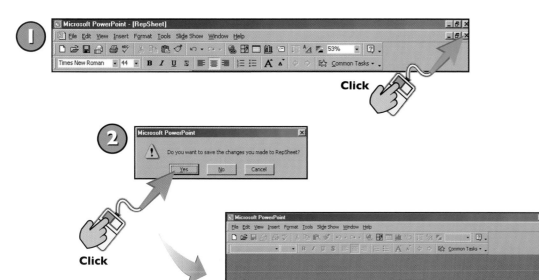

Click

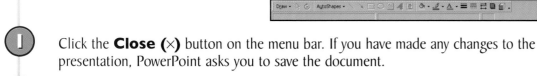

Click

Finishing Work on a Presentation

You can have more than one presentation open at one time in PowerPoint. As you finish with a presentation, you may no longer need to have it open anymore. You can close it and continue to work in PowerPoint.

✓ No Save

If you don't want to save your document when Word asks, two options are available. If you decide you want to continue working in the document, click **Cancel**. Click **No** if you want to close your document but don't want to save your changes; in this case your presentation will revert to the previously saved version.

✓ Ctrl+F4

As with most Windows applications, PowerPoint provides many ways to close a presentation. For example, you can press **Ctrl+F4** to close the active presentation.

① Click the **Close** (×) button on the menu bar. If you have made any changes to the presentation, PowerPoint asks you to save the document.

② Click the **Yes** button if you want to save any recent changes. PowerPoint closes the presentation.

Starting a New Template Presentation

PowerPoint gives you the opportunity to begin a new presentation each time you start the application, but you can create another new presentation at any time. For example, after you have saved and closed one presentation, you might want to begin a new one. In addition, PowerPoint gives you the option to begin a new presentation with a little template help.

A New, Blank Presentation
If you want to create a new, blank presentation, click the **New** button on the standard toolbar and select a slide AutoLayout.

Task 8: Creating a New Presentation Template

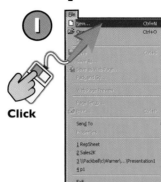

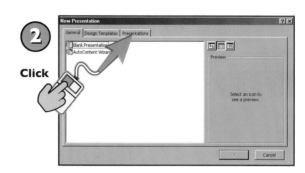

Click

Click

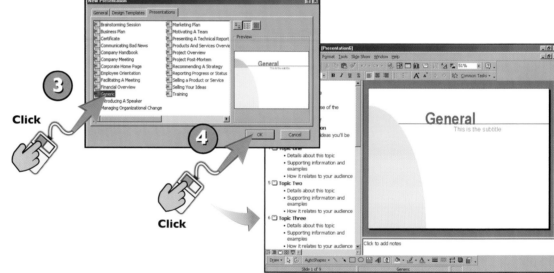

Click

Click

① Choose **File**, **New** to open the New Presentation dialog box.

② Click the **Presentations** tab.

③ Click a presentation template (for example, **Generic**). The Preview area shows an example of what it will look like.

④ Click the **OK** button. PowerPoint opens the Generic presentation template.

Task 9: Opening a Presentation

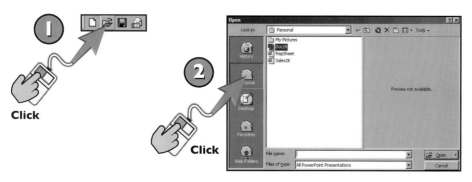

Click

Click

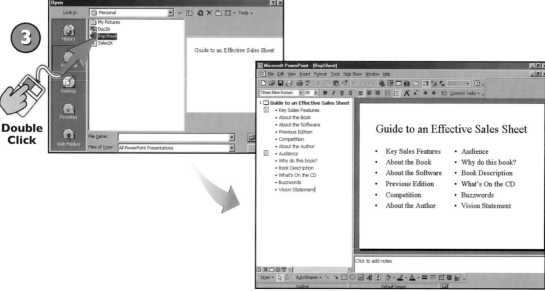

Double Click

Click the **Open** button on the Standard toolbar; the Open dialog box appears.

Click the **Personal** icon on the Places bar (you might have a **My Documents** icon instead).

Double-click the file you want to open (for example, **RepSheet**), and PowerPoint opens the presentation.

Choosing a Presentation to Work With

Eventually, you'll have to close PowerPoint and any presentations you have created. If you saved your work, you can continue working at any time by opening the saved presentations. You also need to save your presentations so you can use PowerPoint to show your slides to others.

 Alternate Look In Locations
If necessary, click the **Look In** drop-down arrow and select the folder from the list. To move up a folder level, click the **Up One Level** button on the Open toolbar.

 Existing Presentations
If you want to open an existing presentation and you just started PowerPoint, click **Open an Existing Presentation** on the PowerPoint opening dialog box.

Task 10: Adding Slide Text

Slide Information

After you create a presentation, whether by starting from scratch (see Task 3, "Starting a Blank Presentation"), using the AutoContent Wizard (see Task 1, "Starting a Presentation with the AutoContent Wizard"), using a design template (see Task 2, "Starting a Design Template Presentation"), or using a presentation template (see Task 8, "Creating a New Presenta-tion Template"), you need to put in the information you want to present. In the Normal view, you can add text in the Outline pane or the Slide pane.

✓ Adding Text in Outline View

Another way to quickly add text is to use Outline view. This view enables you to add text without the clutter of other objects on your slide. See Task 5, "Working in Different Views," for information about using Outline view.

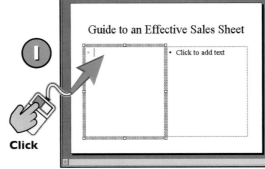

Click

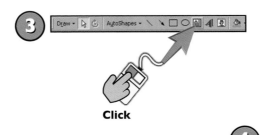

Click

 Click in the **Slide** pane to begin adding text (for example, in a bulleted list).

 Type your text into the text box. Notice that the Outline pane in the Normal view fills in automatically.

 Click the **Text Box** button on the Drawing toolbar.

 Click in the **Slide** pane and begin typing text into the text box.

End Task

Task 11: Formatting Slide Text

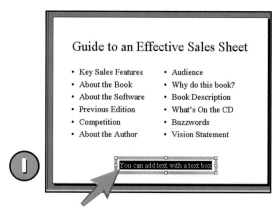

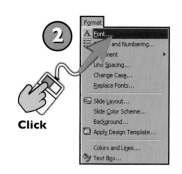

Click

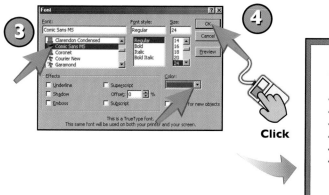

Click

Altering the Appearance of Text

An effective presentation gets your point across while maintaining the audience's attention. You can keep attention focused on your presentation by making the information on the slides stand out. One way to do this is to format the text. PowerPoint gives you many different options to format your text, such as changing its font, style, size, and effects.

✓ The Font Dialog Box

The Font dialog box gives you many different options of ways to format your text. Instead of formatting the text and then seeing what it looks like, you can click the **Preview** button and make changes before you click the **OK** button to accept the settings.

---

1 Select the text you would like to format.

2 Choose **Format**, **Font** to open the Font dialog box.

3 Select the options you would like to apply to your text (for example, **Blue** color, **Comic Sans MS** font).

4 Click the **OK** button to accept your changes and see the results.

Task 12: Working with Numbered and Bulleted Lists

Organizing Slide Information

You can select text and make it into a numbered or bulleted list. In addition, you can use a text box to begin typing a numbered or bulleted list. In this task we are going to make a bulleted list into a numbered list and format a regular bulleted list to have graphical bullets.

✓ Multilevel Lists

A new feature in PowerPoint 2000 is that you can automatically create multilevel bulleted and numbered lists by default. When typing text into a list, pressing the **Tab** key automatically indents the list to a new level.

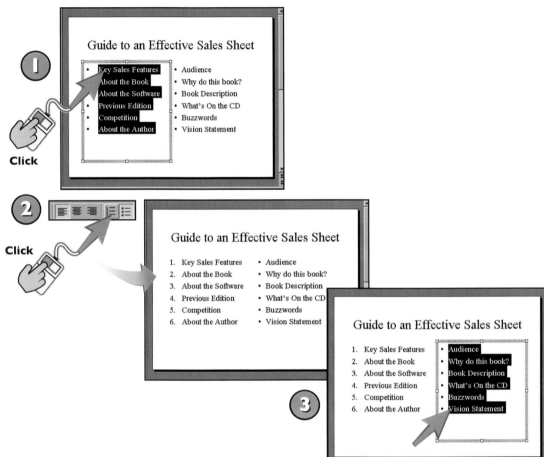

① Select the list or text you would like to make into a numbered list.

② Click the **Numbering** button on the Formatting toolbar.

③ Select the bullets you would like to alter.

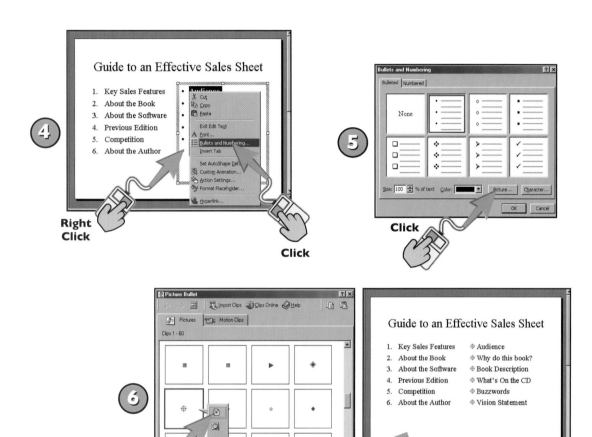

Changing Number Styles

You can change the numbered list style—for example, from Arabic (1, 2, 3) to Roman (I, II, III)—by choosing **Format, Bullets and Numbering**. Click the **Numbered** tab, select from the list of styles, and click the **OK** button.

Creating a New List

If you haven't yet created the list you want to number or bullet, click the **Numbering or Bullets** button on the Formatting toolbar, and then start typing the information. When you press **Enter** to start a new line, PowerPoint adds the number or bullet automatically. To stop adding bullets or numbers, press the **Enter** key more than once.

④ Right-click the bullets and choose **Bullets and Numbering** from the shortcut menu.

⑤ Click the **Picture** button on the Bullets and Numbering dialog box.

⑥ Click the clip and choose **Insert clip** from the pop-up menu.

Task 13: Adding and Deleting Slides

Inserting and Removing Slides

If you think of a new topic you want to include in your presentation, you might need to insert a new slide. On the other hand, you might determine that your presentation runs a bit long and need to delete a slide.

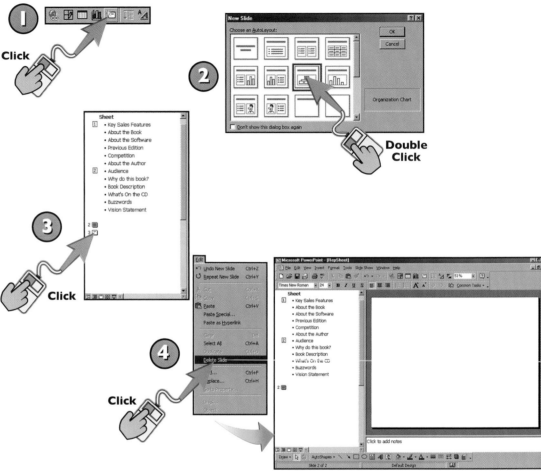

Start Here

Click

Click

Double Click

Click

Click

✔ **Drag Delete**
Another way to delete a slide is to click the slide number in the outline and drag it off the Outline pane.

① Click the **New Slide** button on the Standard toolbar.

② Double-click the kind of slide you want in the New Slide dialog box (for example, **Organization Chart**). Notice that PowerPoint adds the new slide to the Outline pane.

③ Click a slide or a slide number in the Outline pane.

④ Choose **Edit**, **Delete Slide** to delete the slide.

End Task

Task 14: Duplicating Slides

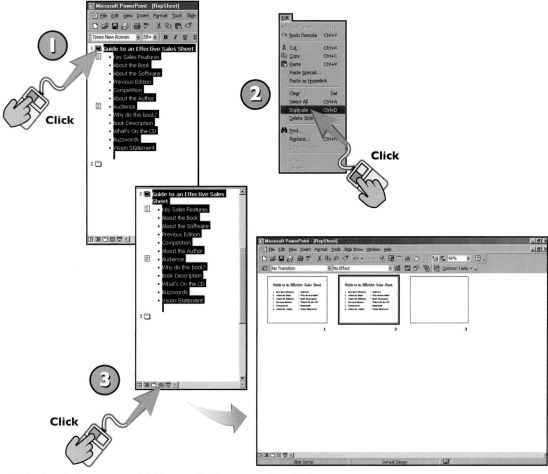

Click

Click

Click

Re-creating the Same Slide

If you have created a slide you really like, and you want to re-create the same look and text on another slide, you can duplicate it in Outline or Slide Sorter view. For example, if you have too much information for one slide, you might want to duplicate the slide and place the extra text on the additional slide.

✓ **Duplicating Layout and Design**

Another reason you might want to duplicate a slide is because you already applied a slide layout or a slide design template. You have created the slide exactly the way you want it and would like other slides to be formatted the same way. See Tasks 15, "Changing the Slide Layout," and 16, "Changing the Slide Design," for more information about applying slide layouts and design templates.

---

1 Click the slide you would like to duplicate in the Outline pane.

2 Choose **Edit**, **Duplicate** to duplicate the slide outline.

3 Click the **Slide Sorter View** button to see a visual image of the duplicated slide.

Task 15: Changing the Slide Layout

Applying Different Layouts to Slides

To add visual interest to your presentation, you can vary the layout of your slides. You can choose from 21 slide layouts (called AutoLayouts), including many that let you add visually interesting features such as clip art, tables, and graphs.

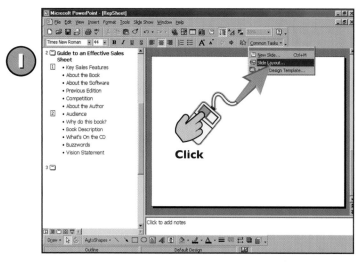

Click

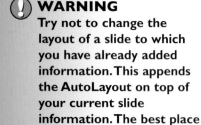

Double Click

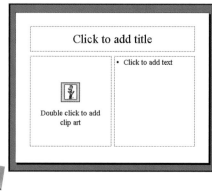

Click to add title

• Click to add text

Double click to add clip art

⚠ WARNING

Try not to change the layout of a slide to which you have already added information. This appends the AutoLayout on top of your current slide information. The best place to alter the layout is in a new slide.

✓ Clip Art and Tables

For more information on adding clip art and tables to your slides, see Part 8, Tasks 1, "Inserting a Table," and 2, "Inserting a Chart."

① Click **Slide Layout** from the **Common Tasks** drop-down list on the Formatting toolbar.

② Double-click the type of slide you want in the New Slide dialog box (for example, **ClipArt & Text**).

End Task

Task 16: Changing the Slide Design

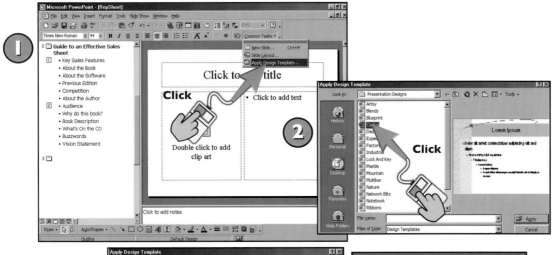

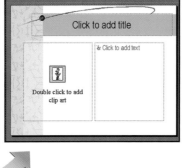

Changing the Look of Your Slides

You can alter the look of individual slides, and PowerPoint also provides numerous design templates that you can immediately apply to your presentation to give it a certain look. In addition to changing slide design while you are working in a slide, it can be convenient to set your slide design before you begin working.

1. Click **Apply Design Template** from the **Common Tasks** drop-down list on the Formatting toolbar.

2. Click the design you would like to apply from the **Presentation Designs** list box (for example, **Cactus**).

3. Click the **Apply** button on the Apply Design Template dialog box.

⚠ WARNING

When you apply a design, keep in mind that it will be applied to all the slides in your presentation. If you apply a design after you have finished your slides, some of the design formatting might overlap some of the information on your slides.

Enhancing PowerPoint Presentations

You can insert many different elements—such as tables, clip art, and other objects—into your presentations to help keep the audience's attention and interest in the information you are presenting. In addition, you can add special features such as animation effects, transitions, and action buttons to enhance your presentation.

Your PowerPoint presentation file contains everything you need—an outline of your presentation, your slides, audience handouts, and even your speaker's notes. You can prepare this file to give at a presentation using the Pack and Go feature. This allows you to give your presentation on a computer that doesn't have PowerPoint installed.

You can even rehearse the timing of the presentation to make sure it isn't too long or too short. And finally, you can print your outline, speaker's notes, and audience handouts to use and distribute.

Tasks

Using Tables

Many times you need to add more to your presentation than just words. Maybe you want to display data or show relationships between numbers or totals. Creating a table in PowerPoint is one way to do this. You can insert a table directly into your slide and format it just as you would a Word table.

✓ **Table Information**
For more information on how to work with and format tables, see Part 4, "Advanced Word Features." There you will learn how to manage columns and rows.

✓ **Adding Tables and Worksheets**
You can also add Word tables and Excel worksheets to your presentations as objects. See Task 3, "Inserting Linked Objects," for more information.

Task 1: Inserting a Table

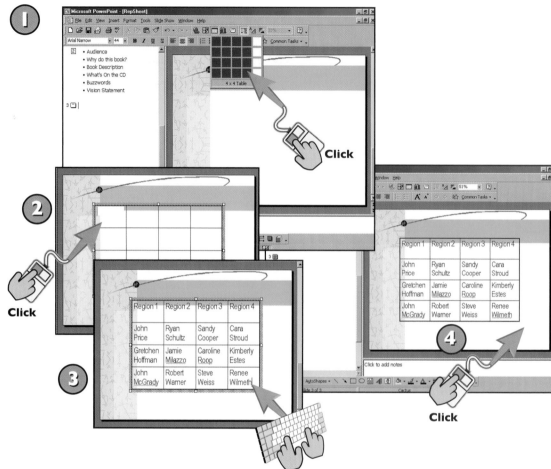

1 Click the **Insert Table** button on the Standard toolbar and select the number of rows and columns you want the table to have (for example 4×4).

2 Click in the table.

3 Type the text you would like to have in the table (using the **Tab** and arrow (→, ←, ↑, ↓) keys to move between the table cells, just like in Excel).

4 Click anywhere in the presentation outside the Word table.

Task 2: Inserting a Chart

Start Here

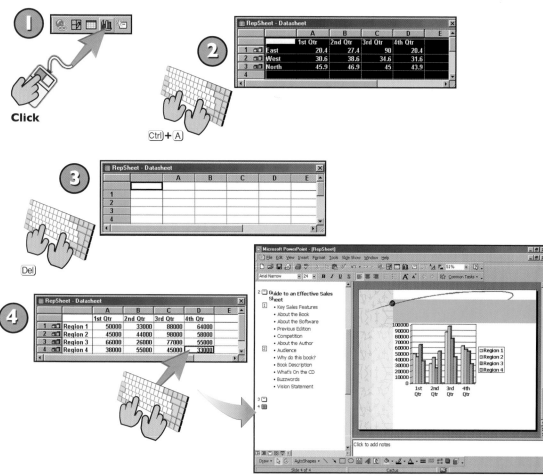

Click

Ctrl + A

Del

Graphing Information

Charts can be one of the best ways to get your point across in a presentation because they present data visually. For example, instead of including a worksheet or table, you could use a graph that shows the comparison between your sales regions by quarter.

✓ **Working with Charts**
If you double-click your chart, you see a new **Chart** menu, **Chart** toolbar, and the datasheet ready for you to use to edit your chart. If you have forgotten how to work with charts, see Part 6, Tasks 20, "Inserting Charts," through 23, "Moving a Chart."

① Click the **Insert Chart** button on the Standard toolbar.

② Press the **Ctrl+A** shortcut key to select the entire datasheet.

③ Press the **Delete** button.

④ Type the data you want into the datasheet and click anywhere in the presentation outside the chart. Notice that the chart color scheme matches that of the design template.

End Task

Task 3: Inserting Linked Objects

Adding Information You Created Elsewhere

Instead of creating a new table or inserting a new chart, you can insert a worksheet or chart that you have created in a different application. You can *link* the object to your PowerPoint presentation so that if you make any changes to the object in the future, the change will be made to your presentation. In addition, you can add numerous types of objects—besides just worksheets—to your presentations.

✓ Browse Versus Open

The Browse dialog box is the same as the Open dialog box and can be used the same way. If necessary, click the **Look In** drop-down arrow and select the folder from the list. To move up a folder level, click the **Up One Level** button on the Browse toolbar. If you double-click a subfolder, its contents appear in the list of files and folders.

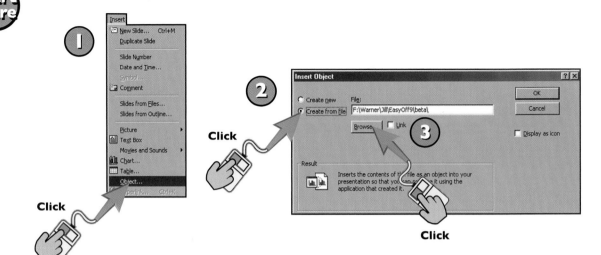

Click

Click

Click

Double Click

① Choose **Insert**, **Object** to open the Insert Object dialog box.

② Click the **Create from File** option to use a file that's already created.

③ Click the **Browse** button to open the Browse dialog box.

④ Double-click the file you want to insert (for example, the **Sales01** worksheet you created in the Excel section).

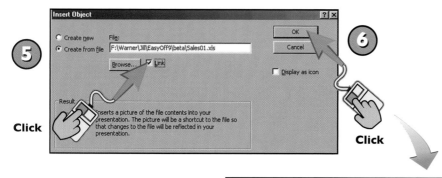

Click

Click

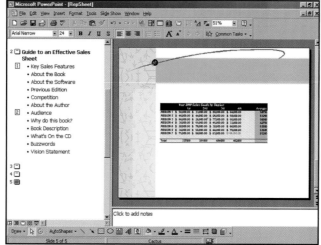

Updating the Worksheet
You can double-click the inserted worksheet to open the application in which it was created. This way you can make changes to the worksheet that directly affect your presentation.

Updating Links
You can right-click your linked object and select **Update Link** to update the information to include any changes you might have made to the original file.

No Link
If you don't check the option to link the objects to your presentation, a copy of the object is made and pasted in your presentation. If you change the original file, PowerPoint can't automatically bring in those changes. You have to enter the changes manually.

5 Click the **Link** checkbox in the Insert Object dialog box. This ensures that any updates made in the file are linked to the presentation.

6 Click the **OK** button to see the linked object in your presentation.

Task 4: Inserting Clip Art

Adding Pictures to Presentations

Clip art adds visual interest to your PowerPoint presentations. With Microsoft Clip Art, you can choose from numerous professionally prepared images, sounds, and movie clips. After you have added graphics, you can move them around in the document and even assign text wrapping.

✓ **The Picture Toolbar**
When you insert a picture, the Picture toolbar appears with tools you can use to crop the picture, add a border to it, or adjust its brightness and contrast.

✓ **Resizing and Repositioning Clip Art**
Clip art usually fills the slide. You can shrink it and move it anywhere on the slide. Task 5, "Resizing or Moving Objects," provides more information on this.

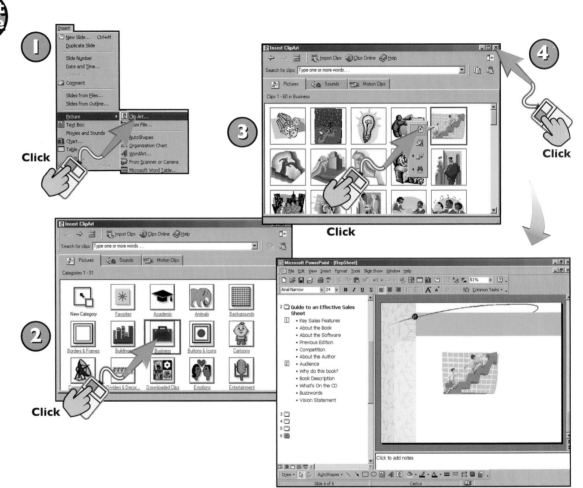

1. Choose **Insert**, **Picture**, **Clip Art** to open the Insert ClipArt dialog box.

2. Click the category of clip art in the **Pictures** tab (for example, **Business**) and scroll through the options.

3. Click the piece of clip art and choose **Insert Clip** from the pop-up menu, which inserts the clip art into your document.

4. Click the **Close (✕)** button to close the Insert ClipArt dialog box.

Task 5: Resizing or Moving Objects

Start Here

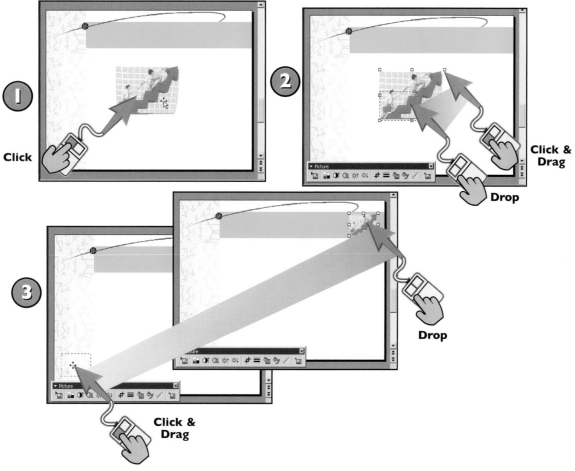

Click

Click & Drag

Drop

Click & Drag

Drop

Manipulating Objects

You can easily move or resize objects on the same slide, or you can move them to another slide. You can move and resize any object—text, art, a table, or a chart. In addition to resizing and moving, you can cut, copy, and paste objects (refer to Part 2, Task 11, "Cutting, Copying, and Pasting Text," for more information).

✓ **Keeping Correct Proportions**
Using the corner border handles to drag the size of an object so that it's larger or smaller increases or decreases the horizontal and vertical size proportionately. If you use the side border handles, you increase the horizontal and vertical size separately, possibly making the object look out of proportion.

1 Click the object you want to resize. Notice that sizing handles appear around the edges of the object.

2 Click a handle and drag the object to a new size, and then release the mouse button.

3 Click the object. Hold down the mouse button and drag the object to where you want it to appear. Then release the mouse button to drop the object in its new location.

End Task

Task 6: Reordering Slides

Rearranging Slides in Your Presentation

You can easily and quickly reorder the arrangement of your PowerPoint slides. For example, you might decide you want to place your graphical slides earlier in your presentation to draw the attention of the audience.

Undoing an Action
If you move a slide to an incorrect location, click the slide and move it again. Another action you can take is to click the **Undo** button on the Standard toolbar (or press **Ctrl+Z**). This undoes your last action of moving the slide.

Click

Click & Drag

Drop

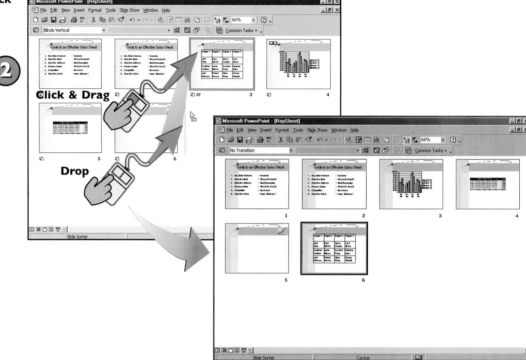

1 Click the **Slide Sorter View** button.

2 Click the slide and drag the mouse pointer to the desired location. Then release the mouse button to drop the slide in the new location.

Task 7: Viewing a Slide Show

Start Here

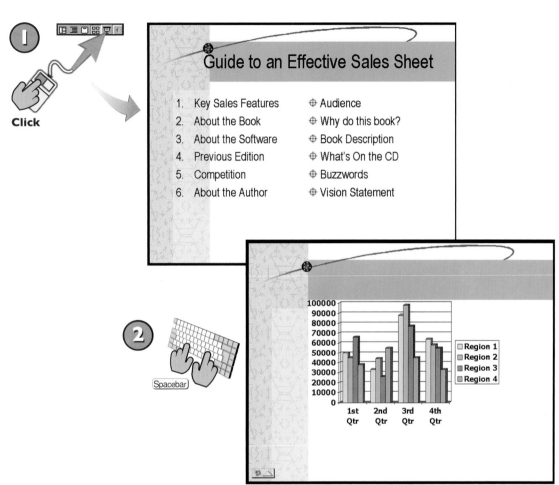

Click

Spacebar

Click the **Slide Show** button on the View toolbar with your presentation open.

Press the **spacebar** to display the next slide. You can press the **Esc** key to stop the slide show anywhere in the presentation.

Looking at Your Presentation On Screen

Perhaps the best way to test your **PowerPoint** presentation is to view the presentation on screen. Your slides appear in vivid color and full screen (as they would in an actual presentation). You can use the mouse pointer or press the **Page Up** and **Page Down** keys to advance the slides and try any action buttons you have established. (See Task 10, "Adding Action Buttons," for more about action buttons.)

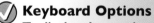

Keyboard Options

To display the previous slide, press the **Backspace** key. To display a particular slide, press the number of the specific slide on the keyboard and press the **Enter** key. To stop the slide show, press the **Esc** key.

Task 8: Adding Slide Transitions

Setting the Look for Moving Among Slides

Slide transitions can make your presentations look more professional and interesting. For example, having each slide appear to open like a vertical blind draws the attention of the audience. It's generally best to use only one kind of transition in a presentation—using more can distract the audience from your message.

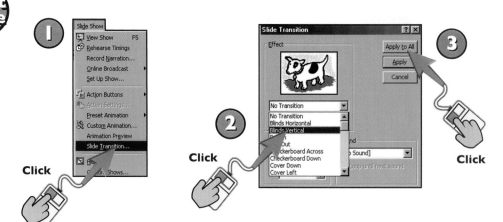

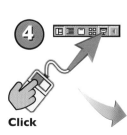

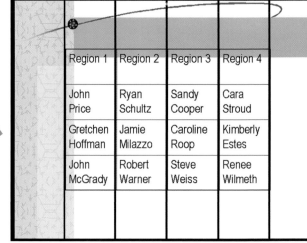

Working with Effects
If you want a special transition effect for a single slide, open the slide, select the effect, and select to apply it to the slide instead of to all slides.

(1) Choose **Slide Show**, **Slide Transition** to open the Slide Transition dialog box.

(2) Click the **Effect** drop-down arrow and choose the transition you want to use (for example, **Blinds Vertical**).

(3) Click the **Apply to All** button to apply the slide transition to all slides in the presentation.

(4) Click the **Slide Show** button to see what the effect will look like.

Task 9: Adding Animation Effects

Start Here

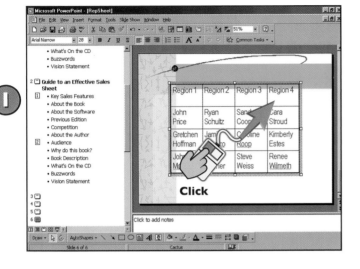

Click

Click

② **Click**

③ **Click**

Click

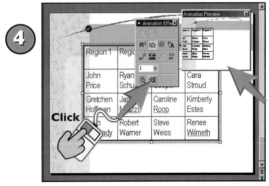

④

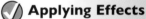

Animating Objects

In today's multimedia world, text and graphics sometimes aren't enough to keep an audience's attention. PowerPoint's animation effects can bring presentations to life, making it hard for people to ignore information. You can apply animation to draw attention to especially relevant information. Keep in mind that effects on slides that aren't beneficial to the presentation can distract your audience instead of apply emphasis in a positive way.

✓ **Applying Effects**
Animation effects are limited by the type of object to which you are applying them. For example, more effects are available for text than for a piece of clip art. In addition, not all effects are installed with Office 2000 by default, so you may need the installation CD to add some effects to your presentations.

① Click the object to which you want to add a slide animation.

② Click the **Animation Effects** button on the Formatting toolbar.

③ Click the effect you want to apply to the object (for example, **Drive-In Effect**).

④ Click the **Animation Preview** button to see what the effect will look like in the slide-miniature window.

End Task

Working with Button Controls

Action buttons are elements you can add to your PowerPoint presentations to provide information or draw attention to your presentation. You can set up any type of action: opening a document, linking to a URL, or even playing a sound or movie clip. For example, you can add an action button that makes a sound when you click the button during the presentation.

⚠ WARNING

Each action button should be independent of other objects on your slides. Action buttons do not work properly if you group them together.

Task 10: Adding Action Buttons

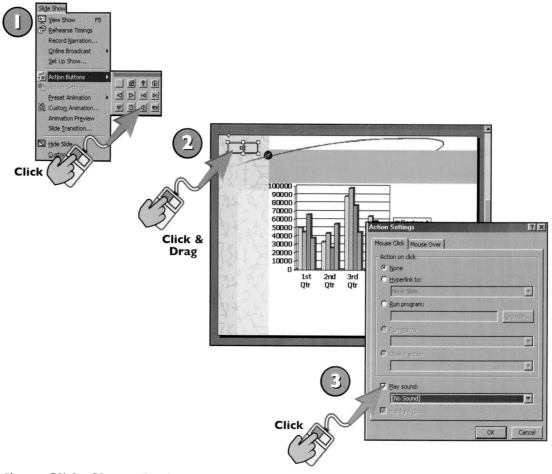

Start Here

Click

Click & Drag

Click

1 Choose **Slide Show**, **Action Buttons**, **Sound**.

2 Click and hold the mouse button in the location where you want the action button. Drag to the appropriate size and then release the mouse button.

3 Click the **Play Sound** checkbox option.

Next Step

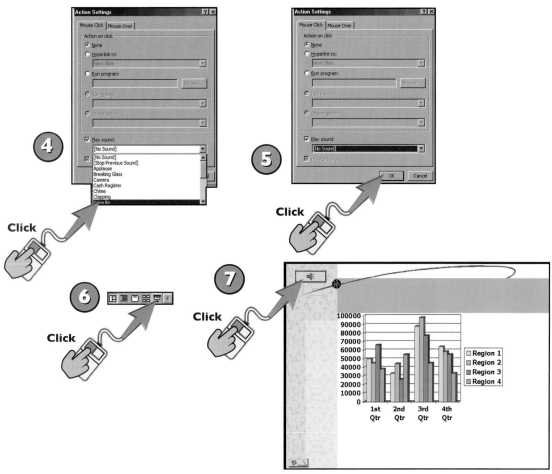

✓ **Multiple Action Buttons**
You can place several action buttons on a slide. For example, assign one that makes a sound, one that takes you to a Web site, and one that pops up visual information for the audience.

✓ **Hyperlink Buttons**
Adding a hyperlink button to your presentation can be a convenient resource for information. For example, if someone in the audience has a question about where your information came from, you could click a hyperlink button and immediately go to the Web site where you obtained your information (assuming, of course, that your PC is connected to the Internet during the presentation).

4 Click the **Play Sound** drop-down list box and select the sound you want to play when you click the action button (for example, **Drive By**).

5 Click the **OK** button.

6 Click the **Slide Show** button to see what the effect will look like.

7 Click the **Action Button** button to see how the action works. Press the **Esc** key to return to Slide view.

End Task

Using Pack and Go

Perhaps someday you'll need to give a presentation using someone else's computer. If you're not sure PowerPoint is on that computer, you can create a Pack and Go presentation to view your presentation from any computer, even one that does not have PowerPoint installed.

Task 11: Preparing the Presentation for Another Computer

Start Here

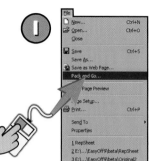

Click

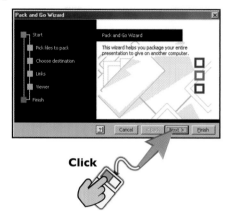

Click

Click

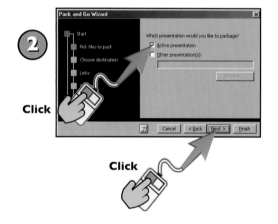

Click

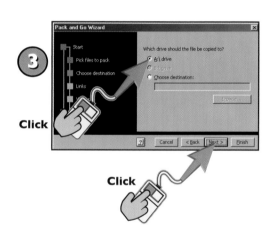

Click

Click

✓ Network Files

If your company allows you to place files on a network drive, and the conference room computer is connected to the network, you can access your files from there.

1 Choose **File**, **Pack and Go** to open the welcome information on the Pack and Go Wizard dialog box, and then click **Next**.

2 Click the **Active Presentation** option, and then click **Next**.

3 Click the **A:\ drive** option, and then click **Next**.

Next Step

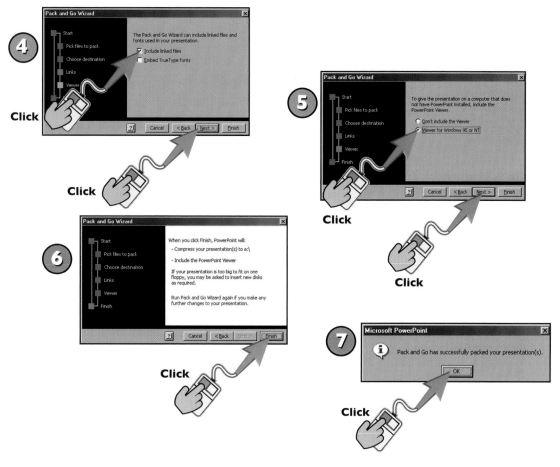

4   Click the **Include Linked Files** check box, and then click **Next**.

5   Click the **Viewer for Windows 95 or NT** option, and then click **Next**.

6   Read the Finish information, place a disk in the A:\ drive, and click **Finish**.

7   Click the **OK** button when a message appears, letting you know that the presentation has been packed successfully.

✓ PowerPoint Viewer
If you don't have the PowerPoint Viewer installed on your hard disk, you might be asked to insert the **Office 2000 CD-ROM** before you can complete the Pack and Go. If you decide not to include the Viewer in your pack, simply click the **Cancel** button so Pack and Go can continue packing without the Viewer. Remember that you'll need the Viewer if the computer you'll use to deliver the presentation doesn't have one.

Task 12: Rehearsing a Presentation

Timing Your Presentation

When people create presentations, they usually have a specific time limit they need to stick to. Instead of using your watch and trying to time the show yourself, why not let PowerPoint do the work for you? If you need to stop and make some notes, you can pause the time recorder. If you get off to a bad start or need to repeat the rehearsal, you can click the **Repeat** button. When you get to the end of the slide show, PowerPoint asks if you want to record the slide times. If you do, Slide Sorter view shows recorded times with each slide.

✅ **Canceling the Rehearsal**
You can click the **Close** (×) button on the Rehearsal toolbar to cancel a rehearsal and return to working in the presentation.

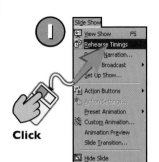

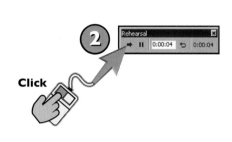

Click

Click

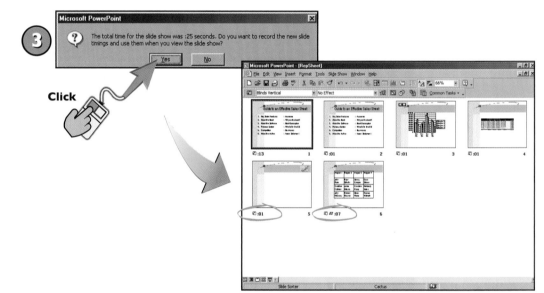

Click

(1) Choose **Slide Show**, **Rehearse Timings**.

(2) Click the **Next** button on the Rehearsal toolbar to rehearse your slide show as you would perform it. PowerPoint will notify you when you click through the last slide.

(3) Click the **Yes** button to record your slide show times. These are then displayed in the Slide Sorter view.

Task 13: Printing a Presentation

Start
Here

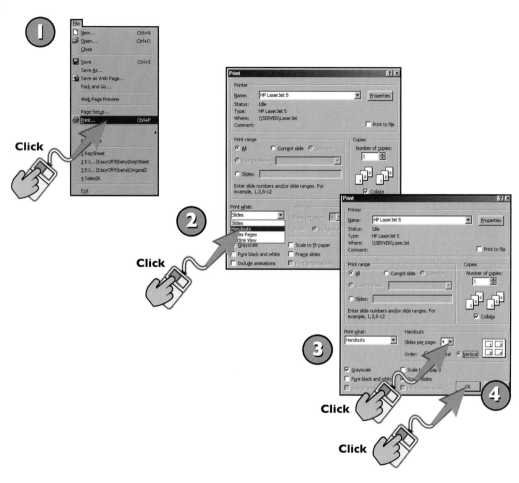

Click

Click

Click

Click

Getting Hard Copy

In PowerPoint you can print copies of your presentation as you need them. For example, you might want to print copies of your presentation so the audience can follow along, print your presentation in outline view for your boss to review, or print speaker notes for yourself.

✓ Additional Printing Options

In the **Print Range** area of the Print dialog box, you can choose to print all slides, the current slide, or specific slides. In the **Copies** area, you can select the number of copies to print or have PowerPoint collate the slides.

---

(1) Choose **File**, **Print** to open the Print dialog box.

(2) Click the **Print What** drop-down arrow and choose the printing option you want (for example, **Handouts**). You can print the slides, handouts for your audience, notes pages, or the outline.

(3) Click the number of **Slides per Page** you want (for example, **4**). This option is only available if you print handouts.

(4) Click the **OK** button, and the presentation prints.

End
Task

Outlook 2000 Basics

Microsoft Outlook is an email *client*, an appointment calendar, a journal, and other tools, all rolled into one personal information management (PIM) application. Outlook is similar to a three-ring-bound organizer with folders that you might tote around during your business day.

With Outlook, you can keep track of email, daily appointments, and meetings. Whether you are working on an individual computer or computers linked together in workgroups, you can use Outlook to prioritize your work and manage your time.

You can easily access all these features using the Outlook Today view. From this view you can see items in your calendar, tasks, contacts list, and even mail folders.

Outlook mail folders let you read, create, and send messages. When you receive a message, it goes in your Inbox. When you create and send a message, it goes in your Outbox until you actually connect to the Internet. After you have connected to the Internet and sent the message, Outlook puts a copy of the message in your Sent Items folder.

To use Outlook's email features, you need to have access to the Internet. You might have an account with an online service (for example, America Online), with a local Internet service provider (ISP), or in a corporate setting, where you have to log in to the network to gain Internet access. In any case, it would be a good idea for you to connect to the Internet to perform the tasks in this part, although to understand the tasks you don't need to.

Tasks

Task 1: Moving Around in Outlook Today

Working with Windows and Shortcuts

Outlook manages many different folders for your email and information management. These folders can be accessed by clicking the icons on the Outlook bar. The Outlook bar is divided into Outlook Shortcuts, My Shortcuts, and Other Shortcuts. Outlook 2000 also offers an Outlook Today view that summarizes your appointments, email, tasks, and a contact search.

✓ Shortcut Icons

Notice that the shortcut icons on the Outlook Shortcuts bar are larger than those on the My Shortcuts bar. To alter the icon sizes, right-click the shortcut bar and choose either **Large Icons** or **Small Icons**.

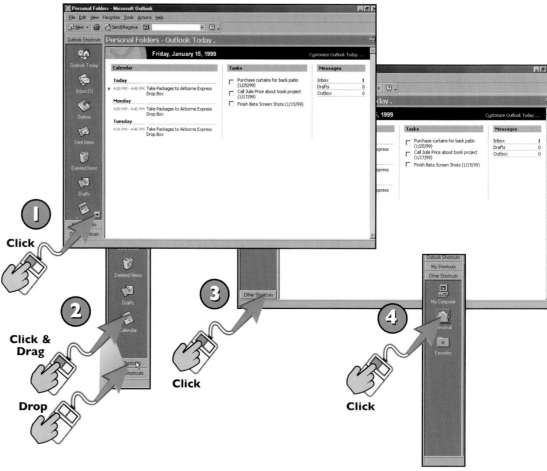

Click

Click & Drag

Drop

Click

Click

① Click the down arrow on the Outlook Shortcuts bar to see the other shortcuts available at the bottom of the bar.

② Click the **Calendar** icon and drag it over the **My Shortcuts** bar and drop the icon; the icon's new location is displayed.

③ Click the **Other Shortcuts** bar.

④ Click the **Personal** folder icon.

Next Step

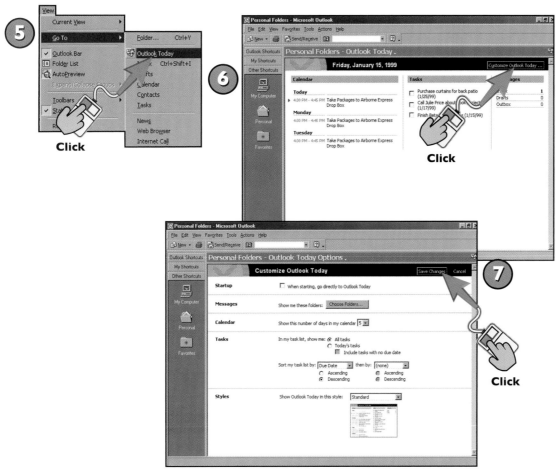

5 Choose **View, Go To**, **Outlook Today** to return to Outlook Today view.

6 Click **Customize Outlook Today** to change the various ways you can organize information presented in Outlook Today.

7 Click **Save Changes** to accept any options and return to Outlook Today view. Click **Cancel** if you don't want to keep any changes.

Reviewing Messages

The Inbox enables you to send and receive messages as well as read email and faxes. You can preview messages before you open them and open and close messages in the various Outlook Mail folders. You can have multiple messages open at the same time by double-clicking each message. In addition, you can close each message by clicking the **Close** (×) button on the title bar. An unread message looks like the back of a sealed envelope; a read message looks like the back of an envelope with the flap open.

Task 2: Reading Email Messages

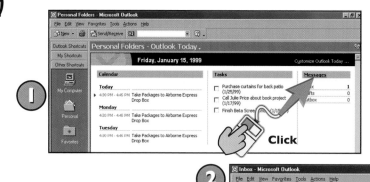

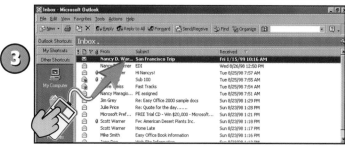

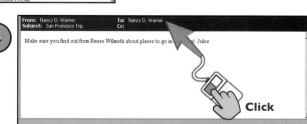

(✓) **Reading Message Attachments**
You can open and review the attached files while you are in Outlook. Choose **Open** when prompted to either open or save the attachment.

1. Click the **Messages** option in Outlook Today.

2. Click the **Send/Receive** button on the Standard toolbar to see if you have any new messages.

3. Click the message you would like to read; the message is displayed in the Preview pane.

4. Click in the **Preview Pane** and move through the message with the arrow (→, ←, ↑, ↓) keys.

Task 3: Saving Mail Attachments

Start
Here

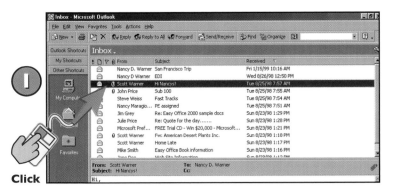

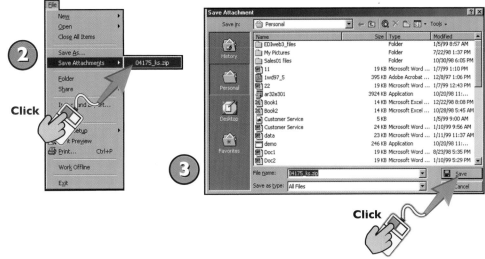

Email Messages with Icons

Many times you receive messages that contain attachments. These are usually files the sender wants you to use. You can double-click any attachment icon in the message to launch its application (for example, if you just want to quickly view a Word document's contents). To save the attachment, you save it using the same kind of dialog box you use to save any other Office document.

⊘ Saving Multiple Attachments

You can save multiple attachments at the same time and to the same location. Outlook asks you which attachments you want to save to a particular location. If you want to save them one at a time to different locations, you can do that, too.

① Click a message with an attachment (one with a paperclip in the header).

② Choose **File**, **Save Attachments**, and select the file (or files) you want to save.

③ Click the **Save** button to save the attachment with the same name the sender assigned it.

Task 4: Replying to a Message

Sending a Message Back

After you open and read a message, you probably want to reply to it. You can reply to the person who sent you the message (the sender), to the sender plus additional recipients, or even to a completely different set of recipients.

✓ Replying to All

If you receive a message that also went to other people, you may want to respond to the sender as well as the other recipients. Clicking the Reply to All button is an efficient way of sending your reply to everyone included in the original message.

✓ Message Information

After you reply to or forward a message, the original message icon contains an arrow indicating that you replied to or forwarded the message.

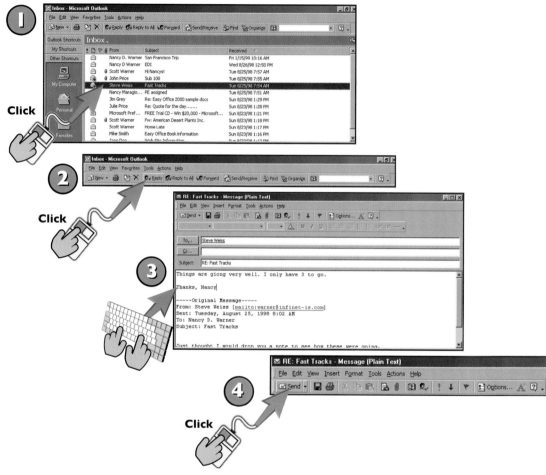

1. Click the message you want to reply to.

2. Click the **Reply** button on the Standard toolbar.

3. Type your reply to the message.

4. Click the **Send** button on the Standard toolbar to send the message.

Task 5: Forwarding a Message

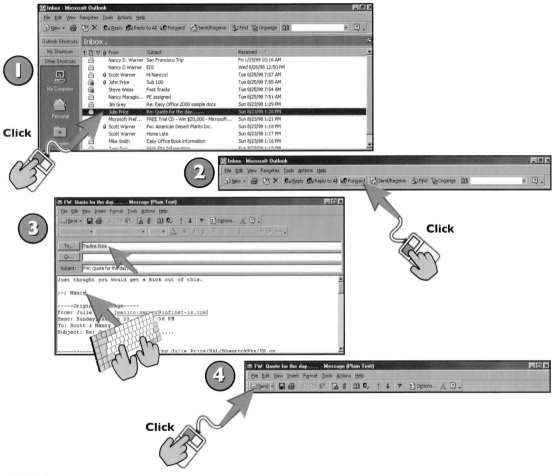

①

Click

②

Click

③

④

Click

Sending a Message to Someone Else

Sometimes when you read a message, you find that the information would be pertinent to another individual. In that case, you can forward the message to that person. You usually want to add a sentence or two that explains why you're forwarding the message.

✓ **Altering Information**
You can alter the information in the Message window by selecting the text and deleting it or typing over it. For example, you might want to alter the Subject line to be more understandable to the person you are forwarding the message to.

① Click the message you want to forward.

② Click the **Forward** button on the Standard toolbar to open the message in a new window.

③ Type the email address of the person to whom you want to forward the message. Press the **Tab** key three times, and type the message.

④ Click the **Send** button on the Standard toolbar to send the message.

Task 6: Creating a Message

Writing an Email Message

Creating email messages is perhaps the most common thing you'll do in Outlook. Fortunately, creating a new message is easy. It is also simple to attach a file to your messages. This task teaches you how. You will also learn how to alter the level of a message's importance. This can help the recipient distinguish which messages to read first.

✓ **Message Recipients**
You can click the **To** or **Cc** buttons to the left of their text boxes in an email message. This opens the Select Names dialog box, where you can add message recipients by typing contact names and selecting them from the Contacts list. Then, click the **To→**, **Cc→**, or **Bcc→** (for blind carbon copy) button to add the recipients to the message.

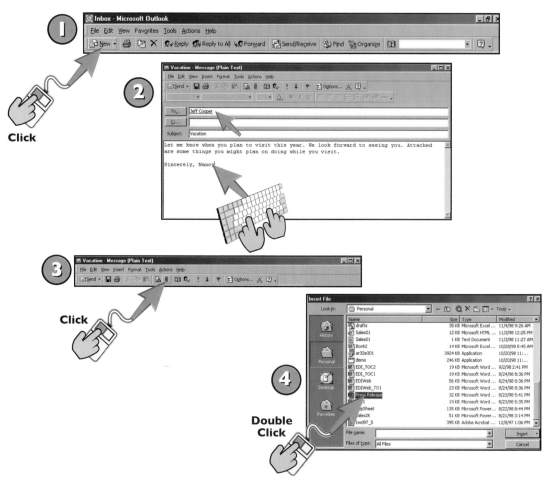

Start Here

Click

Click

Double Click

1 Click the **New Mail Message** button on the Standard toolbar.

2 Type the recipient's email address in the **To** area (you can also add recipients in the **Cc** area) and press the **Tab** key twice; then type a **Subject** and the text of the message.

3 Click the **Insert File** button (if you want to include an attachment with your message).

4 Double-click the file you want to attach (for example, **EDI**).

Next Step

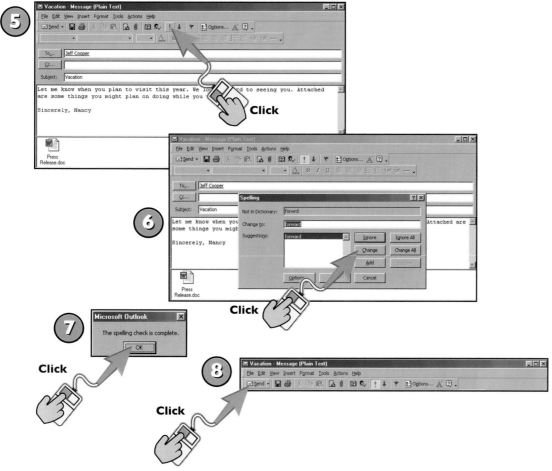

Click

Click

Click

Click

Click

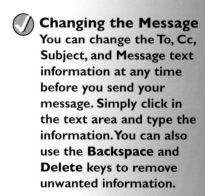
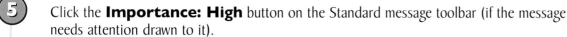

⑤ Click the **Importance: High** button on the Standard message toolbar (if the message needs attention drawn to it).

⑥ Press the **F7** key to check the message's spelling. Outlook highlights any misspelled words, and the Spelling dialog box suggests other spellings; use the **Change** or **Ignore** buttons as appropriate.

⑦ Click the **OK** button if the spelling check is complete.

⑧ Click the **Send** button to send your message.

Getting Rid of Unwanted Messages

Just like regular mail, email has *junk* mail you do not want to keep in your Inbox. For example, you might want to delete the Welcome message Microsoft sends you the first time you use Outlook. Or perhaps you want to delete a message that is in your Outbox waiting to be sent.

✓ **Locating the Deleted Items Folder**
If you moved the Deleted Items folder to a different location, simply click the Outlook Shortcut bars to find the icon.

✓ **Alternate Mail Folders**
If you decide you want to keep the message but don't want it in your Inbox, you can click the message and drag it into a different folder.

Task 7: Deleting a Message

Click

Click

Right Click

Click

Click

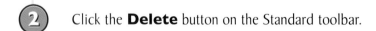

① Click the message you want to delete.

② Click the **Delete** button on the Standard toolbar.

③ Right-click the **Deleted Items** folder and choose **Empty "Deleted Items" Folder** from the shortcut menu.

④ Click the **Yes** button to permanently delete the message.

Task 8: Finding a Message

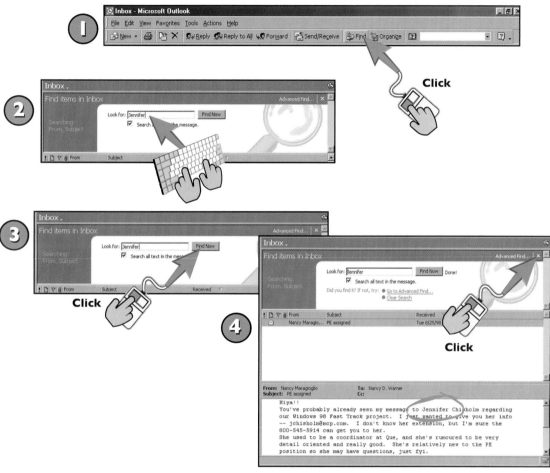

Click

Click

Click

Searching for Messages

Perhaps you received an email message that had information you need, but you cannot remember which message it was in. For example, you were sent contact information on a person, didn't add it to your contacts, and now need to get in touch with that person. Using the Find feature in Outlook will help you.

✓ **Advanced Find**
If you don't find the message on your first find, you can try an advanced find. Click the **Advanced Find** button in the Find Message pane and narrow the scope of your find with more selection criteria.

---

1. Click the **Find** button on the Standard toolbar.

2. Type in the key word or words that will help find the message.

3. Click the **Find Now** button.

4. Click the **Close (×)** button when you finish using the Find feature.

Managing Appointments

In Date Navigator, you can switch the view from today's schedule to a different day, a week-at-a-glance, and a month-at-a-glance. You can schedule appointments and events in any view, as well as move the appointments and events.

Task 9: Viewing Your Schedule

Start Here

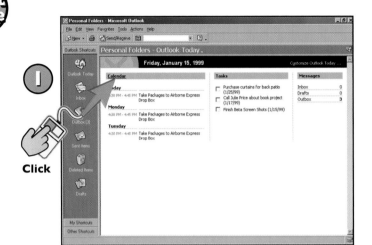

Click

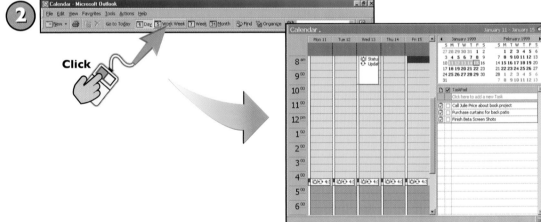

Click

✓ **Long Appointments**
If your appointment is too long to read in Week or Month view, you no longer have to click the Day view or Go to Today button on the Calendar toolbar to read it all. You can simply move the mouse pointer over the appointment, and the complete description appears in a ScreenTip.

1 Click **Calendar** on the Outlook Today opening window.

2 Click the **Work Week** button on the Calendar toolbar.

Next Step

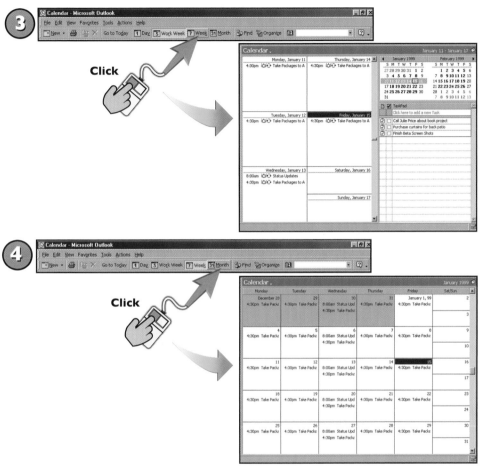

③ Click the **Week** button on the Calendar toolbar.

④ Click the **Month** button on the Calendar toolbar.

✅ **Go To Today**
If you need to immediately go to today's calendar, you can click the **Go To Today** button on the Standard toolbar. This takes you to today's date, no matter what view you are in. To see only today's events, click the **Day** button.

✅ **Organizing Your Calendar**
If you would like to see suggestions for how you can better organize your calendar, click the **Organize** button on the Standard toolbar. Outlook shows you how to use categories and views to manage and organize your information.

Task 10: Scheduling an Appointment

Adding Appointments

You can fill in daily and weekly appointments in your schedule. For example, you might want to schedule a meeting, doctor and dentist appointments, and conferences. The time schedule displays a 24-hour day, starting at 12 a.m. You can assign a reminder for an appointment so you don't miss the appointment.

✅ Selecting a Conference Room

If you work in a corporate environment, conference rooms may have been added to the central Outlook database. You can select them without having to type or remember their names. Go to the **Attendee Availability** tab and click the **Invite Others** button. Many companies place the rooms in the Contacts list.

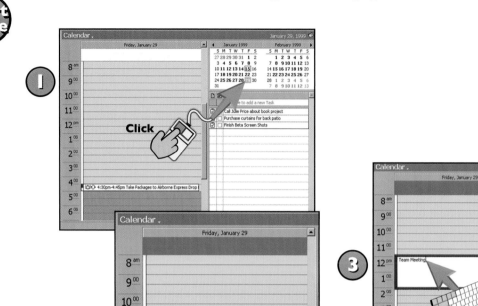

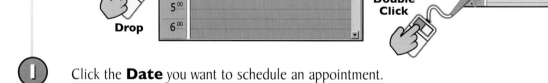

① Click the **Date** you want to schedule an appointment.

② Click the **12 p.m.** time slot and drag the pointer down to the bottom of the **1 p.m.** time slot; then release the mouse button.

③ Type **Team Meeting** and press the **Enter** key.

④ Double-click the border of the **Team Meeting** appointment to open the appointment options.

Next Step

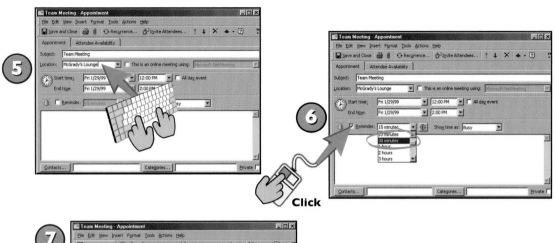

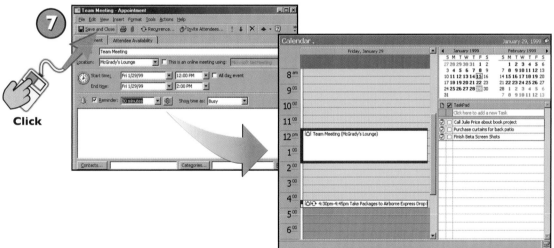

Click

Click

✓ **Moving an Appointment**

To move an appointment to a different time slot, move the mouse pointer to the blue vertical bar on the left end of the appointment's or event's text. Drag the appointment or event to the new location.

✓ **Viewing with ScreenTips**

If you cannot read the entire line of a scheduled appointment, move the mouse pointer over the appointment, and the entire appointment information line appears in a ScreenTip. This is a new feature in Outlook 2000.

⑤ Type the location of the meeting (for example, **McGrady's Lounge**).

⑥ Click the **Reminder** option and select an earlier **Reminder** time to notify you about the appointment (for example, **30 minutes**).

⑦ Click the **Save and Close** button, and you see what the appointment looks like in your calendar.

✓ **Removing an Appointment**

To remove an appointment, click the appointment and click the **Delete** button on the Standard toolbar.

Task 11: Planning a Meeting

Inviting Others to a Meeting

Outlook's Meeting Planner enables you to plan a meeting from start to finish with other attendees. You specify the attendees, determine a meeting time, check for any schedule conflicts, and then schedule a room. You also can send an email to the other attendees, inviting them to the meeting.

Inviting Others
In a corporate setting, you can click the **Invite Others** button and choose attendees and resources from your company's list.

WARNING
Keep in mind that you should offer meeting attendees alternate meeting times in case they have scheduling conflicts.

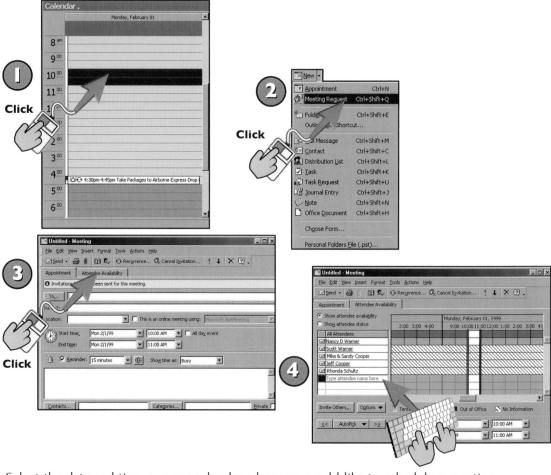

Select the date and time on your calendar when you would like to schedule a meeting.

Choose **Meeting Request** from the **New Appointment** drop-down list.

Click the **Attendee Availability** tab on the Meeting dialog box.

Type the name of the attendees in the **Type Attendee Name Here** box. Press the **Enter** key and repeat this for each attendee.

Next Step

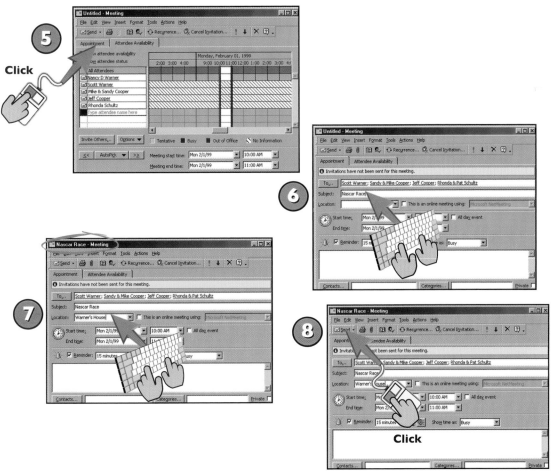

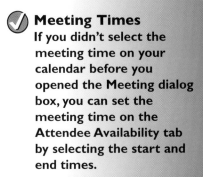

✓ Meeting Times

If you didn't select the meeting time on your calendar before you opened the Meeting dialog box, you can set the meeting time on the Attendee Availability tab by selecting the start and end times.

✓ Meeting Icons

In Calendar view, choose the meeting's date on the current month calendar and then click the **Day** button on the Calendar toolbar. Notice that the meeting is scheduled, with a **Meeting icon** (two people) next to it.

✓ Meeting Responses

Many workplaces set up Outlook so that recipients of meeting requests can choose to accept, tentatively accept, or decline your meeting. This comes back to you as email messages noting the responses. When a recipient accepts or tentatively accepts, Outlook automatically puts the meeting on that person's calendar.

5 Click **Appointment** tab to add information about the meeting.

6 Type the **Subject** of the meeting; notice the new title bar name.

7 Type where the meeting will be held in the **Location** text box.

8 Click the **Send** button on the Meeting toolbar, and the meeting notification is sent via email and listed on your calendar.

Managing Your Tasks

Creating a to-do list helps you organize tasks and projects that are significant to the dates and appointments on your schedule. You can build lists of things you need to do each day and items you must work on to complete a project. Any item you list in the to-do list is called a *task*.

✓ Deleting Tasks
You can right-click any task and press the **Delete** key to delete it.

Task 12: Working with Tasks on Your To-Do List

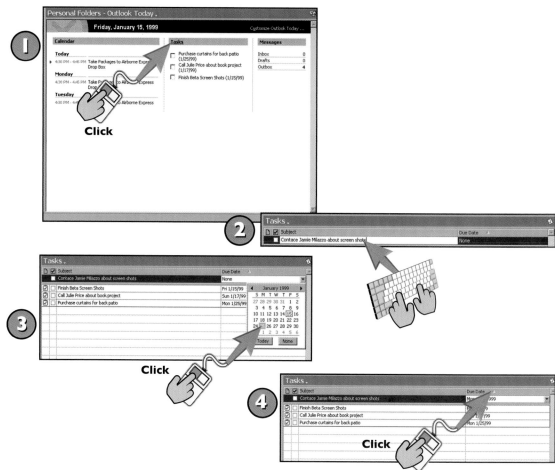

Click

Click

Click

① Click **Tasks** on the Outlook Today opening window.

② Type a new task in the **Click Here to Add a New Task** list box.

③ Click the **Due Date** drop-down arrow next to any task and select a due date for that task.

④ Click the **Due Date** header to sort the tasks by date.

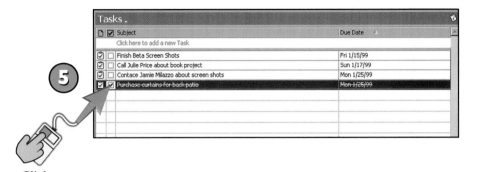

Click

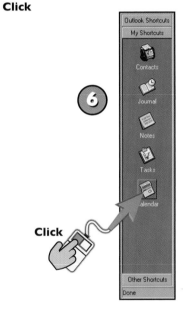

Click

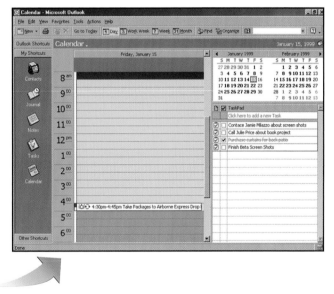

 Due Dates
You don't have to assign
due dates to your tasks,
but doing so can help you
keep track of when tasks
need to be done and
whether you have passed
the completion date.

 Past Due
If you don't complete a
task by a certain date, the
task appears in a red font,
indicating that the task
wasn't completed and is
past the due date.

 Click the empty check boxes to the left of any task descriptions you have recently completed. A line is drawn through the task, indicating that the task is complete.

 Click the **Calendar** button on the Outlook Shortcuts bar to return to Calendar view. The tasks are now listed on the TaskPad on the right side of the schedule.

Task 13: Creating a Contact

Keeping Track of People

You can create a contact list that contains business and personal contact information. The list is an electronic version of an address book or card file. After you set up the names, addresses, phone numbers, and email addresses, you can use the contacts to create mailing lists and dial up other computers with a modem.

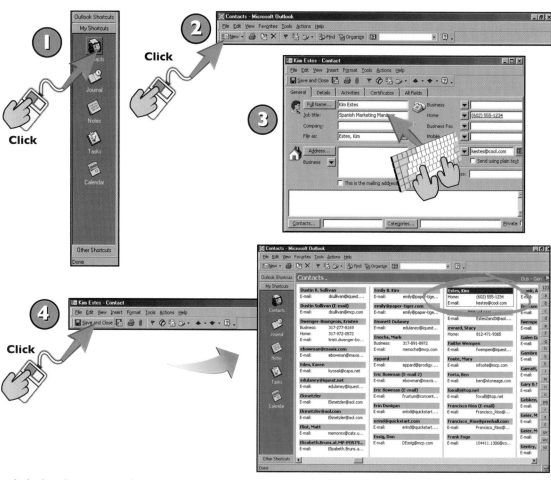

✓ **Deleting a Contact**
To delete a contact, click the contact to select it, and then click the **Delete** button on the Contacts toolbar.

✓ **Finding a Contact**
You can quickly search for a contact while in the Outlook Today window. Type the name of the contact in the **Find a Contact** text box and click the **Go** button.

① Click the **Contacts** button on the Outlook bar.

② Click the **New Contact** button on the Standard toolbar.

③ Type the contact information, pressing the **Tab** key to move between text boxes.

④ When you finish, choose the **Save and Close** button on the Contacts toolbar.

Task 14: Creating Notes

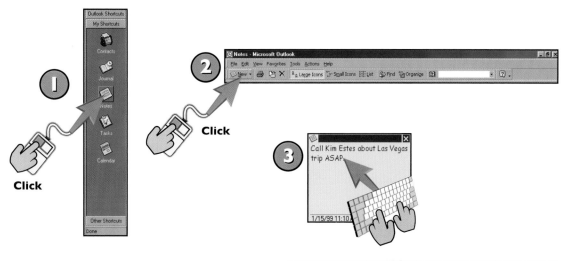

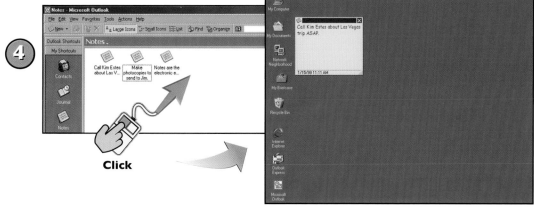

Working with On-Screen Sticky Notes

You can use Outlook's Notes feature to jot down ideas, questions, reminders, directions, and anything you would write on paper. You can leave notes visible onscreen as you work.

Click the **Notes** button on the Outlook Shortcuts bar.

Click the **New Note** button on the Standard toolbar.

Type your note in the Note box.

Click in the Notes window to see the note. Any active notes also appear in your workspace.

✓ Editing Notes

To open a note in Note view, double-click the note. To resize an open note, drag the lower-right corner of the note. To delete an open note, click the **Note** icon in the upper-left corner of the note and then choose **Delete** on the shortcut menu.

End Task

Task 15: Creating a Journal Entry

Tracking Activity

The Journal feature gives you a place to record information that is important to you. You can record activities such as talking to a contact, writing a mail message, or working on a file, as well as appointments, tasks, and notes. The Journal feature also automatically keeps track of work you perform in other Office 2000 applications.

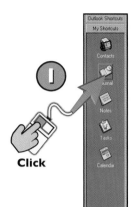

Start Here

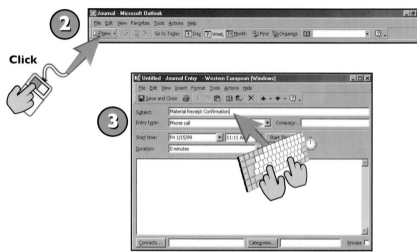

Click

Click

Click

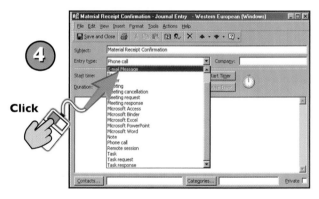

Click

✓ Entry Types

Selecting the Entry Type is very important because this is what the Journal feature keeps track of. For example, if you select Microsoft Word, the Journal feature tracks the amount of time and documents you work on.

1. Click the **Journal** icon on the Outlook Shortcuts bar.

2. Click the **New Journal** button on the Standard toolbar.

3. Type a subject in the **Subject** text box.

4. Click the **Entry Type** drop-down arrow to select the kind of thing you're doing; for example, **E-mail message**.

Next Step

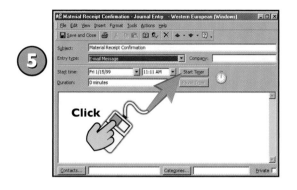

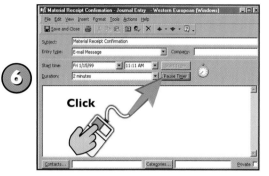

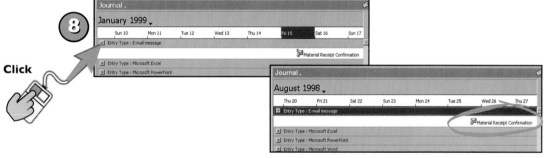

Deleting a Journal Entry
To delete a journal entry in Journal view, right-click the journal entry you want to delete and choose **Delete** on the shortcut menu.

Timer Buttons
The Stop Timer and Start Timer buttons enable you to track the duration of the journal entry (from beginning to end). That time duration is then displayed in the Duration list box.

⑤ Click the **Start Timer** button to begin creating your email to track the duration.

⑥ Click the **Pause Timer** button when finished writing the email.

⑦ Click the **Save and Close** button.

⑧ Click the **+** sign for **Entry Type: E-mail Message** to review the journal entry assigned; it will then become a **–** sign.

PART 10

Office 2000 and the Web

Numerous Office 2000 features can make working with the Internet and the Web easier and more convenient. You learned how to save an Office document as a Web page, use Web Page Preview, and use other Office Web options such as frames, themes, and backgrounds in Part 4, "Advanced Word Features."

This part covers general Office Web features, not those that benefit most from using Microsoft Word. These tasks can be done in Word, Excel, and PowerPoint. We even show you how to get Outlook into the act.

You can view your Office documents in a *browser* to see how they will look if you put them on a Web page. You will learn how to save a Web page as an Office document and open it up in an Office application. You can add *URLs* and all kinds of *hyperlinks* to your documents. In addition, you can edit, assign ScreenTips to, and remove hyperlinks using the Hyperlink dialog box. You can even add email hyperlinks and send your documents as email messages.

To use the Web and Internet features in Office 2000, you need to have access to the Internet. You might have an account with an online service (for example, America Online), with a local Internet service provider (ISP), or in a corporate setting, where you have to log in to the network to gain Internet access. In any case, it would be a good idea for you to connect to the Internet to perform the tasks in this part.

Tasks

Task 1: Activating the Web Toolbar

Working with the Web Toolbar

You can use the Web toolbar in Office 2000 applications to open documents on the Internet; browse Web documents; jump to other documents, objects, or pages using hyperlinks; or even share your documents on the Web. If you have ever used a Web browser (such as Microsoft Internet Explorer or Netscape Navigator), this toolbar should look familiar.

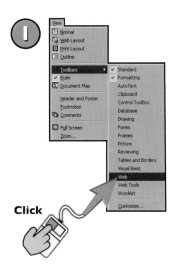

Click

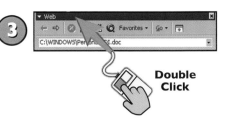

Double Click

Click

✓ **Closing the Web Toolbar**
Choose View, Toolbars and click the **Web** toolbar option. The Web toolbar disappears.

 Choose **View**, **Toolbars**, **Web** to open the Web toolbar in an Office application (for example, Microsoft Word).

② Move the mouse pointer over the buttons on the Web toolbar to see a ScreenTip name of each button.

③ Double-click the Web toolbar name to dock it with the other toolbars (Standard and Formatting).

④ Click the drop-down arrow of the **Address** list box to see Office documents and Web pages you visited recently.

Task 2: Viewing the Start Page

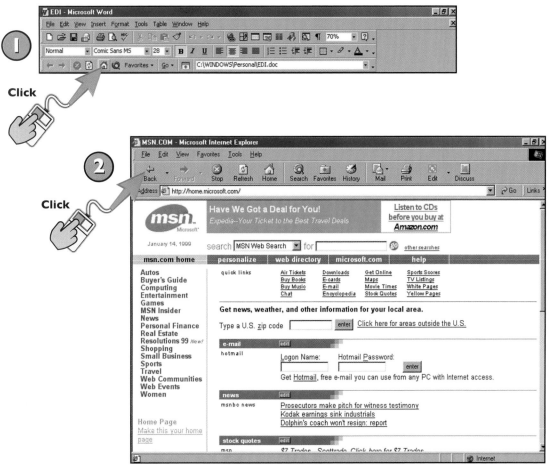

Click

Click

Browsing the Web from Office Applications

Office 2000 applications let you immediately access the Internet and browse Web pages from your Office applications. For example, you might be working on a document in Word and need to look up information on a particular Web page. You can do this in Office without having to open your Web browser.

✓ Web Browsers

Keep in mind that as soon as you go to a Web page, you are in a Web browser. From there you can go to any other Web pages you want. In addition, instead of using the **Back** button to return to your Office document, you can click the document on the Windows taskbar to switch from the browser application to the Office application.

1 Click the **Start Page** button on the Web toolbar.

2 Click the **Back** button on the Standard toolbar to return to the previous document; in this case, you return to the original document.

Searching the Web from Office Applications

Say you are working on a document in Excel and need to search for data pertaining to what you are writing about. Instead of opening your Web browser, you can simply use the Web toolbar in your Excel application to start the search page automatically.

✓ Alternative Search Engines

Instead of using Microsoft's search page, sometimes it is faster to go directly to the search engine page you want. Try typing one of the following: www.yahoo.com or www.lycos.com.

Task 3: Viewing the Search the Web Page

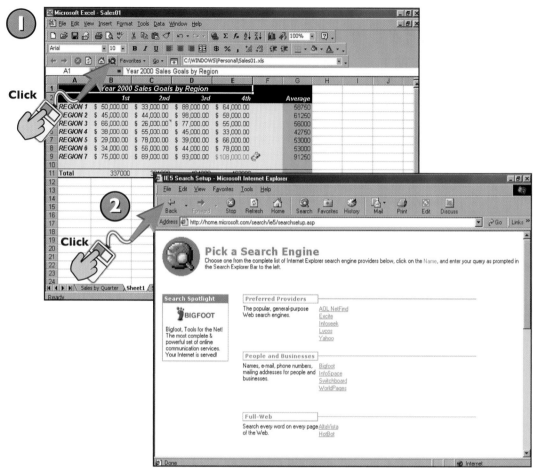

Click

Click

① Click the **Search the Web** button on the Web toolbar.

② Click the **Back** button on the Standard toolbar to return to the previous hyperlink; or in this case, you return to the original Office document.

Task 4: Opening an Internet Address

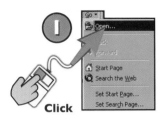

Click

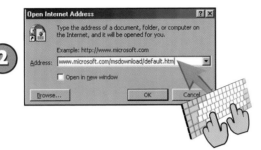

Using the Go Menu

When you want to go to a specific Web page, but you don't want to go to your start or search pages first, you can use the **Go** menu. This menu gives you several options to begin browsing Web pages.

Click

1. Choose **Go**, **Open** to open the Open Internet Address page.

2. Type the Internet address you would like to go to (for example, `www.microsoft.com/msdownload/default.htm`).

3. Click the **OK** button; your default browser opens automatically to the address you typed in.

Recent Locations and Files

Files and Web pages that you have recently visited are listed at the bottom of the Go menu; if you choose one of them, you are immediately taken back to it.

Saving Files from the Web to Your Hard Drive

In many situations you need to download software, data, or information from a Web site. This is a simple task and one you should try on different Web sites to become familiar with the procedure. Basically the files you want to download need to be saved from the Web site to your computer hard drive.

✓ Saving Locations

Your Windows settings probably select the default location `c:\Windows\Downloads` as the place where the files will be saved. However, you can save your downloaded files to any location you want on your hard drive.

Task 5: Downloading Information from the Web

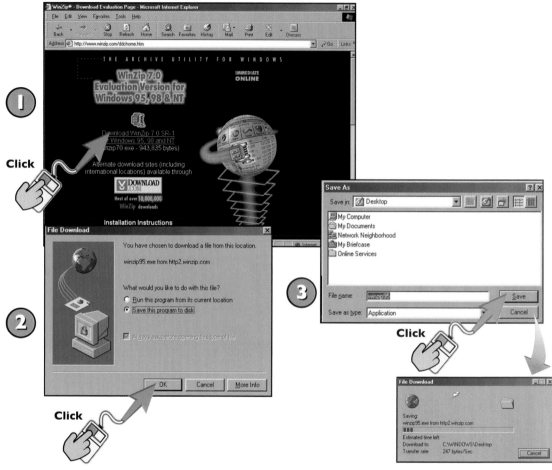

Open an Internet address (for example, **www.winzip.com**; refer to Task 4, "Opening an Internet Address," if necessary) and click the download hyperlink.

Click the **OK** button to save this application to disk.

Click the **Save** button and a File Download dialog box will display the download status.

Task 6: Adding a Favorite Web Page

Start Here

Click

Click

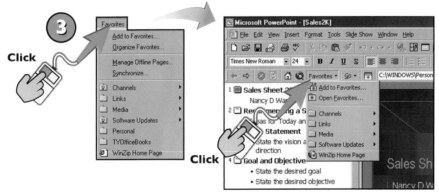

Click

Click

Adding to Your Favorites List

When you are comfortable with visiting Web sites and browsing Web pages, you will find that there are certain ones you want to visit regularly. For example, perhaps you want to locate information about Office 2000 or a link to a site where you want to download software updates.

① Open an Internet address (for example, **www.winzip.com**; refer to Task 4, "Opening an Internet Address," if necessary) and choose **Favorites, Add to Favorites**.

② Click the **OK** button to accept the default page name.

③ Click the Favorites menu option to see the new addition. Notice that this is also available in the Office document Favorites menu.

✓ Favorites Names
You can assign any name you want to a Web page Favorites listing. You don't have to select the default name. Simply type in the new name at Step 2 in this task.

End Task

Saving and Opening Web Pages in Office

There are times when you find some information on a Web page and you want to save the information for reference. Office 2000 lets you save the Web page as an Office document and allows you to edit this page in an Office application. This can be convenient because previously when you saved a Web page, many unnecessary objects were saved in the file and sometimes rendered it unreadable. Now after you save these pages, you can open them and they look almost identical to the original Web pages.

✓ Editing a Web Page

As an alternative to saving the Web page and working with it in an Office application, you can choose **File**, **Edit** with a Microsoft Office application. This automatically opens the Office application that is best suited to edit that Web page.

Task 7: Saving a Web Page as a Document

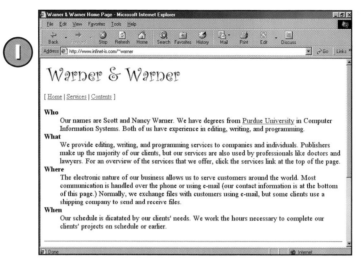

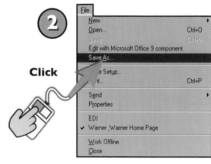

Click

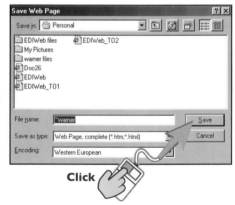

Click

 Open an Internet address (for example, **www.infinet-is.com**/~**warner**; refer to Task 4, "Opening an Internet Address," if necessary).

 Choose **File**, **Save As** to open the Save Web Page dialog box.

3 Click the **Save** button to save the file with the default file name in the **Personal** folder.

Next Step

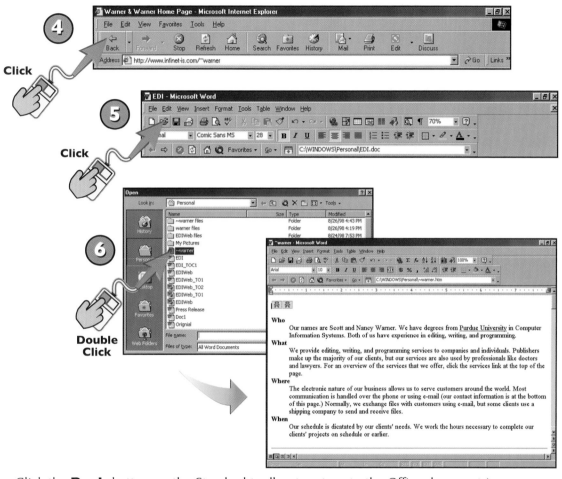

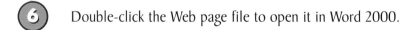

Click

Click

Double Click

4 Click the **Back** button on the Standard toolbar to return to the Office document in which you started.

5 Click the **Open** button on the Standard toolbar.

6 Double-click the Web page file to open it in Word 2000.

Browsing Office Documents

Not only can you use the Web toolbar to quickly open Web pages, but you can use it to quickly switch to other files and Office documents. This can be convenient when you are working in multiple files and don't want to have to use the Windows 98 taskbar. In addition, it helps you keep track of the files you have recently worked on.

Task 8: Viewing Documents with the Web Toolbar

Start Here

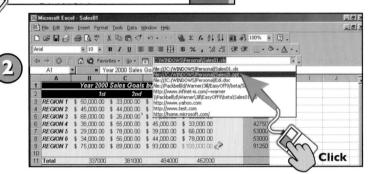

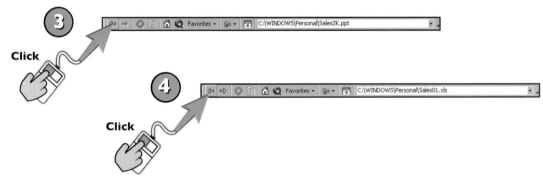

✅ **The Address List Box**
The Address list box can be a convenient way to keep track of the location of the document you are currently working on. For example, if you share files on a network drive, the drive letter and folders are listed.

① Click the drop-down arrow of the **Address** list box and select an Office document you have worked on recently (for example, **C:\WINDOWS\Personal\Sales01.xls**).

② Click the drop-down arrow of the **Address** list box and select another Office document you have worked on recently (for example, **C:\WINDOWS\Personal\Sales2k.ppt**).

③ Click the **Back** button on the Web toolbar to move back one link.

④ Click the **Back** button on the Web toolbar again to move back to your original link.

Task 9: Typing a URL into a Document

Start Here

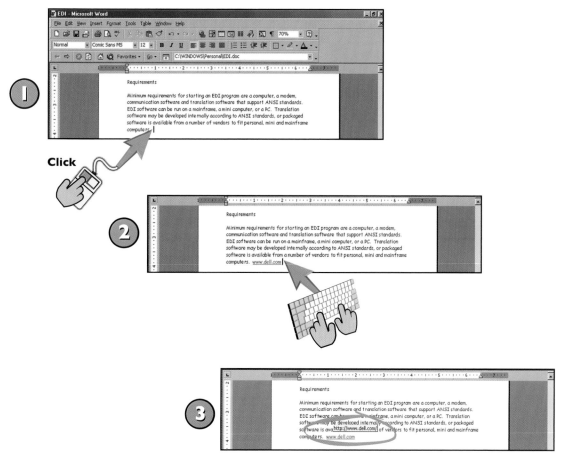

Click

Adding Hyperlinks to Documents

A URL (uniform resource locator) is a link to an addressable location on the Internet. Word 2000 lets you type these into your documents and automatically establishes a link. Notice that this link is a different color and underlined; it is referred to as a *hyperlink*.

✓ **Non-automatic Hyperlinks**
If you type a URL into your document and Office 2000 doesn't recognize it automatically as a hyperlink, see Task 11, "Inserting a Web Hyperlink," to make it one.

✓ **Removing Hyperlinks**
If you are typing a hyperlink into a document as an example and don't want it to be an active link, see Task 16, "Removing a Hyperlink."

① Click the mouse pointer in the document where you want to add the URL.

② Type the URL into your document (for example, **www.dell.com**), and the address automatically becomes a hyperlink.

③ Move the mouse pointer over the hyperlink, and the location displays in a ScreenTip.

End Task

Task 10: Clicking a URL in a Document

Document Links to the Web

If you click a hyperlink in a document, you are immediately taken to the URL address in your application (if you are connected to the Internet) in a read-only document. If you click any link, Office takes you to the specific Web site with your default Web browser.

✓ Returning to Your Document

If you have finished browsing the Web, you can click the × close button to close the Web browser or the **Back** button until you return to your Office document. You could instead click the document in the Windows taskbar to make it the active document.

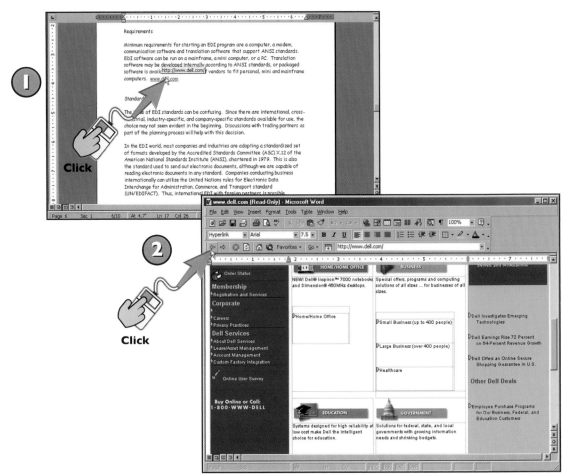

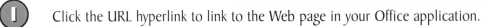

Click the URL hyperlink to link to the Web page in your Office application.

Click the **Back** button on the Web toolbar to move back to your original link.

Task 11: Inserting a Web Hyperlink

Start Here

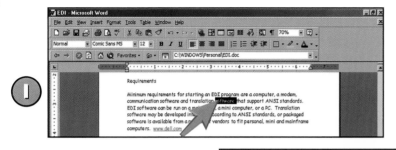

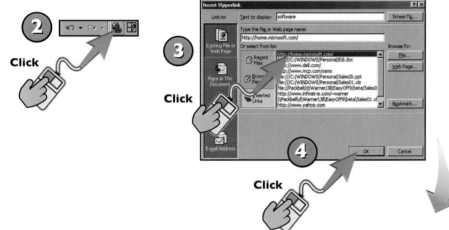

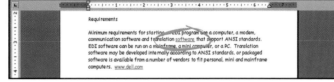

Click

Click

Click

Adding Web Links to Your Documents

If you cannot remember the name of the hyperlink you want to add to your document, you can use the **Insert Hyperlink** button on the Standard toolbar to help you out. From the Insert Hyperlink dialog box, you can browse Web pages or use recent links to locate and add the correct address.

✓ Inserted Links

If the link you want to add to your document isn't listed in the **Inserted Link** list box, simply type the Web page name directly into the Insert Hyperlink dialog box.

✓ Graphics

In addition to making text into a hyperlink, you can click any other object and create a link. For example, you could make a piece of clip art, a chart, or a worksheet cell into a hyperlink.

---

1 Select the text that you want to make into a hyperlink.

2 Click the **Insert Hyperlink** button on the Standard toolbar to open the Insert Hyperlink dialog box.

3 Click an **Inserted Link** from the list box (for example,
`http://home.microsoft.com/`).

4 Click the **OK** button to accept the link.

End Task

Task 12: Inserting a Document Hyperlink

Adding Document Links to Your Documents

When creating an elaborate document, worksheet, or presentation, you may want to add a link that takes you or the intended reader to some other pertinent file. For example, you could add a sales worksheet link to your monthly report document so that the data updates automatically.

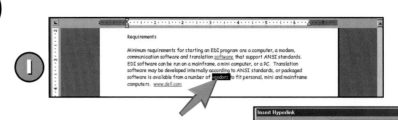

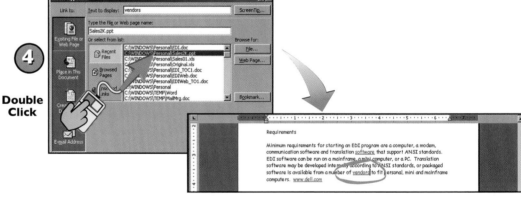

Click

Click

Double Click

✓ **Recent Files**
If the Recent Files list doesn't show the document you want to link to, click the **File** button to browse and select the correct document.

① Select the text that you want to make into a document hyperlink.

② Click the **Insert Hyperlink** button on the Standard toolbar to open the Insert Hyperlink dialog box.

③ Click the **Recent Files** button to see files you recently worked on.

④ Double-click an **Inserted Link** from the list box (for example, `C:\WINDOWS\Personal\Sales2K.ppt`).

Task 13: Inserting an Email Hyperlink

Start Here

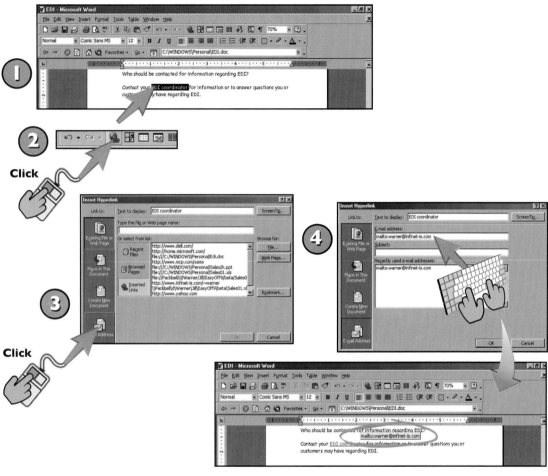

Click

Click

Adding Email Links to Your Documents

When creating a document, you may want to add your email address for the reader to access immediately. For example, say you create a report for your customers, and you want them to email you as soon as they read the report, to let you know their thoughts. You can set up an email link in the document so that the readers can email you immediately, without having to leave the document to go to their email application.

① Select the text that you want to make into an email hyperlink.

② Click the **Insert Hyperlink** button on the Standard toolbar to open the Insert Hyperlink dialog box.

③ Click the **E-mail Address** button to make the link an email address.

④ Type in the email address (for example, `mailto:warner@infinet-is.com`) and press the **Enter** key. When you move the mouse pointer over the text, the email link displays.

✓ **Emailing a Document**
Perhaps you want to email the actual document instead of adding an email address to a document. For more information on this, see Task 17, "Sending a Document as an Email."

End Task

Altering a Hyperlink

People aren't perfect, and you will invariably type an incorrect hyperlink and end up needing to edit it. In addition, some Web page addresses change frequently; you need to update your hyperlinks to those pages.

Task 14: Editing a Hyperlink in a Document

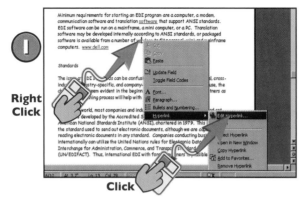

Right Click

Click

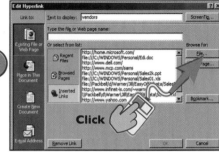

Double Click

Click

✓ **Removing Links**
Not only can you update a hyperlink in the Edit Hyperlink dialog box, but you can remove the hyperlink if you decide to. **Click the Remove Link** button, and then click the **OK** button to close the Edit Hyperlink dialog box.

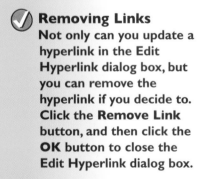

1 Right-click a hyperlink and choose **Hyperlink**, **Edit Hyperlink** to open the Edit Hyperlink dialog box.

2 Click the **File** button to select a different linked document.

3 Double-click the document you want to link to.

4 Click the **OK** button to accept the edits.

Task 15: Editing Hyperlink ScreenTips

Start Here

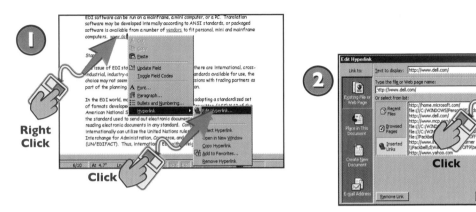

Right Click

Click

Click

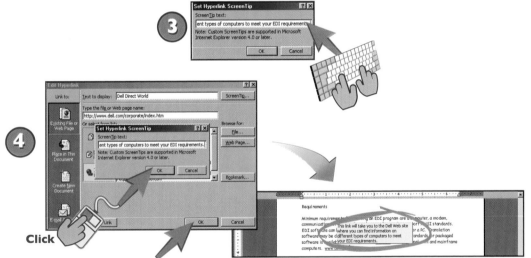

Click

Click

Changing the ScreenTip a Hyperlink Displays

When you first type a hyperlink into a document, the ScreenTip text that is displayed is the Web page link. Sometimes this isn't the information you want to display.

✅ **Text to Display**
In addition to altering a ScreenTip associated with a hyperlink, you can alter the text that is displayed in your Office document. For example, you can have the www.microsoft.com hyperlink actually appear in your document as "Microsoft" and the ScreenTip display "Microsoft Home Page." You do this by altering the **Text to Display** box in the Edit Hyperlink and Insert Hyperlink dialog boxes.

1 Right-click a hyperlink and choose **Hyperlink**, **Edit Hyperlink** to open the Edit Hyperlink dialog box.

2 Click the **ScreenTip** button.

3 Type the text you want the hyperlink ScreenTip to display.

4 Click the **OK** button twice to accept the changes. When you move the mouse pointer over the hyperlink, the new ScreenTip displays.

End Task

Task 16: Removing a Hyperlink

Deleting a Hyperlink

If you decide you no longer want a particular hyperlink in your document, you can remove it. One reason you might want to remove a hyperlink is because you didn't really intend for the document to contain a hyperlink. Perhaps you were just referring to a particular Web page in a report so that you could easily check up on the information you needed, but didn't want people to use a link to it.

Start Here

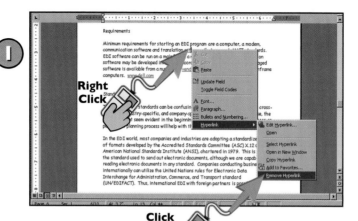

Right Click

Click

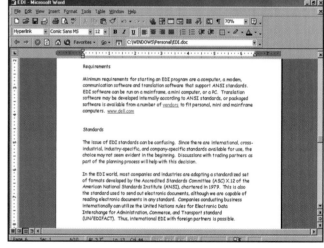

✓ **Using Undo**

If you remove a hyperlink and decide you want it back in your Office document, you can click the **Undo** button on the Standard toolbar, and the hyperlink is restored.

Right-click a hyperlink and choose **Hyperlink**, **Remove Hyperlink** to remove the hyperlink.

End Task

Task 17: Sending a Document as an Email

Start
Here

① Click

②

③ Click

④

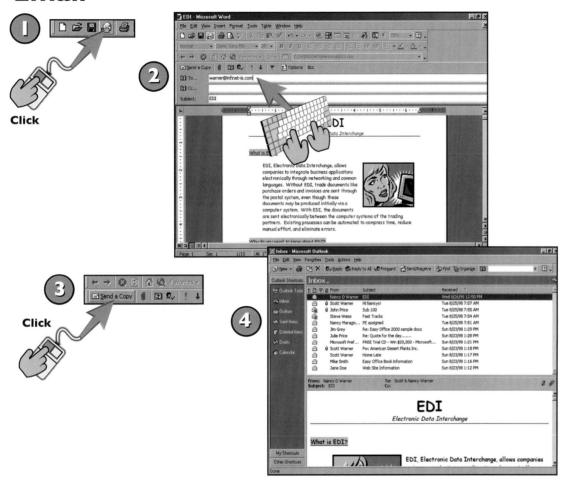

Emailing Documents

The feature for emailing documents is now a button on the Standard toolbar in all Office applications. This feature is fun to use if you want to get feedback on a report you are working on with a colleague in a different location.

✓ Subject File Names
Notice that the file name of the document becomes the Subject line in the email. You can change that by clicking in the subject area and typing a different subject.

✓ Document Links
Notice that the hyperlinks that were in the document are also accessible from the Preview pane in Outlook.

① Click the **Email** button on the Standard toolbar.

② Type the recipient name in the **To** area (try sending it to yourself).

③ Click the **Send a Copy** button to mail the document.

④ Check the messages in your email client (for example, use Outlook; see Part 9, Task 2, "Reading Email Messages," for more information), and you should see this document waiting for you.

End
Task

Publisher 2000 Basics

Microsoft Publisher is a business *desktop publishing* application that lets you create high-impact *publications*. These publications can consist of newsletters, Web sites, brochures, catalogues, flyers, signs, all kinds of cards, letterhead, envelopes, forms, banners, calendars, advertisements, certificates, labels, menus, programs, paper airplanes, and even origami.

Although you can create many different types of publications, we can't cover them all in a single part. This part only covers the new Publication Wizard and how to save your publications, move around in your publication, insert design gallery objects, add additional pages, and print your publications.

Tasks

Using a Wizard to Create a New Publication

When you first start Publisher, the Catalog dialog box appears onscreen to allow you to begin working in Publisher. You can create a blank publication, use an existing publication design, or use the Publication Wizard—as you will learn in this task.

✅ **Personal Information**
If this is one of the first times you have worked in Microsoft Publisher, you might be asked to enter your personal information so that Publisher can automatically add your business or other information to your publications.

Task 1: Creating a New Publication with the Wizard

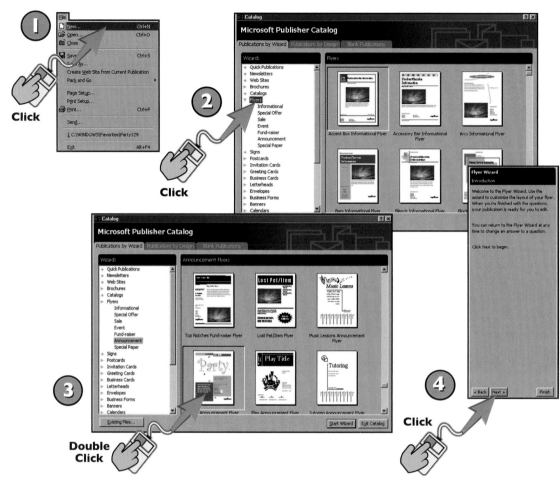

Start Here

Choose **File**, **New** to open the Catalog dialog box if it is not already open.

Select the type of publication wizard you want to create in the **Wizards** list box (for example, **Flyers**).

Click the publication subtopic if there is one (for example, **Announcement**), and double-click the announcement flyer preview (for example, **Party Announcement Flyer**).

Click the **Next** button after you read the Flyer Wizard Introduction.

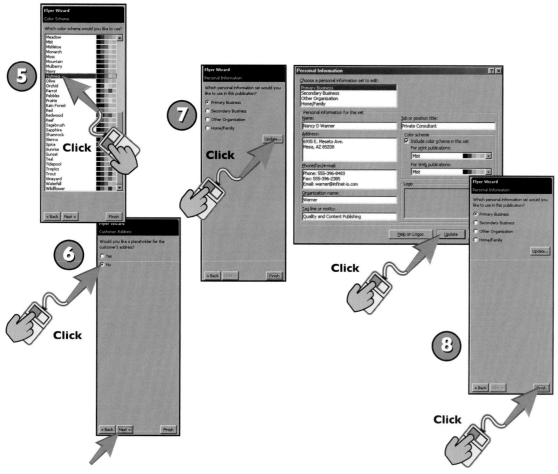

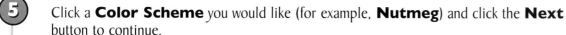

5 Click a **Color Scheme** you would like (for example, **Nutmeg**) and click the **Next** button to continue.

6 Click **Yes** or **No** to whether you want a **Customer Address** placeholder and click the **Next** button to continue.

7 Select which set of **Personal Information** you want entered on your flyer. Click the **Update** button to set personal information, enter the information, and click the **Update** button again to save.

8 Click the **Finish** button to begin working in your publication.

✓ **Saving Publications**
While you are working in the wizard, Publisher will periodically ask you to save your work. When you see a message box asking if you want to save, click the **Yes** button and assign a file name as you would in any other **Office** application. For more information, see the next task on saving publications.

✓ **Finish Button**
You can click the Finish button at any time during the wizard to begin working in your publication.

End Task

Task 2: Saving Publications

Storing a Publication on Disk

Save the publication you are working in to store it on disk. A good practice is to save your publications frequently as you work in them. After you save a publication, you can retrieve it later to work on. The Save As dialog box includes a Places bar with icons to immediately take you to recently saved History files, Personal files, files on your Desktop, files in your Favorites folder, and Web folders.

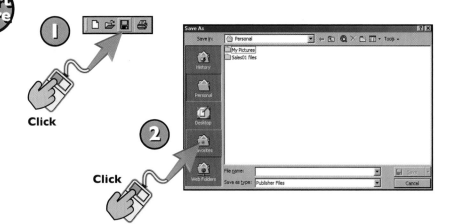

Start Here

Click

Click

✓ Saving As a Different Name

If you want to save your file with a different name than you already assigned it, choose **File, Save As,** and you can type a different file name.

✓ Changing Dialog Box Views

You can view different file information in the Save As dialog box by clicking on the **Views** button on the dialog box toolbar.

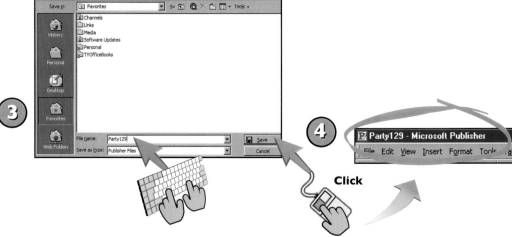

Click

1 Click the **Save** button on the Standard toolbar; the Save As dialog box appears.

2 Click the **Favorites** icon on the Places bar.

3 Type a different document name in the **File name** list box if you want (for example, `Party129`).

4 Click the **Save** button, and the document saves. The file name you assigned now appears in the title bar.

End Task

Task 3: Changing Publication Views

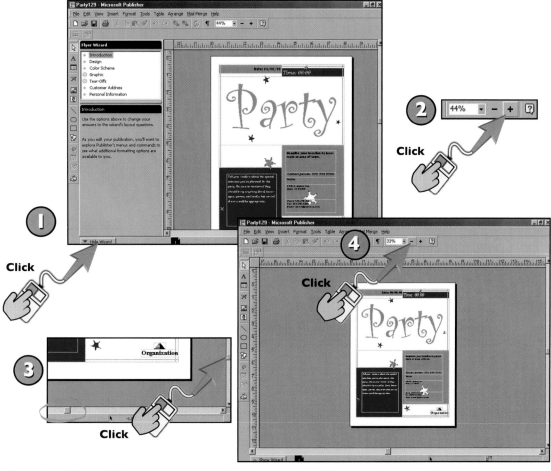

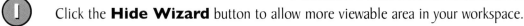

Working with Views

You will find it necessary at times to move through your publication and zoom in and out to view your information. Publisher lets you easily view your document by using the scrollbars and the Zoom In and Zoom Out buttons on the Standard toolbar.

---

① Click the **Hide Wizard** button to allow more viewable area in your workspace.

② Click the **Zoom In** button a couple of times to view your publication in more detail.

③ Click the scrollbars to move around in your publication and see the different text frames that you can edit.

④ Click the **Zoom Out** button to view your publication more as a whole and see how it looks.

✓ Showing Wizard Options

You can show the wizard options at any time if you click on the **Show Wizard** button and select the different wizard options, such as **Design, Color Scheme,** and **Personal Information.** See Task 4 for more information on editing your publications.

End Task

Making Changes to Publications

You can edit your publications to make them look how you want. You can change and realign the text, change the colors of frames, and even rotate objects.

✓ **Changing Colors**
To change the color of any of your publication objects, right-click the object and choose **Change (*object name*)**, **Fill Color**, and select from your original scheme colors or more colors to select a different one.

Task 4: Editing Publications

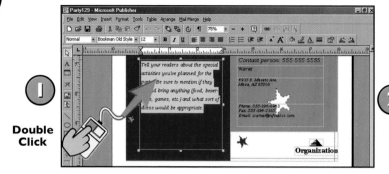

Double Click

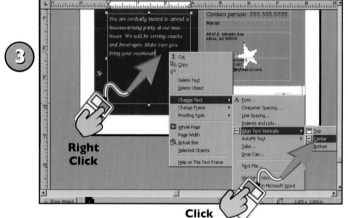

Right Click

Click

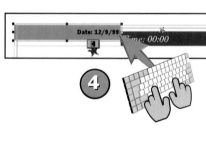

① Double-click directly on an object in your publication (for example, a **Text Frame**).

② Type the text you want entered into the text frame.

③ Right-click on an object in your publication whose alignment you want to alter and choose **Change Text**, **Align Text Vertically**, **Center**.

④ Click an object and type in information to alter the text (for example, the date and time).

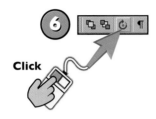

Click

Click

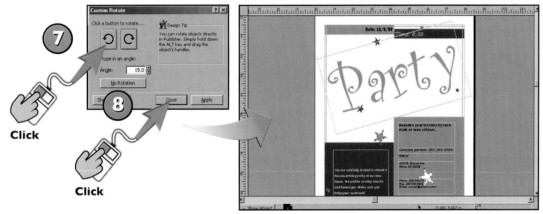

Click

Click

Click

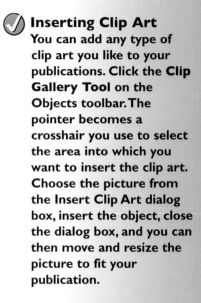

Inserting Clip Art
You can add any type of clip art you like to your publications. Click the **Clip Gallery Tool** on the Objects toolbar. The pointer becomes a crosshair you use to select the area into which you want to insert the clip art. Choose the picture from the **Insert Clip Art** dialog box, insert the object, close the dialog box, and you can then move and resize the picture to fit your publication.

The Objects Toolbar
You can insert numerous objects into your publications by using the Objects toolbar: text boxes, tables, WordArt, pictures, clip art, lines, circles, rectangles, custom shapes, and design gallery objects. You'll learn more about the design gallery tool in the next task. In addition, you can review Part 8, Task 3 to learn more about adding objects.

⑤ Click on an object whose rotation you would like to alter.

⑥ Click the **Custom Rotate** button on the Standard toolbar to open the Custom Rotate dialog box.

⑦ Click the **Counterclockwise** button three times to rotate the object 15 degrees.

⑧ Click the **Close** button to see how the button appears in your publication.

Task 5: Inserting Design Gallery Objects

Adding Design Elements to Publications

There are many different types and styles of objects that you can add to your publications. Along with adding gallery objects, you can move them around, resize them, and even move them to the *front* or *back* of your publication so that they overlap or are over-lapped by other objects.

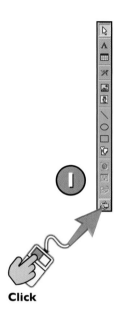

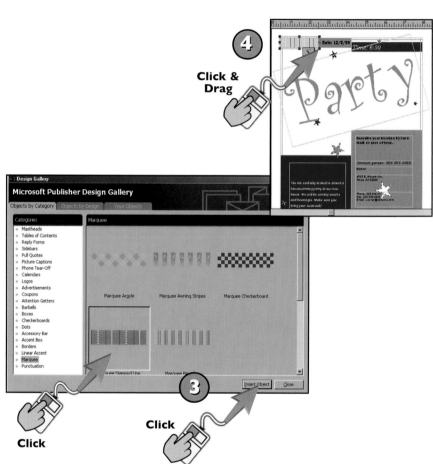

Click & Drag

Click

Click

Click

Click

✓ The Undo Button

Remember that if you alter any objects or aspects of your publication that you decide you don't want, you can click the **Undo** button on the Standard toolbar to remove that action.

1 Click the **Design Gallery Object** button on the Objects toolbar to open the Design Gallery dialog box.

2 Select an object **Category** and subtopic (for example, **Marquee** and **Marquee Diamond Line**).

3 Click the **Insert Object** button to place the object in your publication.

4 Click and drag the object and release the mouse button at the location you desire.

Next Step

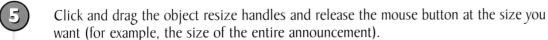

Drag

Drop

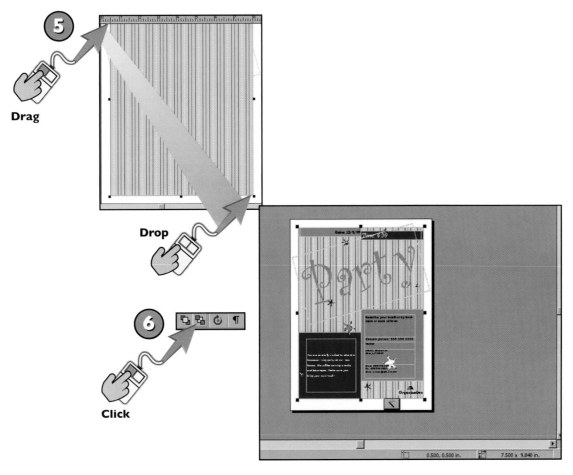

Click

0.500, 0.500 in.   7.500 x 9.840 in.

5 Click and drag the object resize handles and release the mouse button at the size you want (for example, the size of the entire announcement).

6 Click the **Send to Back** button on the Standard toolbar. This will send the object behind all other objects in your publication.

✓ **Bringing to Front**
If you want an object to be in front of another object (or on top of it), click the **Bring to Front** button on the Standard toolbar.

✓ **Objects by Design**
In addition to adding objects by category, you can click the **Objects by Design** tab in the Design Gallery dialog box to insert design set objects such as arcs, bars, blocks, and bubbles.

End Task

Adding Pages to Publications

When working in your publication, you might find that you need to add more pages. You can add as many as you like—blank pages, text frames, or duplicate pages. You can delete unnecessary pages just as easily.

✓ Deleting Pages

You can delete pages in your publications as easily as you can add new pages. Select the page you want to delete by clicking on the specific page number in the status bar area and choose **Edit, Delete Page**. A message box will ask if you indeed want to delete a page. Click the **OK** button if you want to delete the page, or click the **Cancel** button to return to working in your publication.

Task 6: Inserting Additional Pages

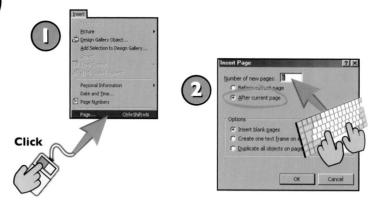

Click

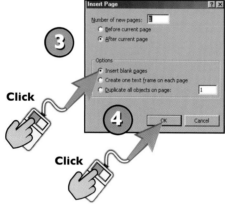

Click

Click

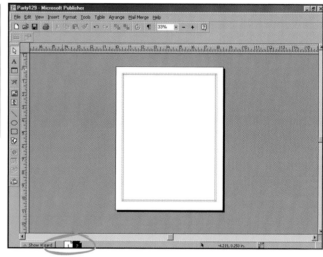

1. Choose **Insert**, **Page** to open the Insert Page dialog box.

2. Type the number of new pages (for example, **1**) and choose whether you want the new page(s) to go before or after the current page.

3. Click one of the **Options** to insert blank pages, create one text frame on each page, or duplicate all objects on the page you specify (for example, you can insert pages identical to the page you are viewing).

4. Click the **OK** button, and Publisher inserts the new page(s) into your publication.

End Task

Task 7: Printing Publications

Click

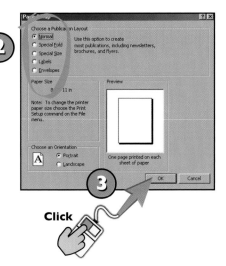

Click

Click

Sending Publications to the Printer

Publisher makes it easy to print a publication and enables you to select the print and page setup options from the File menu. This task covers the **Page Setup** options; the **Print Setup** options allow you to switch the printer you are sending the publication to; the **Print** options allow you to choose a print range and the number of copies you send to the printer.

✓ **Taking Publications to a Printer**
Publisher has a feature that allows you to prepare your files for commercial printing. Choose **File, Pack and Go, Take to a Commercial Printing Service.** The Pack and Go Wizard will walk you through the questions about files, fonts, and graphics and create a packed file that you can take to a professional printer.

① Choose **File**, **Page Setup** to open the Page Setup dialog box.

② Select a **Publication Layout** if you need a special fold or size, or you want to create labels and envelopes.

③ Click the **OK** button.

④ Click the **Print** button on the Standard toolbar.

End
Task

FrontPage 2000 Basics

With FrontPage 2000 installed, you are ready to start making your own Web pages and Web site. This part's goal is to familiarize you with FrontPage and show you how to create a basic Web page. The last task tells you how to publish a Web site on the Internet.

You need to obtain server space from your *ISP* (Internet service provider) in order to have a location to place your Web site and link your URLs (uniform resource locators). You will need a server name and password to access your Web space.

Tasks

Designing a New Web Page

FrontPage lets you easily create all different types of Web pages with the many templates to choose from. You simply open one of the templates and replace the sample text with text that you want on your Web page.

Task 1: Creating a New Web Page

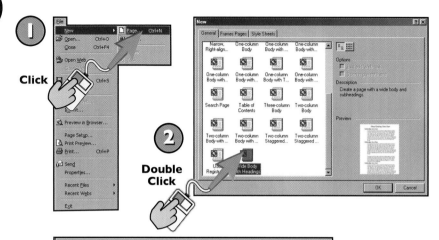

Click

Double Click

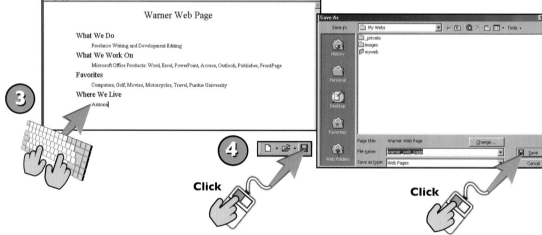

Click

Click

✓ Saving As
You can save your Web page as any name you like. It will default to the page title of the Web page you are working in.

1 Choose **File**, **New**, **Page** to open the New dialog box.

2 Double-click on a Web page template (for example, **Wide Body with Headings**).

3 Type the text you want to appear on your Web page.

4 Click the **Save** button on the Standard toolbar and click the **Save** button in the Save As dialog box to save the default file name.

Task 2: Adding a Web Page Theme

Start Here

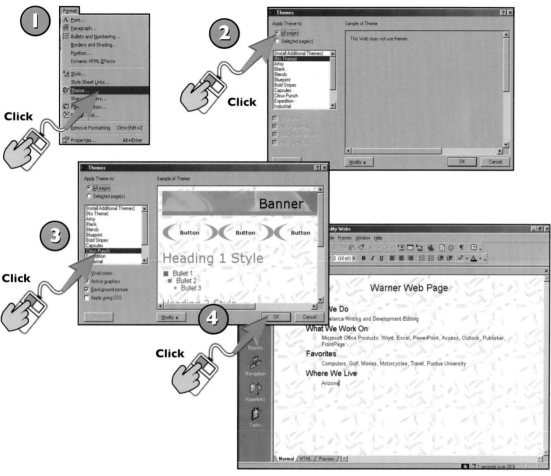

Formatting a Theme on Your Web Page

Instead of adding background color and then altering the style and color of additional objects (such as bullets, separator bars, and so on), you can apply a document theme. These help create consistent-looking Web pages.

① Choose **Format**, **Theme** to open the Themes dialog box.

② Click the **All pages** option to apply the selected theme to all Web pages.

③ Click the theme you want to apply (for example, **Citrus Punch**).

④ Click the **OK** button to see how your text will look with the applied theme.

 Modifying Themes
You can click the Modify button in the Themes dialog box to alter the colors, graphics, and text in a sample theme.

End Task

Page
255

Task 3: Inserting Pictures and Tables

Adding a Web Page Picture and Table

Most Web pages you view contain pictures and tables. The pictures can be clip art, scanned image files, or even video clips. In addition, the tables can be as small or long as you like. Keep in mind that you should make sure your pictures and tables are necessary and aesthetically pleasing, or you might lose your Web readers.

✅ **Modem Time**
You might notice that the status bar updates the modem time when you add something else to your Web page. This tells you how long it will take to download your Web page.

Start Here

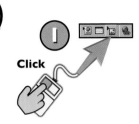

Click

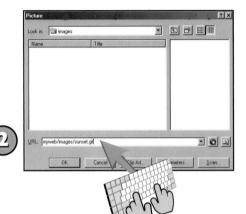

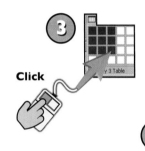

Click

1 Click the **Insert Picture from File** button on the Standard toolbar to open the Picture dialog box.

2 Type the location of the image file (for example, `myweb/images/sunset.gif`) and press the **Enter** key.

3 Click the **Insert Table** button on the Standard toolbar and choose the table dimensions (for example, **3 by 3 Table**).

4 Type some text into the table just as you would in a Microsoft Word table.

End Task

Task 4: Adding Hyperlinks

Start Here

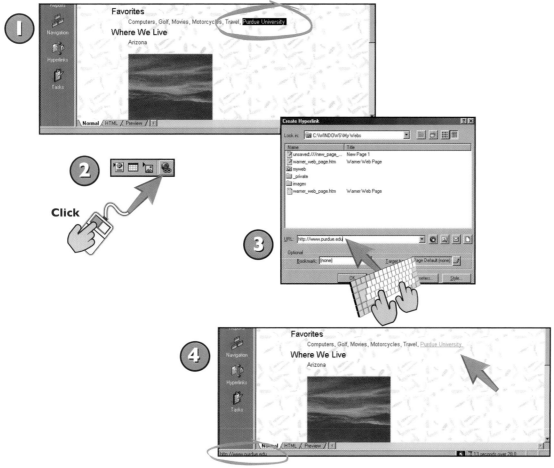

Inserting a Hyperlink in Your Web Page

Your Web pages would be pretty boring if you didn't link to other sites or pages. You can assign text already on your page as a hyperlink, type in a new hyperlink, or even assign an object as a hyperlink.

Click

✓ **Hyperlink Objects**
You can make any object on your Web page into a hyperlinked object. For example, you could click on the picture or table and add a URL address to it.

✓ **Viewing Hyperlinks**
You can view the hyperlinks associated with your Web site by clicking the Hyperlinks button in the Views bar on the left.

1. Select the text or object you want to have a hyperlink.

2. Click the **Hyperlink** button on the Standard toolbar to open the Create Hyperlink dialog box.

3. Type the URL you want to link to (for example, **http://www.purdue.edu**) and press the **Enter** key.

4. Move the mouse pointer over the newly created hyperlink, and the URL will display in the status bar.

End Task

Task 5: Adding FrontPage Components

Inserting Web Page Components

Numerous types of FrontPage components allow you to add all kinds of Web features. This task only covers a few, but you can try them all.

Start Here

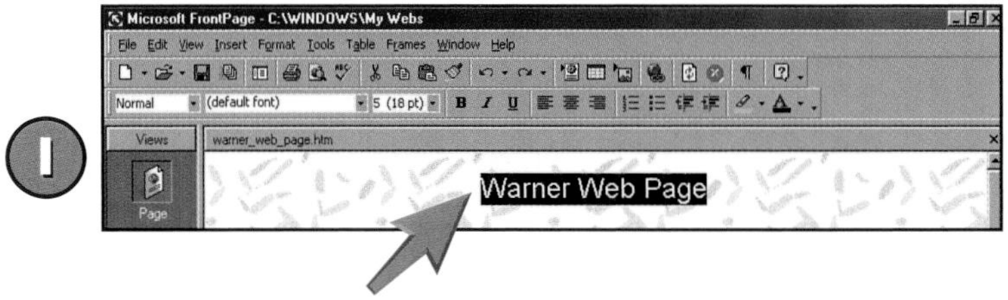

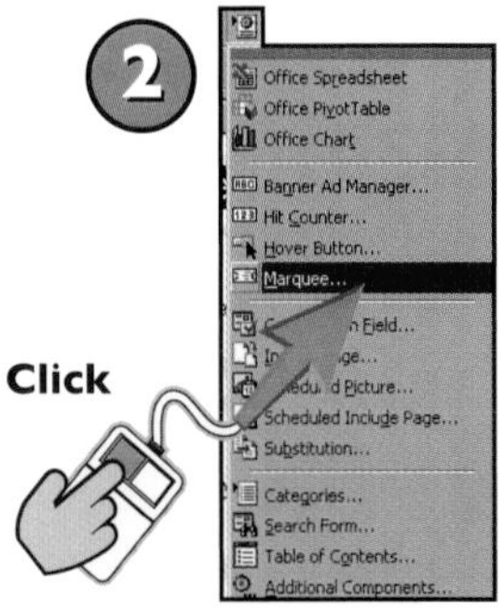

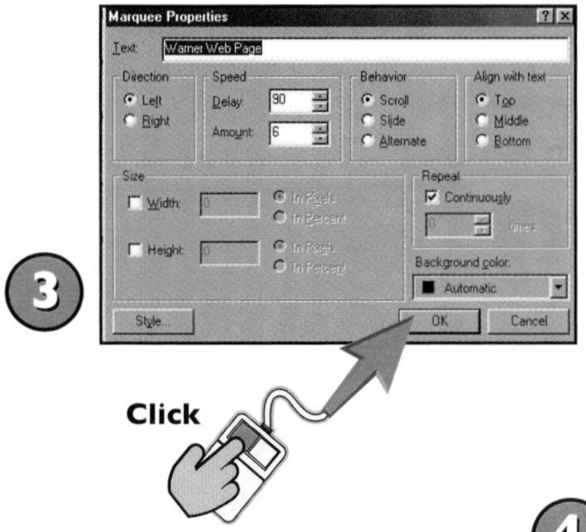

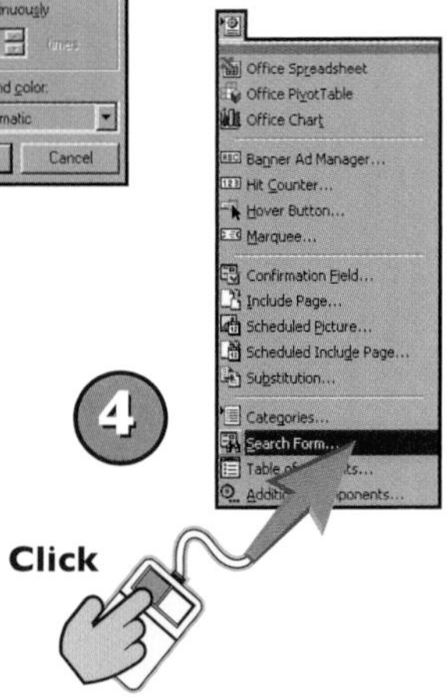

1. Select the text you want to make into a marquee.
2. Choose **Insert Component**, **Marquee** from the Standard toolbar.
3. Click the **OK** button to select the default options on the Marquee Properties dialog box (or you can alter them as you like).
4. Choose **Insert Component**, **Search Form** from the Standard toolbar.

Marquee Text

You can change the marquee text or create new text by typing what you want into the Text box in the Marquee Properties dialog box.

Search Forms

A search form allows Web site visitors to search for specific words or phrases. FrontPage reviews the text index and provides the visitor with a list of hyperlinks to pages that contain the text they are searching for.

Next Step

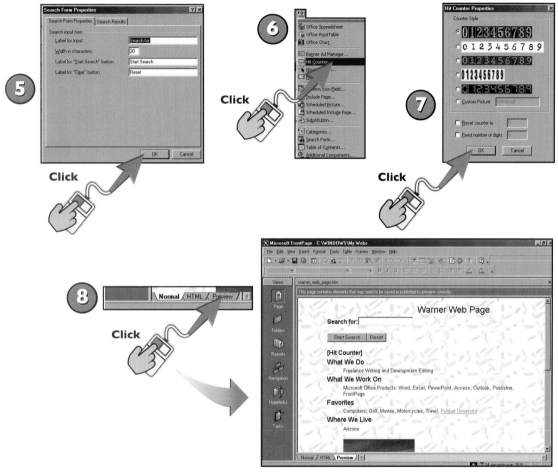

FrontPage Server Extensions
Keep in mind that certain components require you to have FrontPage Server Extensions, if your Web is server based, in order for them to work. The Search Form and Hit Counter are examples of these components. If you wonder about a particular extension, look it up in FrontPage Help.

Hit Counters
A hit counter keeps track of the number of times a page has been visited by users and displays the results in odometer-like fashion.

Viewing HTML
You can click the **HTML** tab to view the actual HTML that is generated to create the Web page.

5. Click the **OK** button to select the default options on the Search Form Properties dialog box (or you can alter them as you like).

6. Choose **Insert Component**, **Hit Counter** from the Standard toolbar.

7. Click the **OK** button to select the default options on the Hit Counter Properties dialog box (or select a different Counter Style option).

8. Click the **Preview** tab to see what the Web page and components look like.

Task 6: Creating a New Web Site

Creating a Personal Web Site

For this task, you are going to simply create a Web site on your hard drive, not on your service provider's Web server. Because this is just a test, you can save it and change it later, before you publish the Web site.

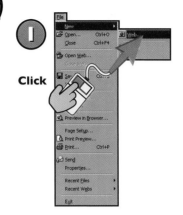

Click

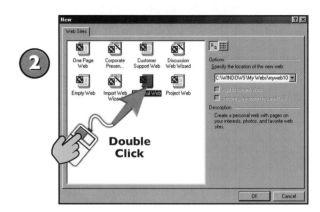

Double Click

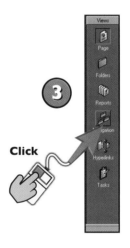

Click

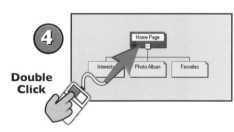

Double Click

✓ **Server Addresses**
If you know the address of your service provider's host name, type that into the **Specify the Location of the New Web** drop-down list box in the New dialog box.

(1) Choose **File**, **New**, **Web** to open the New dialog box, with the Web Sites tab showing.

(2) Double-click on the Web Sites **Personal Web** option. FrontPage then takes some time to create the Web.

(3) Click on the **Navigation** icon in the Views pane.

(4) Double-click on **Home Page** to view the Normal tab defaults that FrontPage has given to this Web Site template.

Next Step

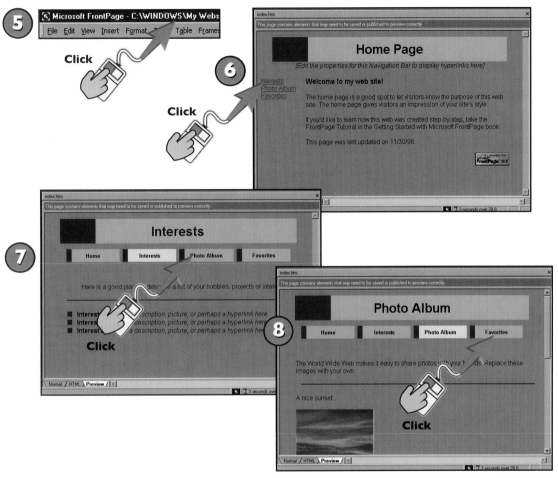

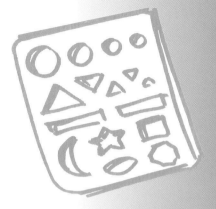

Editing Template Pages

You can edit any of the text or objects in a Web site template. Be careful when you edit objects that are in banners or navigation bars because they might affect the appearance of other Web pages in the site.

End Task

Task 7: Uploading Your Web Site

Publishing Your Web Site

Now that you have created a Web site, added Web pages, and found an ISP to store your new Web site, you need to dial in to your ISP and move the entire Web site from your local computer to your remote server. This task shows you how to upload the site on your hard drive; you simply replace the destination server address with your remote server address.

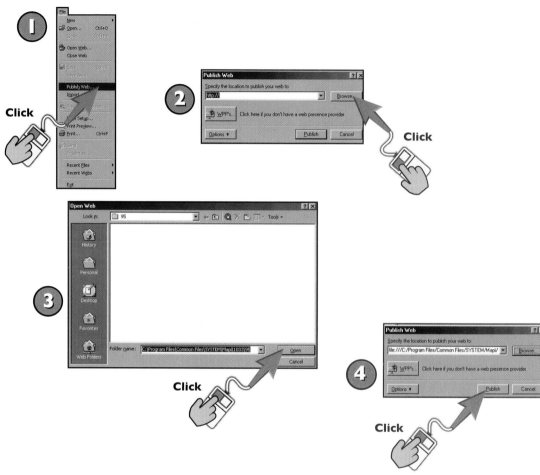

Click

Click

Click

Click

✅ The Destination Server

You might need to include a specific directory with the server name when you enter the destination server, depending on the server you are uploading to. Ask the system administrator of the server you are connecting to.

1. Choose **File**, **Publish Web** to open the Publish Web dialog box.

2. Click the **Browse** button.

3. Click the **Open** button to select the default publishing location on your hard drive.

4. Click the **Publish** button.

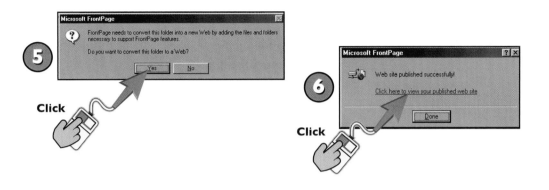

Click

Click

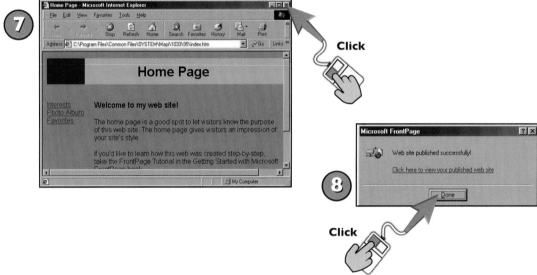

Click

Click

⚠ WARNING

Make sure you check with your ISP and its system administrator so that you know how much space you are allowed to upload to your Web site. The ISP might have a particular limit you cannot exceed.

5️⃣ Click the **Yes** button to convert the selected folder to a Web.

6️⃣ Click the **Click Here to View Your Published Web Site** hyperlink.

7️⃣ Click the **Close (×)** button on the Internet Explorer window to return to FrontPage.

8️⃣ Click the **Done** button to finish.

End Task

absolute cell reference   An entry in a formula that does not change when the formula is copied to a new cell. In certain formulas, you might want an entry to always refer to one specific cell value.

active document   The document currently selected in the application you're using.

alignment   The way text lines up against the margins of a page. For example, justified text lines up evenly with both the left and right margins.

animation effect   An illusion of movement during a PowerPoint slide show that is accomplished by controlling how text is displayed.

AutoContent Wizard   A tool in PowerPoint that guides you through the steps of a proposed presentation and includes suggested content.

AutoText   A feature that automatically corrects mistyped text. You can also use AutoText to specify a string of characters that will automatically correct itself to a word or phrase. For example, Word comes with AutoText that automatically corrects "teh" to "the."

background   A color or picture you can add to your Office documents or objects contained in them such as tables, charts, or clip art.

browser   A tool that lets you view documents on the Internet.

bullet   An object, such as a circle or square, used to set off items in a list.

carriage return   When the cursor in an Office document moves to the next paragraph after pressing the **Enter** key.

cell   An area in an Excel worksheet or a Word table that holds a specific piece of information.

chart   A graphic representation of a selection of Excel workbook cell data.

client   Software that uses resources available from other computers. For example, an email client uses the resources available for running a mail server.

Clip Gallery   A collection of clip art, pictures, sound files, and video clips you can use to spruce up Office documents.

Clipboard   A location in Windows that holds the information that is cut or copied. New to Windows 98 and Office 2000 is the ability to place up to 12 items on the Clipboard and use any of them you want at any time.

color scheme   A set of eight coordinated colors you can use in your PowerPoint presentations.

column   (1) In a table, a vertical set of cells. (2) In a document, the vertical

arrangement of text and graphics so the document looks like a newspaper.

conditional statement   A function that returns different results depending on whether a specified condition is true or false.

context menu   See shortcut menu.

cursor   The location where you last entered text. This is a flashing bar in some applications.

data   The information you work with in an Excel spreadsheet, including text, numbers, and graphic images.

datasheet   A grid of columns and rows that enables you to enter numeric data into a chart.

demote   To indent a line of text more than the previous line, indicating a lower level of importance.

dialog box   An information box that appears during the installation or use of an application and requires input from the user.

docked toolbar   A toolbar that is attached to one of the four sides of an application window.

document map   A vertical display of the headings in a Word document. You can click an entry to move quickly to that part of the document.

drag-and-drop   To move an object (an icon, a selection of text, a cell in an Excel worksheet, and so on) by selecting it, dragging it to another location, and then releasing the mouse button.

drop-down list   A list of choices presented when you click the arrow to the right of a field in a dialog box.

embedded object   An object that is physically included in the document to which it belongs. The source and destination file aren't linked, which means that when one object is updated, the other is not.

Endnotes   A Word feature in which a note number is placed within the document, and reference information about the noted word or phrase is automatically placed at the end of the document.

file   Information you enter in your computer and save for future use, such as a document or a workbook.

filter   A feature in Excel for controlling which records are extracted from the database and displayed in the worksheet.

floating toolbar   A toolbar that is not anchored to the edge of the window, but instead is displayed in the document window for easy access. You can drag a floating toolbar out to your Windows desktop.

font   The typeface, type size, and type attributes of text or numbers.

footer   Text or graphics that appears at the bottom of every page of a document or worksheet.

Footnotes   A Word feature in which a note number is placed within the document and reference information about the noted word or phrase is automatically placed at the bottom of the page.

format   To change the appearance of text or numbers.

formatting   Attributes of text and data that determine the appearance of information.

formula   In Excel, a means for calculating a value based on the values in other cells of the workbook.

frame   A means for sectioning a window to allow it to show multiple documents. You can navigate each part of a frame separately.

function   A built-in formula that automatically performs calculations in Excel.

graphic   An image that can come in many shapes and sizes. Typical graphics include clip art images, drawings, photographs, scanned images, and signature files.

handles   The small black squares around a selected object. You use these squares to drag, size, or scale the object.

header   Text or graphics that appears at the top of every page of a document or a workbook.

hyperlink   Text formatted so that clicking it "jumps" you to another, related location.

highlight   A band of color you can add to text by using the Highlight tool on the Word toolbar. In addition, when you select text to format or move, for example, you are selecting or "highlighting" the text.

I-beam   The shape of the mouse pointer when you move over a screen area in which you can edit text.

indent   An amount of space that an object, usually text, is moved away from the left margin.

insert mode   A mode in which the new text you enter moves the text that was previously in the same location over to the right.

insertion point   The blinking vertical bar that shows where text will appear when you type. The insertion point is sometimes called a cursor.

Internet A system of linked computer networks that facilitates data communication services such as remote login, file transfer, electronic mail, and newsgroups.

justify To align text so that it fills the area between the left and right margins.

link A connection between a linked object and a source object. If one of the objects is altered, the other is altered as well.

macro A method of automating common tasks you perform in applications such as Word or Excel. You can record keystrokes and mouse clicks so that they can be played back automatically.

margins The space around the top, bottom, left, and right sides of a page. This space can be increased or decreased as necessary. This can also be the location where elements such as headers and footers are located.

merge A feature that enables you to combine information, such as names and addresses, with a form document, such as a letter.

mixed cell reference A single-cell entry in a formula that contains both a relative and an absolute cell reference. A mixed cell reference is helpful when you need a formula that always refers to the values in a specific column, but the values in the rows must change, and vice versa.

Office Assistant An animated Office Help system that provides interactive help, tips, and other online assistance.

overtype mode A mode in which the new text you type replaces the text that was previously in the same location.

page setup The way data is arranged on a printed page.

path A map to the location of the folder that contains a file. For example, **My Documents\Letters\ Mom.doc** means the document **Mom.doc** is stored in the **Letters** folder, which is stored in the **My Documents** folder.

personalized menu A menu that changes to show the commands you use most often.

PIM Personal Information Manager. Software (such as the Contacts folder in Outlook) in which you track information about contacts and keep notes on your interaction with those contacts.

pop-up menu See shortcut menu.

presentation A group of related slides you can create by using PowerPoint.

promote To indent a line of text less than the previous line, indicating a greater level of importance.

range A cell or a rectangular group of adjacent cells in Excel.

reference A means for addressing something in a specified context. For example, in Excel, "AI" is a reference to the cell at column A, row I.

relative cell reference A reference to the contents of a cell that Excel adjusts when you copy the formula to another cell or range of cells.

Replace A command on the Edit menu that you can use to automatically replace text with different text. This feature can also be used with special characters such as tabs and paragraph marks.

revision marks The tracked changes you see onscreen.

row A horizontal set of cells in Excel.

ruler A tool for measuring distances of where objects are in relation to the page. Appearing horizontally across the top of a page and vertically along the side of a page in Word, rulers also display page margins and tab settings.

sans serif Fonts that don't have "tails" on the letters (for example, Helvetica and Arial).

ScreenTip   A note that displays on screen to explain a function or feature.

search criteria   Defined patterns or details used to find matching records.

select   To define a section of text so you can take action on it, such as copying, moving, or formatting it.

serif   Fonts that have "tails" on the letters (for example, Times New Roman and Courier).

shortcut key   A keyboard combination that provides a quick way to execute a menu command. For example, **Ctrl+S** is a shortcut key for **File**, **Save**.

shortcut menu   A menu that pops up when you right-click an object. This menu changes according to the context of the task you are trying to accomplish.

slide transition   A special effect used to introduce a slide during a PowerPoint slide show.

sort   A function that rearranges the data in a list so it appears in alphabetic or numeric order.

speaker notes   Notes that help you document and give a presentation in PowerPoint.

status bar   A place at the bottom of each Office window that tells you information about your documents and

applications, such as whether you are in insert or overtype mode.

strikethrough   A font option in which the text is marked out with a line (for example, ~~strikethrough~~).

style   A named collection of formatting settings that you can assign to text. For example, the Normal style might use the Times New Roman font at II points with standard margins.

submenu   A list of options that appears when you point at some menu items in Windows 95 and in applications designed for use with Windows 95. A small, right-pointing arrowhead appears to the right of menu items that have submenus.

tab   An element that allows you to separate objects with a precise amount of space (such as one inch), which using the spacebar can't do.

tab stop   An element that you place in your ruler to allow you to add space and alignment between your tabs. For example, you could add a right, center, or left-aligned tab stop.

table   A series of rows and columns. The intersection of a row and column is called a cell, which is where you type text and numbers.

TaskPad   In Outlook, a list of tasks that displays when you use the Calendar view.

template   Available in Word and Excel, it provides predesigned patterns on which documents and workbooks can be based.

text wrapping   Text automatically flows to the next line without having to insert a carriage return using the Enter key.

theme   A consistent visual in a document that may include colors, icons, bullets, figures, background colors, and so on.

transition effect   Movement that occurs between slides in PowerPoint to smooth the passing of one slide to another.

URL   Uniform Resource Locator. A link to an addressable location on the Internet.

Web   Also known as the World Wide Web; a hypertext-based document retrieval system with machines linked to the Internet. This allows you to view documents, especially ones that are graphical in nature.

workbook   An Excel document that contains one or more worksheets or chart sheets.

worksheet   In Excel, the workbook component that contains cell data, formulas, and charts.

A

B

finding

Paragraph dialog box (Word)

Get FREE books and more...when you register this book online for our Personal Bookshelf Program

http://register.quecorp.com/

 Register online and you can sign up for our *FREE Personal Bookshelf Program*—immediate and unlimited access to the electronic version of more than 200 complete computer books! That means you'll have 100,000 pages of valuable information onscreen, at your fingertips!

 Plus, you can access product support, including complimentary downloads, technical support files, book-focused links, companion Web sites, author sites, and more!

 And, don't miss out on the opportunity to sign up for a *FREE subscription to a weekly email newsletter* to help you stay current with news, announcements, sample book chapters, and special events, including sweepstakes, contests, and various product giveaways!

 We value your comments! Best of all, the entire registration process takes only a few minutes to complete, so go online and get the greatest value going—absolutely FREE!

Don't Miss Out On This Great Opportunity!

QUE® is a brand of Macmillan Computer Publishing USA. For more information, please visit *www.mcp.com*